Disarmament and the Economy

A PUBLICATION FROM THE
CENTER FOR RESEARCH IN CONFLICT RESOLUTION AT THE
UNIVERSITY OF MICHIGAN

DISARMAMENT AND THE ECONOMY

EDITED BY

EMILE BENOIT & KENNETH E. BOULDING

GREENWOOD PRESS, PUBLISHERS
WESTPORT, CONNECTICUT

Library of Congress Cataloging in Publication Data

Benoit, Emile.
    Disarmament and the economy.

    "A publication from the Center for Research in
Conflict Resolution at the University of Michigan."
    Reprint of the ed. published by Harper & Row, New
York.
    Includes bibliographical references and index.
    1. United States--Economic policy. 2. United
States--Military policy. I. Boulding, Kenneth Ewart,
1910-   joint author. II. Title.
HC110.D4B44 1978   338.973   77-25966
ISBN 0-313-20076-9

338.973
B473

Reprinted in 1978 by Greenwood Press, Inc.
51 Riverside Avenue, Westport, CT 06880

Printed in the United States of America

Contents

v

Preface

This volume is the final report of the Program of Research on Economic Adjustments to Disarmament (READ), sponsored by the Center for Research on Conflict Resolution at the University of Michigan. It was financed by grants from the Carnegie Corporation, supplemented by grants from the Ford Foundation, the Christopher Reynolds Foundation, the AFL-CIO, and the Institute for International Order.

The origins of this study trace back to some informal conversations among a group of economists associated with the Society of Friends at meetings of the American Economic Association some years ago. The project was first formulated in detail by Emile Benoit as part of the program of research of the Institute for International Order, sponsored by the Committee on Research for Peace under the chairmanship of Dr. Harold Taylor. The Center for Research on Conflict Resolution obtained and administered the original grant from the Carnegie Corporation. A board of advisors under the chairmanship of Kenneth E. Boulding of the University of Michigan exercised broad supervision over the study,* and Emile Benoit acted as project director.

* The other members of the advisory board were Roy Blough, Neil W. Chamberlain, Gerhard Colm, Eli Ginzberg, Walter Isard, Klaus Knorr,

The study was organized and maintained its office in New York, but a large part of the research was contracted to individuals in various parts of the country, most of whose contributions appear in this volume. All the contributors are professional economists, whose work had to meet the highest professional standards. Nevertheless, the editors and the contributors have taken pains to make the conclusions accessible to the general audience concerned with the problem. The editors are grateful to the contributors for their willingness to allow extensive editorial revisions of their manuscripts, in the interest of making the book accessible to as wide a public as possible. Some of the preliminary results of our study have already been made available to the United States government and to the United Nations to assist in their research in this general area.*

We should like, at this time, to acknowledge a particular debt of gratitude to the late Mrs. Ada Wardlaw of the READ staff, who not only participated in the administration and research, but also did a large part of the preliminary editing of the papers. Her faith in the program, her unstinting efforts in its behalf, her unfailing cheerfulness, and her exceptional editorial skills contributed more to the project than we can readily find words to express. Miss Mary Painter, another member of our staff, did much of the basic research, and Mrs. Sylvia Schuman has been extremely helpful in the final checking and editing of the manuscript. We have also been aided by the research contributions of Jack Atlee, Jack Behrman, Mannie Kupinsky, Theodore Mesmer, and Thomas O'Sullivan, by the prior or parallel research of Doris Ikle and George A.

Theodore J. Kreps, Wassily Leontief, Paul W. McCracken, Marshall A. Robinson, Thomas C. Schelling, Arthur Smithies, George E. Steiner, Ralph J. Watkins. Lincoln Gordon and Thomas K. Finletter were also members until their appointment as United States Ambassadors.
* See, for example, "The Economic Impacts of Disarmament" published in January 1962 by the United States Arms Control and Disarmament Agency. The report was prepared by a panel of economists, the chairman and three of the members of which were associated in the READ program. Our gratitude is expressed to John J. McCloy, William C. Foster, and Alexander Kiefer for making this fruitful collaboration possible.

Steiner, and by the technical advice and criticism of John J. Mc-
Sweeny and C. Locke Anderson, as well as by the thoughtful papers
and discussions of the economists who participated in the READ
conference on "West Coast Adjustments to Disarmament" in Santa
Barbara in May 1961.*

Our deep appreciation must be expressed to the foundations and
organizations which supported the project, and to the staffs of the
Center for Research in Conflict Resolution and the Institute for
International Order who saw us through the complexities of its
financial administration. The project director also wishes to acknowledge his personal gratitude to Dean Courtney Brown of the
Columbia University Graduate School of Business for his encouragement and support, and for his approval of the academic leave
required to undertake the research, and also to the Ford Foundation for a recent grant which will make possible the continuance of
research in this general area, with special attention to the *international* economic repercussions of arms agreements, and to the
problems of East–West economic competition and coexistence in
a warless world.

We are under no illusions that disarmament is easy or close, or
that the economic adjustments are the major problem involved.
The political problems of disarmament are the most difficult and
the most important, and the economic problems will rise in importance only as the political problems are solved. It is essential, however, to know that we *can* solve the economic problems concerned;
otherwise, our fears in this regard, even though they are below the
surface, may operate as a serious handicap in our efforts to solve
the political problem. If we have succeeded in making even the

---

* These included: Robert Arnold, John T. Booth, Sterling Brubaker, Eugene
Brussell, Russell Bryan, Richard Cartwright, Edward Chambers, Jr., Robert
W. Child, Alfred Conrad, Pierre Crosson, Stahrl W. Edmunds, Robert E.
Freeman, Robert A. Gordon, Lee W. Hansen, Arch D. Hardyment, Francis
Hoeber, Neil Houston, Doris Ikle, Dudley Johnson, Dale W. Jorgenson,
Fremont Kast, Theodore J. Kreps, D. Kybal, Robert Lawrence, Everett
Lennon, Michael MacDonald, Roderick MacIver, Jim Rosenzweig, G. N.
Rostvold, William Royce, Hal Shean, Stanley Sheinbaum, Leon Sloss, Paul
L. Smith, Robert Spiegelman, Daniel B. Suits, Charles M. Tiebout, Carl G.
Uhr, Leonard Wainstein, Robert M. Williams, Elmer Wohl.

smallest contribution toward the establishment of that stable peace for which we all long, this in itself would be the richest kind of reward.

EMILE BENOIT
KENNETH E. BOULDING

PART I

Defense Industry and the Pattern of Disarmament

1

The World War Industry as an Economic Problem

Kenneth E. Boulding*

The world war industry is the total sum of human effort and resources devoted to preparation for war or its actual conduct. The annual expenditure on, or income generated by it, may be estimated as something between $100 and $120 billion, depending to some extent upon the narrowness of its definition. This is roughly equal to the total income of the poorer half of mankind, assuming that the per capita income of the poorest billion and a quarter is still under $100 per year. Because of the very large income of the rich countries, however, it represents something less than 10 per cent of the gross world product. Assuming the $120 billion figure, the United States accounts for a little more than a third of this, the Soviet Union for a little less than a third, and the rest of the world for about a third.

This chapter looks at the world war industry with the eye of an economist; that is, one who selects and abstracts from the complexity of the social system those elements which relate to commodities, exchange, transactions, bargains, and negotiations. The economist's eye does not necessarily see the whole truth. It is, nevertheless, useful to look at the world scene through the colored

* KENNETH E. BOULDING is Professor of Economics at the University of Michigan and Co-director of its Center for Research on Conflict Resolution. He is author of *Conflict and Defense: A General Theory, Economic Analysis, The Image, The Organizational Revolution, Economics of Peace,* etc.

lens of a single abstraction. Indeed, where there is a good deal of glare, we may see more through colored glasses than we can with the naked eye. I make no apology, therefore, for attempting to bring the methods of the economist to the study of a part of the world system which is usually regarded as being outside his fold.

The first thing which an economist asks himself when he contemplates an industry is, "What commodity does it produce and whence comes the demand for this commodity?" The economist conceives the economic problem fundamentally as one of the allocation of scarce resources among a number of different industries, each of them producing a commodity or a group of commodities which are then exchanged for the products of other industries. It is a legitimate question for the economist, therefore, to ask what commodity the war industry produces, and whence comes the demand for it.

THE TIME-SPACE PERSPECTIVE

Suppose we begin by looking simply at the physical consequences of the world war industry over, shall we say, a hundred years. We would find, of course, that its activity is somewhat sporadic and there are times ("peace") in which it seems to do very little except develop potential. Then, in its times of activity, that is, during wars, it devotes itself to diminishing the durability of capital. If we include the human person as capital, the notion of diminishing the durability of capital seems to cover almost every purely physical aspect of the world war industry. It diminishes the durability of human capital and reduces the age of death. It also diminishes the durability of physical capital, not only of the war industry itself, but also of civil society as embodied in cities, bridges, works of art, and so on. The observer from outer space who did not have the advantage of understanding the human organism because of his inability to experience empathy with an alien form of intelligence might conclude that the principal aim of the world war industry was to prevent the undue accumulation of capital. He might devise several positive theories to account for this phenomenon. He might conclude, for instance, that the main interest of the human race was not the enjoyment but the accumulation of capital; and as the act of accumulation unfortunately always leads to the development of stocks of capital, it was necessary to devise an industry devoted to reducing this stock, hence permitting a continued and perpetual accumulation. In this view, production would be regarded as the fundamental human activity; and the war industry would, therefore, be seen as a device for augmenting consumption by the destruction of capital in order to prevent overaccumulation and the diminution of production which might follow.

THE PRODUCER-DESTROYER MODEL

This theory, attractive as it may seem at first sight, would soon be challenged by further investigation. The basic fallacy of the theory is, of course, the assumption that mankind is both homogeneous and rational. Our investigator from outer space would soon find that this is not so. A second tentative hypothesis that might emerge, therefore, is that mankind is in fact divided into two social species, the producers and the destroyers—the producers, whose object is the accumulation of capital and the increase in its durability, and the destroyers, whose main interest is the decumulation of capital and the lessening of its durability. This theory has to overcome the difficulty that the destroyers are supported by the producers in the sense that the producers provide the food and other necessary commodities which the destroyers need in order to be able to live. At this point, perhaps, the concept of the threat might be introduced and the theory put forward that the destroyers are able to compel the producers to feed, clothe, and house them because the destroyers control the means of destruction and, consequently, are able to threaten the producers with further destruction of their beloved products. This essentially would be an exploitation theory. The producers produce a surplus of products beyond what they need to sustain themselves. The destroyers are able to take this surplus away from the producers and sustain themselves with it, and because they can sustain themselves, they can produce the means of destruction by which they can coerce the producers into yielding up a certain proportion of their produce. This has all the elements of a stable social system, and our alien observer would clearly be inching toward the truth.

Closer investigation, however, would undermine the simple exploitation theory. It would be observed, for instance, that the producers and the destroyers were not, in fact, independent social species. At times, large numbers of producers join the destroyers' organization; and at other times, large numbers of destroyers go back to being producers. The person from outer space would observe, moreover, that on frequent occasions, the destroyers receive praise and adulation from the producers. He would observe that even though the support of the destroyers comes, on the whole, from the quasi-coercive institution known as taxation, the organization which coerces the producers into paying taxes is usually not part of the organization of the destroyers. The police and the courts, that is to say, are not part of the military organization. Now our observer would begin to perceive that the social heterogeneity of the human race cuts across the more obvious distinction between destroyers and producers. A microscopic examination of the world social system would reveal the existence of nations and national boundaries, entities which are, of course, quite invisible even from the height of five miles.

THE NATION-STATE MODEL

This phenomenon our space visitor might find very puzzling. He would not be able to identify the division of the world into nations with any other division of mankind, for a partition of mankind based on language, skin color, religion, wealth, marriage customs, or any other variable we might mention would not correspond to the partition into nations. Some language areas, for instance, are divided into many nations; some nations have many languages. The same proposition holds for race, religion, or any other characteristic of men or men's culture that we might like to mention. The division of mankind into nations, therefore, can only be accounted for by a historical process in which there is a strong relationship between the division into nations and the division of the world war industry into separate organizations. If he thinks, as an economist, of the division of the world war industry into "firms," then the armed forces of each nation constitute a firm, and it is these firms which, more than anything else, define a nation. One hesitates to add another word to an already overburdened jargon, but we do need a word relative to the world war industry which corresponds to the concept of the firm in other industries. The word I suggest is "milorg," which is short for *military organization*. The Department of Defense of the United States then takes its place as the largest world milorg, followed closely in size by the milorgs of the Soviet Union and those of Great Britain, France, etc.

THE MILORG

It is interesting now to compare and contrast the milorg with the firm—the firm, that is, in non-war industry as it is generally conceived by economists. There are, of course, many important similarities arising out of the fact that both milorgs and firms are organizations. They both have a hierarchical structure. They both consist of a set of roles tied together by lines of communication. They are both divided into departments and subdepartments. They are both organized internally largely through the device of the budget. They both develop elaborate rules and procedures, but the individuals in these organizations also develop defenses against these rules and procedures, whether these go by the names of soldiering, goldbricking, blat, bribery, and corruption, or more dignifiedly, of informal channels of communication and influence. The financial and accounting procedures of the two organizations are likewise very similar. Each organization, for instance, has a through-put of dollars or other monetary unit. The total budget corresponds roughly to the total receipts; these filter down through the organization through subbudgets and eventually disappear as expenditures. A milorg purchases inputs in much the same way as a firm, with one exception. The firm ordinarily has to purchase labor in the open market, whereas a milorg usually employs conscript labor. This can be thought of, if we like, as a form of taxation in kind; but the fact that the soldier does not usually have the right to quit, as the employee of a firm does, makes for certain very important differences in organization. Many of the images and stereotypes, for instance, that we associate with the word "military" arise out of this characteristic of the milorg. It is an organization which lies somewhere on the continuum between the slave plantation and the free enterprise. The conscript is not quite a slave, because there are elements of consent in conscription as there are in taxation. His freedom, however, is much more limited than that of a free laborer.

In the purchase of other commodities, the milorg is not very different from the firm. The great difference from the economic point of view lies, of course, in the source of the revenue. In the case of the firm, revenue is derived almost entirely from the sale of commodities on the open market; in the case of the milorg, the revenue is derived from a budget allocation from government, financed ultimately from the sources of government revenue, that is, taxation or the creation of money.

MILORGS AS ECONOMIC UNITS

Although the differences between the budget-oriented organization and the market-oriented organization are large, they must not blind us to certain fundamental similarities, even in the acquisition of revenue. Both the milorg and the firm, for instance, have a sales problem. Both have specialized resources devoted to salesmanship. In the case of the firm, of course, the salesman works ultimately with the customer who buys the product. In the case of the milorg, likewise, salesmanship is an important part of the organization. In this case, however, the salesmen consist of the officers who work with the legislators and legislative committees which command the appropriations. There are also public relations officers who work with the general public who pay the taxes. The almost unfailing appearance of some kind of external threat in the news stories just before the appropriations for milorgs are to be passed is a phenomenon strongly related to some things which go on in Madison Avenue. The product which the milorg is selling is a psychological product called national security. Because of its very nature, it is hard to put a price on it, simply because we do not know its quantity. We know pretty well the quantity of money that is expended, but we do not have any very good measure of the quantity of product that is produced.

Another very obvious difference between the milorg and the firm —which may, however, be smaller than it seems—is that the firm is supposed to be a profit-making (and in economics, a profit-maximizing) institution, whereas the milorg is in some sense "nonprofit." The firm is interested in the difference between its total revenue and its total costs in a way that the milorg is not. This difference is unquestionably reflected in the sociological and psychological distinction between the two forms of organization. The milorg is somewhat like a church in the sense that its professional managers, insofar as they are not mere organization men, are in the business not merely for what they can get out of it, but also because they believe in it. There is about the milorg a certain ideology of service which is not complete humbug. The fact that the common euphemism for employment by a milorg is "in the service" reflects a widespread popular image which is, at least not consciously, deceitful. Nevertheless, from a strictly economic point of view, the difference between the nonprofit and the profit organization is very tenuous. Under ideal conditions of perfect competition, all profit organizations are, in fact, nonprofit in the sense that their total revenue is only just adequate to attract the resources which are necessary to keep them in being. Thus, from this point of view, there is no real difference between an efficient milorg and an efficient firm under conditions of perfect competition. Under conditions of monopoly, of course, it is possible for the firm to attract revenues from the sale of its product which are larger than what are necessary to attract the resources which it needs. The same is true, however, of the milorg, which, like the firm, may find itself, and in fact usually does find itself, in a monopoly position. As a result, it is able to extract from society a larger revenue than is strictly necessary to attract the resources which go toward it. This larger revenue, it is true, does not generally go to line the pockets of the entrepreneurs; it is reflected, however, in waste and extravagance and in the exercise of arbitrary power. The efforts of Charles Hitch and other economists to introduce concepts of efficiency and economy into the American milorg are received with as little enthusiasm as the efforts of the anti-trust division of the Department of Justice are received in the large corporation. It can be argued, therefore, that it is only at the psychological and sociological levels that the difference between a profit and a nonprofit organization really shows up, and that from this point of view, the milorg is not different from the large corporation.

THE SOCIAL SYSTEM OF MILORGS

We now come to the most important difference between the milorg and the firm. It is that the main demand for the product of the milorg is provided by the existence of another and competing milorg. Firms compete with each other in the provision of commodities to a common market. Milorgs compete only *against* each other. This, I think, is the source of the real distinction between the world war industry and commercial industry. War industry produces its own demand, which no single commercial industry is able to do. The only justification for the existence of a milorg is the existence of another milorg in some other place. This is not true of any other social organization. It is a unique property of the milorg and of the war industry. We must distinguish the milorg sharply from such institutions as police forces and courts of justice, even though these, like the milorg, are essentially budget-oriented organizations financed out of the revenues of government. A police force is not justified by the existence of a police force in another town, that is, by another institution of the same kind. Rather, it is justified by institutions of a different kind, that is, law violators. The operations of police forces are qualitatively different from those of milorgs; they are engaged in apprehension rather than destruction; they operate on individuals rather than on groups; and they operate as agents of law and, theoretically at least, are not supposed to be concerned with punishment.

In spite of the unique property of self-generation which is characteristic of the demand for the product of the world war industry, the interrelations and competition of milorgs are not wholly unlike the interrelations and competition of firms. We can learn a good deal, therefore, from the model of economic competition and especially from the models of economic oligopoly. Anything like perfect competition among milorgs is virtually impossible because of the essentially spatial nature of their operations. The number of interacting milorgs also is likely to be small in the sense in which that word is used in the theory of economic competition. The actions of one milorg, for instance, will be perceived and will produce reactions in other milorgs. The situation, that is to say, is one of oligopolistic interaction.

I have developed the theory of the interaction of milorgs in some detail in my book *Conflict and Defense*.[1] I will, therefore, summarize in this chapter the basic assumptions, parameters, and re-

[1] New York: Harper & Row, 1962.

sults of this theory as far as possible without the use of diagrams. The basic assumption is that the milorg is producing something called "strength." In the theory this can be left as a loosely defined variable almost like "utility." It must be capable, however, of establishing a dominance relationship at any point in the field. Strength is so defined, that is to say, that if one milorg is stronger than another at any given point in the field, it is said to be dominant. For each milorg, we now postulate a strength function over the field of operation, which is, of course, the geographical field of the world. In our theoretical constructions, we can begin with a homogeneous field, but we can perfectly well put real geography into it. The theory would suggest, for instance, that over the globe we could draw "isovis" lines, that is, contours of equal strength for any given milorg. This strength function depends on the nature of the military techniques and on the amount of economic resources devoted to the milorg itself. In what we might call the classical system of national defense, it is reasonable to postulate a "loss-of-strength gradient." That is to say, the strength of any milorg diminishes as we go away from its home base. The isovis lines will be roughly circular around the central location of the milorg, with the highest contour at the location of the milorg itself. In the simplest model, we suppose that there is some "home strength" at the location of the milorg and that the strength in the field diminishes in a linear fashion as we go away from the central location. This is the great military principle of "the further, the weaker." It arises, of course, because strength, whatever it is, has a certaint cost of transport, just as ordinary commodities have cost of transport. The economist will immediately perceive the analogy between the isovis lines of a milorg and the contours of equal selling price of the firm. In the case of the firm, also, we have the principle of "the further, the weaker." That is, the further from home a firm sells its commodity, the higher the price it must charge in order to return a given price at the mill, and the weaker, therefore, its power to attract customers.

THE PROBLEM OF VIABILITY

If we put two milorgs at different points in the field, we may be able to find a boundary of *equal strength* somewhere between them.

This boundary divides the field, assuming only two milorgs, into two regions, each milorg being stronger than the other in the region in which it lies. If one milorg increases its home strength or diminishes its loss-of-strength gradient, the boundary of equal strength is pushed away from it and toward the other milorg. If this process can go on until the boundary of equal strength actually passes through the location of the other milorg, the latter is no longer *unconditionally viable*. That is to say, the first milorg, if it wishes, can eliminate the second milorg altogether. If the second milorg continues to exist, it does so in a state which I call "conditional viability." We now introduce the concept of maximum home strength of the milorg in the simple case of a constant loss-of-power gradient. We could make the concept more complex and talk about a significant maximum of the whole-strength function, meaning by this the strength function over the field which will permit the largest area of domination under given conditions of the other milorgs. The maximum home-strength concept is closely analogous to the concept of minimum average cost in the theory of the firm and interactions of firms. Just as there is some average revenue of the firm below which it cannot go without endangering its existence, so there is some maximum home strength of the milorg which it can extract from the society which pays for it and which is a function, although perhaps a complicated one, of the gross national product of that society and of its demand for strength.

We can now raise the very important question as to how many milorgs can exist in a given field like that of the earth in a condition of mutual unconditional viability. We find that the absolute level of the maximum home strength is virtually irrelevant in this problem. The number of milorgs that can co-exist in the above sense depends upon two parameters of a system. The first might be called the range of critical dominance; the second is the loss-of-power gradient itself. The range of critical dominance is that distance beyond its home base which the milorg must be able to dominate if it is to be secure. This is clearly a function of the range of the deadliest missile. Each milorg, if it is to have unconditional viability, must be able to dominate not only its own "heartland," that is, the area from which it draws its economic support; it must be able to dominate an area beyond this equal to the range of the deadly missile. When the range of the deadly missile was a few yards, in the case of the spear and the slingshot, the walled city was at least a moderately adequate defense against it and the city-state was viable. Even the city-state, however, could not really build a wall around the country that fed it, and it lost its unconditional viability as early as the days of Alexander, though in times of general political disorganization it tended to revive. The use of firearms, however, finished it, just as firearms also made obsolete the feudal baron in his castle.

PROBLEMS OF SIZE AND HETEROGENEITY

The problem is further complicated, like the corresponding problem of the number of firms that can co-exist in a given market, by the phenomenon of nonconstant returns to scale. In the case of the firm, we know that one of the principal conditions for the co-existence of large numbers of small firms is that diminishing returns to scale should set in while the enterprise is still small. If there are economies of scale over a long range of expanding size, then nothing can prevent the large firms from gobbling up small ones; and a situation emerges with a few large firms or even a single monopolist. The problem of returns to scale of the milorg, therefore, is important but also very difficult. Up to a point it is clear that the home strength depends upon the size of the nation which supports the milorg. Big countries are almost *ipso facto* stronger than small ones, at least at home. There are, however, diseconomies of scale as well as economies; beyond some point, these will tend to dominate. We see this, particularly in the milorg, in the phenomenon of social heterogeneity. A nation, for instance, by putting a lot of its resources into its milorg, may acquire an empire. The empire, however, can be as much a source of weakness as of strength. The energies of the milorg are diverted to the threat of internal war and to keeping down the dissident minorities. Austria-Hungary was perhaps a good case in point, for the very size and heterogeneity of the imperial domain made for weakness rather than for strength.

There is a somewhat parallel problem in the theory of the firm in regard to the heterogeneity of its output. As long as the firm sticks to a single commodity or a small group of commodities, its expansion is sharply limited by the difficulties of expanding into the market in the face of the competition of other firms. The firm can nearly always expand, however, by increasing the number of commodities which it produces. Yet, as it does so, it becomes more heterogeneous in its organization, and it loses some of the advantages of organizational specialization. For any given firm, we can postulate an optimum degree of heterogeneity of product. Thus, a steel firm does not generally produce powder puffs, and the milliner does not sell pots and pans. It seems almost as if among the members of any organizational species we get much the same distribution of internal heterogeneity. Thus, among the churches, we find very homogeneous groups like Jehovah's Witnesses, analogous to the one-product firm; at the other extreme, we get the Episcopal church, which produces a wide variety of spiritual products. Among nations, likewise, we get sprawling, heterogeneous agglomerations like the Soviet Union or India; and at the other extreme, we have tight little countries like Norway, with a very homogeneous population and culture.

BREAKDOWN OF UNCONDITIONAL VIABILITY

The above theory of a milorg, sketchy as it is, throws a great deal of light on the nature of the present world crisis. It is my contention that what we are now facing is a fundamental breakdown in the "classical" system of national defense, in which the milorgs of the various nations were, for periods of time at any rate, unconditionally viable. The classical theory of national defense is not wholly unlike the classical economic theory of competition. We postulate a number of nation-states and milorgs large enough and independent enough so that any one nation can regard the field in which it operates as relatively constant. It is true that the geographical structure of the interaction of the milorgs prevents even an approximation to the simple model of perfect competition. At best, we have imperfect competition; the classical balance-of-power system is analogous to the theory of interaction of firms under conditions of monopolistic competition. An increase in the home strength, for instance, does not result in an indefinite expansion of the area of dominance, just as a price cut under monopolistic competition does not give the firm the whole market. The analogy, however, is with monopolistic competition, not with oligopoly or duopoly. The system has inefficiencies which, again, are closely parallel to the inefficiencies of firms under monopolistic competition, but it is not necessarily an unstable system. Under monopolistic competition, as we know, there may be, in some sense, too many firms, and each of them may be a little too small. There is also likely to be a waste of resources on selling cost, which is strictly analogous to expenditure on the war industry. The situation is bearable, however, and it can be argued that there are certain social benefits of monopolistic competition either in the firm or in the milorg, which justify the social costs involved. A superfluity of gas stations is a certain insurance against running out of gas, and a superfluity of brands at least gives us an illusion of choice. Similarly, under conditions of classical national defense, the expenditure on the milorgs may be counter-balanced by certain gains in cultural heterogeneity and variety and in the reduction of internal political problems to a manageable scale. The jumble of gas stations on the old road may be preferred to the slick monotony of the turnpike; and a world of costly little countries, to the cheap uniform grayness of a world-state.

Whatever the costs and benefits of the classical system of national defense, however, it represents a system which is no longer available to the developed world. The dynamic of technical change has destroyed it, both the technical change in weapons and in means of transportation and the technical change in organization. It is highly probable, for instance, that no nation, not even the United States or the Soviet Union, is now unconditionally viable. The range of the deadly missile is now rapidly approaching 12,500 miles. This is the end of an era, on this planet at least. The significant range of the deadly missile cannot go beyond half the circumference of the earth. This means, however, that no nation can now hope to dominate an area around it sufficient to make it unconditionally viable. We have got to learn to live with conditional viability if we are to live at all. That is, we are moving into a situation in which almost any nation can destroy any other, and in which all must refrain from exercising this power.

For some weapons systems, the loss-of-strength gradient now

seems to have become negative; that is, we are stronger away from home than we are at home. This is a fantastic revolution in competitive relationships, and it destroys the whole concept of national defense. It replaces it by a system which has practically no analogue in economic life. This is the system of mutual deterrence. It is a system with which mankind has had very little experience. Perhaps the closest analogy was the cowboy era in personal relationships, after the invention of the Colt revolver. We have many examples of one-sided deterrence in social life, in the relations, for instance, of parent and child, or of police and criminal. The parent makes use of the threat in order to achieve compliance on the part of the child, and society presumably uses the threat of punishment in order to control criminal activities. Even in these cases, a certain ineffectiveness of the system may be traced to the fact that it tends to slip over to two-sided deterrence. The child soon learns that it can use threats, too, and the threat of the parent to spank is often counterbalanced by the threat of the child to throw a tantrum. There is need for a much more thorough theoretical examination of social systems of this kind than they have hitherto received. The economist must confess, however, at this point, that economic theory does not seem to have much comparative advantage, although some insights may be derived from regarding the exchange of threats as analogous to the exchange of negative commodities. The analogy, however, is not a close one, and it should not be pushed far. Exchange is successful insofar as it is done; deterrence is successful only insofar as something is *not* done. A threat that has to be carried out has failed just as much as a threat that failed to deter the behavior that it was supposed to inhibit.

DECLINING VALUE OF EXPLOITATION

The international and military situation is made almost unbearably complex by the fact that the milorg now produces a great variety of weapons and of means of destruction—the variety extending both to range and to destructive power. Consequently, at one level of weaponry, the interaction system may be undergoing radical change, whereas at another level it may not. What we have here, therefore, is a complex pattern of overlaid systems at different levels. It is this complexity, I suspect, which accounts for the paradoxical situation in the world of today. We have, on the one hand, the disappearance of unconditional military viability, even for the largest nations, as a result of the development of intercontinental ballistics missiles (ICBM's) and nuclear warheads; and at the other end, we find the disintegration of empire and a large increase in the number of small, independent countries. The disintegration of empire is a phenomenon with perhaps more of an economic than a military base. The new independent countries which have arisen as a result of the disintegration of empire are certainly not viable in a military sense against the advanced powers. Their existence results from the revolution in the payoff system in economic, political, and military activity which the applications of science and technology have produced. One can express this dramatically by saying that in the twentieth century, one can get a hundred dollars out of nature for every dollar one can squeeze out of an exploited man. The rate of return on exploitation as a use of resources, therefore, has fallen very much below the rate of return on productive use of resources in the application of scientific technology. The payoffs of empire, therefore, have been radically reduced in a relative sense and the payoffs of the milorg likewise. From the sixteenth to the eighteenth century, it is quite likely that empire paid off to the imperial power. That is, investment in the milorg in the beginnings of modern military technology paid off when used against a people that did not possess this technology, in spite of the occasional competition between the milorgs of the advanced powers. A turning point occurred sometime in the nineteenth century, after which imperialism no longer paid off. The most casual inspection of the per capita incomes of European countries, for instance, illustrates the proposition that in the twentieth century, at least, the people who did best were those who stayed home and minded their own business. The Swiss and the Swedes did very well; the Portuguese, with the largest per capita empire, have the lowest per capita income in Europe. The flight from empire, therefore, which is so characteristic of the twentieth century, is not unconnected with this profound shift in the payoff, and it is not necessarily connected with the change in military viability.

ECONOMIC VALUE OF DISARMAMENT

The implication of all this analysis is that disarmament is now no longer a dream of the idealist, but has become a matter of intense practical concern. It represents a social system with very large payoffs, a system which is difficult to achieve, but in which the payoffs are so large that it is well worth devoting major resources to the end of achieving them. This is why a discussion of the economic consequences of disarmament is something more than playing with pipe dreams. It is one small step in a long intellectual process. The fact that the economic consequences of disarmament for the United States, for instance, might be calamitous if the transition were not handled wisely is one small obstacle on the path that leads to a much better state of the world than we have now. Even though a very large stone blocks the entrance to the path, in the shape of the world bargaining problem and the extreme difficulty of achieving a world social contract under present conditions, it is important to work on the path as a whole and to gain experience in removing those obstacles that at least we know how to remove. The main competence of economics lies in the field of the other chapters of this volume, that is, in discussing the economic consequences of disarmament. Even in the discussion of the actual achievement of disarmament, however, the economist has something to say, though the achievement of disarmament is rightly regarded as a political and psychological rather than an economic problem. It is, however, a problem in which bargaining is a prominent system element, and insofar as this is the case, the economist has a contribution. I propose to devote the remainder of this paper, therefore, to a discussion of the bargaining problem in the achievement of disarmament in the light of the economic theory of bargaining.

BARGAINING FOR DISARMAMENT

A bargaining system is possible when there are two states of the world: A, the actual state, and B, a potential or possible state in which the total net payoffs or returns, after deducting the costs of making the transition from A to B, are larger than those in A. It is possible, therefore, in state B for all the parties to the system to be better off than they are in state A. The payoffs here, of course, have to be measured in some kind of utility or generalized unit of value. The only test that is necessary is that all the parties should be better off in their own estimation in state B than they are in state A. If, now, there were only one state such as B, there would not really be a bargaining problem, because there would be no problem of agreement. Each party would do the thing which is necessary in order to get the total system from A to B, and all parties would be better off. The bargaining situation arises when there is not a single B situation but a number of them: B1, B2, B3, etc., each of which conforms to the property that all parties are better off in it, but in which the distribution of the gain differs from situation to situation. Thus, in B1, Party I may have a large gain and Party II a small gain, whereas in state B2, Party I may have a small gain and Party II a large gain. Under these circumstances, in the absence of agreement, Party I may act so as to produce a state B1, and Party II may act so as to produce state B2. The net result of these actions might easily be a state C, in which the parties are worse off than before. Under these circumstances, agreement is necessary in order to move from A to one of the B's, and there may therefore be a failure to reach any of the B's because of difficulty of deciding which one to agree upon.

The dilemma of disarmament is illustrated in the matrix of Figure 1. It is a situation familiar in game theory under the title of "The Prisoner's Dilemma." Suppose we simply have two countries, which we call Column and Row. Each may either arm or disarm, giving us four possibilities corresponding to the four boxes of the diagram. In each of the boxes we put two figures, representing the payoffs to the two countries, the first figure being Column's payoff and the second figure, Row's payoff. We see that if both arm, the payoffs are −1 to each, the total, −2, being the cost of the armaments. If both disarm, the payoffs are +1 to each, this being the economic benefit of the resources released from the arms industry. If one arms and the other disarms, the total payoff is zero, but the distribution is heavily in favor of the one that arms; thus if Column arms and Row disarms, Column is able to extract 2 from Row whose payoff, then is −2. Similarly, if Row arms and Column disarms, Row can get a payoff of +2; Column is left with −2. Under these circumstances, the direction of movement is shown by the arrows. If Column is armed and Row is disarmed, it will pay Row to arm, even though this diminishes the total payoff to both parties. Similarly, if Column is disarmed and Row is armed, it will pay Column to arm. The lower right-hand box, therefore, where the total payoff is largest, is unstable under conditions of nearsighted

FIGURE 1 – THE DILEMMA OF DISARMAMENT

COLUMN

	ARM	DISARM
ROW ARM	−1, −1 ◄──── −2, 2
DISARM	2, −2 ◄──── 1, 1

unilateral action. The two parties always end up in the top left-hand corner, where both are worse off than they could be in the bottom right-hand corner.

There are several possible solutions to this problem. The simplest solution, which is not, unfortunately, always feasible, is that of mutual longsightedness. The movement from the bottom right-hand corner to the top left-hand corner always takes place as a result of shortsightedness. Starting from mutual disarmament, if one party arms, he will be benefited only if the other party does not arm. If he is longsighted, however, he will realize that the other party will react to his action, and he will, therefore, refrain from making it. This is, in fact, not an uncommon situation in human relations. Tacit agreements not to take the first step are highly characteristic of many human situations. The stability of prices under oligopoly, for instance, even in the absence of any formal agreement, is recognition of the fact that though the price-cutter may benefit temporarily, the cut in prices which provokes retaliation will end up with all parties being worse off than they were before. There is great need for empirical analysis of situations of this kind, both historically and experimentally. We need to explore in particular the psychological origins of longsightedness, especially why longsightedness seems to be so much scarcer in international relations than it is in domestic relations.

Another possible solution to the dilemma is an agreement to set up an organization to change the payoffs. What this means, in effect, is that we penalize shortsightedness. In effect, this is what we do when we set up a police system. Suppose, for instance, that in the figure, we replace arm by "dishonest" and disarm by "honest." If both parties are honest, the payoffs are clearly greater to both than if both are dishonest. On the other hand, if one is dishonest and the other is honest, the dishonest may make a relative gain at the expense of the honest. We now use the gains of mutual honesty to set up an organization which will diminish the payoffs of one-sided dishonesty and so discourage shortsightedness. It is perhaps the absence of any such organization in international relations which makes the achievement of mutual disarmament difficult in spite of the mutual gain.

CHANGING THE PAYOFFS

Agreement to change the payoffs of unilateral action is a special case of a general problem in the theory of bargaining, known in the theory of games under the heading of side payments, in welfare economics as compensation payments, and in ordinary speech as bribery. The general form of the system is one in which it is possible to move from A, where we are now, to a position, C, where the total payoffs are larger than they are at A, but where some of the parties are worse off at C than they are at A. Under these circumstances, it should be possible to move from C to a position, B, in which all parties are better off than they are at A, by making side payments, that is, by having those who are better off in situation C bribe those who are worse off and so move in effect to B. This is a system which is peculiarly beset by emotional involvements. There is, for instance, a strong moral prejudice against side payments as reflected by the very reaction which the word bribery evokes. The sentiment "millions for defense but not a penny for tribute" seldom fails to stir a positive response. These non-economic elements of the situation must be neglected in this paper.

It may be, of course, that the side-payment problem can be reduced ultimately to the general problem of selection among the various B's. If the route to one of the B's lies through a C-state, this simply differentiates it from the other B's. In that case, the major problem of bargaining then becomes the selection of a B on which all the relevant parties can agree. Under these circumstances, T. C. Schelling, of the Harvard Center for International Affairs, has pointed to the great importance of "salient solutions." A salient solution is one which exhibits some characteristic, not related to the distribution of payoffs, which differentiates it sharply from the others, and especially from those that surround it. The 50-50 split is a good example of a salient solution which may be accepted by both parties not because it is necessarily "just" but simply because it is salient, in the sense that it possesses a property of symmetry which no other division possesses. If we are trying to decide, for instance, between a 45-55 split and a 46-54 split, there is no sharp differentiation between these two solutions. As between, however, a 49-51 split and a 50-50 split, there is a clear distinction in symmetry.

The fact that symmetry may have nothing to do with the bargain may make it all the more important as a condition of saliency. This is why total disarmament is a more attractive solution than partial disarmament. Zero-zero has a saliency which no other combination of figures possesses. Similarly, total nuclear disarmament has a saliency which partial disarmament lacks, even though small-scale nuclear weapons may not be fundamentally different from conventional weapons in their range and destructive power. The fact that poison gas was not used at all in the Second World War is an example perhaps of saliency of the 0-0 solution at the level of tacit agreement—that is, longsightedness in the sense of Figure 1. Another good example is the extraordinary stability of the disarmament of the United States–Canadian frontier, which has persisted now for more than a hundred years and was achieved long before the final political settlement.

POWER, COSTS, AND PAYOFFS

One of the problems involved in general and complete disarmament is the redistribution of power which this would entail. It is clear, for instance, that general and complete disarmament would lessen the relative power of the large countries. If these countries, then, are to accept general and complete disarmament, there must be some form of compensating payment. Part of the price, for instance, might be the readjustment of voting power in the United Nations by giving the large countries more voting power rather than a veto. Another problem in compensation is, of course, the compensation of military personnel and specialized war-related resource owners for the personal costs of conversion to peacetime uses. It is clear that keeping the whole war industry in sheer idleness would entail no real additional cost to the world, and we could therefore afford to compensate military personnel generously out of the economic savings of disarmament. Such compensation should be included in any disarmament proposal.

The critical problem here, however, on which very little work has been done is the functional relation between power and pay-offs. If, for instance, there is a redistribution of power under disarmament away from the large countries toward the small ones, what does this really mean for the inhabitants of these countries? Would the people of the United States, for instance, be any worse off if the United States were not a great power? There has been no general attempt to compute the costs and returns of the investment involved in becoming a great power. Perhaps such calculations are impossible, although the theoretical problems involved, at any rate, can be thoroughly explored. The milorg is one last refuge of the sacred in modern society. We have reduced religion to a consumer good, and thereby largely drawn its sting at the same time that we have preserved its benefits. It would be interesting to treat sovereignty and national power likewise. One suspects that the pay-offs on investments in national power are very low, and that once people realize this, there will be radical changes in their attitude. If we can get abroad the notion that we might seek an optimum degree of power rather than a maximum degree of power, this in itself would be a powerful solvent of some of our present difficulties.

DISARMAMENT AND IDEOLOGY

Another bargaining problem involved in disarmament which has economic overtones is that of the impact of disarmament on the ideological struggle. General and complete disarmament—that is, the abolition of war as an organized institution—involves the transfer of conflict into other arenas. The willingness of the parties involved to make this transfer depends to a considerable extent, therefore, on their image of their own ability to conduct existing conflicts on a different basis. Thus, the end of the religious wars in the seventeenth century did not mean the cessation of religious conflict. It merely meant its transfer to political and psychological arenas. If one party to a conflict feels that its chance for survival is severely diminished by the transfer of conflict to a nonviolent arena, the willingness of this party to abandon violence is likely to be low. Part of the present difficulty unquestionably arises out of the lack of confidence of the West in its own competence in the ideological struggle. The Russian advocacy of general and complete disarmament depends in no small measure on the Russians' belief that in a disarmed world they would have the advantage in the ideological struggle. They believe, rightly or wrongly, that they have the key to history and that they understand the inner dynamics of any society. What they mean, therefore, by peaceful co-existence is that we all disarm militarily, so that no one can intervene by violence in the internal affairs of any society, and then the sheer logic of the internal development of all societies will bring them eventually into the Communist camp. If nobody cuts down the tree, all the apples will eventually fall into their basket. The fact that they are, to my mind at least, quite wrong in this image of the future does not prevent it from being a powerful determinant of their present actions. The West, on the other hand, is less self-confident about its own ability to manage the future. The conservatives, at any rate, have a sneaking suspicion that the Communists are right and that, therefore, the only way to preserve the values of the West is by maintaining the system of violence. I happen to think that the West is wrong about this, too; but here again a false belief is an important determinant of action. The price of peaceful co-existence and of disarmament in the present world is clearly the better organization of the ideological struggle, to the point where each side feels that it has about an equal chance of winning in the absence of violent intervention. The situation is further complicated by the use of quasi-war by the Communists—guerrilla bands, terror, assassination, and so on—and by the increasing advocacy by the West of the use of these paramilitary methods.

BARGAINERS AND BENEFICIARIES

A feature which plagues this as well as most other social bargaining situations is that the beneficiaries of the bargain are not the same as the parties to the bargain. The people who are most affected by a bargain are seldom represented at the bargaining table. We see this in collective bargaining in industrial relations, where the labor bargain is frequently made at the expense of the consumer, who is not represented at the table by anyone. Similarly, in disarmament negotiations, the people who really stand to benefit by disarmament —the ordinary people of the world—are not directly represented, or are represented only in the dim moral consciousness of the representatives of governments, whereas the people who may be injured by disarmament—especially the professional military people who may have their specialized skills rendered useless—are well organized and well represented at the bargaining table. Under these circumstances, the world's failure to achieve the disarmament bargain is not surprising. It is a striking testimony to the power of the underlying drive toward the ultimate payoffs of disarmament that in spite of two world wars, the hypocrisy of governments, and the weighting of the bargaining organization so strongly against it, the movement toward disarmament refuses to die. Experience also points up the fact, however, that before a bargain can be reached —before, that is, a B-situation can be reached from the inferior A-situation—a preliminary bargain must be reached regarding organization and procedure. We have not paid enough attention in economics or in irenics to these preliminary bargains for organization. It is often more important to bargain for organization than for agreement.

CLUES FROM HISTORY

Another of the elements which must be brought into this very complex situation is the possibility of mutual unilateral action and interaction, leading to disarmament as well as to arms races. We must not think that everything that happens in the world happens as the result of an agreement. Most of the things that happen, happen as a result of the interaction of unilateral actions. A good example of this in the disarmament field is the gradual establishment of personal disarmament. There was a time when all gentlemen carried swords; there was another time in the West when large numbers of people carried guns. Over large parts of the world today, this is rare, and we have established a society in which personal disarmament is the rule. Most people have never owned a weapon, would not know what to do with one, and yet have never been subjected to the slightest inconvenience because of this lack even though some people do have weapons and occasionally use them for armed assault. On the whole, in our society, we do not use violence or even the threat of violence in interpersonal relations. Our conflicts at the interpersonal level are carried on by more subtle, but not necessarily less powerful, means. Personal disarmament, however, was not achieved by agreement. Indeed, there *is* no such agreement. The American constitution explicitly provides against it, and one of the treasured rights of the American citizen is the right to bear arms. Personal disarmament, therefore, has been achieved wholly by unilateral action. A careful study of this process is badly needed. Economic theory can perhaps throw some light on it, although not very much. The closest analogue that we have to this phenomenon in economics is the interaction of firms and the development of what look like tacit agreements through mutual interactions of unilateral behavior. We have an analogy also in the phenomenon of the withdrawal of competition from one field to another. In the case of the firm, for instance, we frequently find that price competition is abjured, not by any formal agreement but because of mutual farsightedness; and some other form of competition—for instance, competition in selling costs—is substituted, the effects of which are more diffuse and seem less likely to lead to an interactive process of mutual impoverishment. We are beginning to find something of the same process in international economic policies. The "beggar-my-neighbor" policies which were unquestioned in the twenties and thirties at least call for a raising of eyebrows now. It is at least not absurd to hope that processes of this kind may operate in military relations. Here again, however, the crucial problem is a deep ignorance of the functional relation between power and payoffs. What, for instance, are the costs and benefits of unilateral disarmament? This we simply do not know. Because we do not know, we reject the whole concept because of our fear of the unknown. In a nuclear age, however, there is a strong case for unilateral disarmament, as there was a case for personal disarmament in the age of the Colt. A system of deterrence has a positive probability built into it of disaster for the deterrer as well as the deterree. Under these circumstances, a decision to remove oneself from the system altogether and to operate in another arena is possible and may well be profitable. The sacred and quasi-religious aspects of the milorg, however, have prevented us from making what essentially are economic studies of this kind.

THE ECONOMIST'S ROLE

As Hitch and McKean say in their brilliant work on *The Economics of Defense in the Nuclear Age,*[2] economics is a way of looking at things rather than a set of precise answers. One may criticize Hitch and McKean on the grounds that they have looked at the problem of national defense too much as if it were still analogous to monopolistic competition, whereas, in fact, it is now like oligopoly or even duopoly—a very different kind of system and a much more unstable one. The economic way of looking at things, however, is a powerful corrosive of the sacred aspects of military policy. It will undoubtedly produce explosive reactions from the defenders of the sacred. The economist may be painted as a man who will barter away such things as honor, integrity, sovereignty, power, glory, and all the other sacred aspects of military systems. There is some point in these criticisms. The economist is not necessarily an enemy of the sacred, nor is his way of looking at things the only way. There is a place for the heroic as well as for the economic aspects of life. Nevertheless, when the heroic and sacred aspects of life threaten to destroy us, as they do at present, it is time for the grubby hand of the economist to signal a halt. The very fact that we are examining in this volume the economics of disarmament therefore is significant. Even though this is a highly complex social system, which involves many noneconomic elements, the contribution of the economist to its understanding and to its transformation is an important one.

2 Cambridge, Mass.: Harvard University Press, 1960.

2

The Disarmament Model

Emile Benoit*

Before projecting disarmament impact or discussing economic adjustments to it, we need to know what we mean by disarmament and what would be its concrete economic contents. The present chapter is devoted to providing and explaining a particular disarmament "model" developed in the READ program (Research Program on Economic Adjustments to Disarmament). Most of the following chapters have utilized this model, or something close to it, as a starting point for their analyses. The reader would be well advised to bear in mind the extent to which a different set of disarmament assumptions might affect the conclusions about economic impacts and adjustment policies.

THE CONCEPT OF DISARMAMENT

In the last few years, the term disarmament has, in some quarters, been largely supplanted by the term "arms control." The latter may

* EMILE BENOIT is Professor of International Business in the Graduate School of Business, Columbia University, and consultant to the United States Arms Control and Disarmament Agency. Formerly attaché to the United States Embassies in London and Vienna, he is the author of *Europe at Sixes and Sevens*. The statistical estimates in this chapter were prepared with the assistance of Mary Painter.

be broadly defined as comprising international agreements to stabilize or limit armaments by changing their composition or deployment or inhibiting their further development, in order to reduce the likelihood of accidental or unintended wars or to limit the scope or destructive effects of war.

While disarmament is sometimes viewed as a type of arms control, we shall regard it here as essentially an alternative, since it aims not to reduce the likelihood or severity of war, but to render it impossible. Under some circumstances, arms control may involve an increase in national military capabilities and, as Professor Schelling and others have demonstrated, an increase in defense expenditures.[1] Disarmament, on the other hand, under almost any realistic assumptions, implies a major reduction in national military capabilities *and* defense expenditures, leaving only residual, minimal, or purely defensive capabilities in national hands.

I believe it is helpful to distinguish three major types of disarmament, which I have entitled unilateral, bilateral, and multilateral disarmament. The first of these, "unilateral disarmament," involves major reductions in national military capabilities without conditions as to reciprocation by other national forces—though perhaps in the hope that such reciprocation will occur. Unilateral disarmament has little political support at this time, although the United States and other countries have, in the past, practiced substantial, if partial, unilateral reductions in military capabilities as a matter of expediency, and without renouncing their freedom to expand them again if it should prove necessary. A second variety is what I call "bilateral disarmament." This involves the agreed, balanced reduction of forces, as between potential combatants, in

---

[1] See T. C. Schelling and M. H. Halperin, *Strategy and Arms Control,* New York: Twentieth Century Fund, 1961, Chapter XI, "The Arms Budget and the Economy." Doris Ikle's paper *How Arms Control Would Affect the National Security Budget,* Santa Monica, Calif.: RAND Corporation, 1961, came to the same conclusions. The rationale is essentially that the high cost of inspection of a limited arms reduction and change-of-arms pattern, plus the possible need to increase the expenditure on low-yield weapons as certain high-yield and relatively efficient weapons were being cut back for arms control purposes, would involve a net increase in over-all expenditure.

such manner as to leave their relative capabilities unchanged, and to leave open (physically, if not legally or morally) the possibility of rearmament by one or both of the protagonists. A third variety is what I call "multilateral disarmament": this involves the establishment of a supranational authority endowed with preponderant force to inspect national compliance with the agreed reductions of national forces and gradually to take over the responsibility for preserving the security of the disarming nations by enforcing agreed restrictions against rearmament and direct and indirect aggression.

We have built our model on the multilateral disarmament concept, which is one of "general and complete" disarmament, with comprehensive and universal reductions of national armaments down to severely limited and essentially defensive capabilities, along with the building up of a supranational peace agency with fully adequate inspection, police, and deterrent capabilities. This model is broadly consistent with the U.S. outline of a draft treaty on general and complete disarmament in a peaceful world presented at Geneva in 1962, although the supranational features in the official program have as yet been little spelled out. Our model clearly implies the progressive abandonment of national capabilities for exercising force in international disputes and the transfer of such force to a world authority capable of settling international disputes by a rule of law, based on pre-existing agreements, and imposing such settlements by force if necessary.[2]

POLITICAL AND MILITARY STEPS TOWARD DISARMAMENT

The politico-military steps included in our disarmament model are shown in Table 1, pp. 32–33. They should be regarded as provisional and hypothetical. While they are, as indicated, broadly consistent with the official United States disarmament proposal, they

[2] This would not necessarily involve what is usually thought of as "world government." What it would involve is not easy to foresee. Some novel suggestions were outlined in this author's "An American Foreign Policy for Survival," *Ethics, International Journal of Social, Political and Legal Philosophy,* July 1946, and in "The Conditions of Disarmament," *Antioch Review,* Fall 1955. These concepts will be further developed in a book, now in preparation.

show divergences on some points and are far more specific than the government's proposals on others. While they have benefited from some discussions with government defense experts, they are solely the responsibility of the author.

The reader should bear in mind that many of the specific provisions mentioned, including some which are of the greatest military and political importance, have little economic significance, but have been included primarily to give the reader a sense of the context in which the economically significant elements fit. This is true, for example, of the provisions for the destruction of weapons or their transfer to the international disarmament organization (IDO). Such measures do not affect the economic impact of disarmament. Only the cessation of national production, research, construction, etc., or a reduction of employment in national defense forces or civilian defense personnel, or the increase in national contributions to world security forces have *economic* significance. Thus, the reader may disagree about the desirability of some of the controversial military measures in the model, without finding the model any less useful for purposes of economic analysis of disarmament impacts.

The above model is based on certain broad politico-military assumptions, which must now be summarily stated, although space is lacking for a detailed discussion of their rationale.[3]

1. It would not be politically and administratively feasible to negotiate and ratify a sound disarmament agreement before 1965, nor fully to implement it—including the necessary supranational inspection and control system—in less than a dozen years after that.[4] Some further build-up in national forces is likely until a definite agreement on disarmament is reached.

---

[3] These could be fully understood only in relation to a particular theory of disarmament—currently under elaboration.

[4] As Schelling has observed, under the highly unstable conditions of "reciprocal fear of surprise attack," a crash disarmament might become necessary to avoid a war (a war in which each side would, as one might say, "try to retaliate first"). In the event of such a traumatic experience, the economic difficulties would seem trivial by comparison. On the other hand, the deliberate choice of a crash disarmament tempo to minimize the problem of safe inspection and balance by practically eliminating the transi-

TABLE 1 – DISARMAMENT MODEL: POLITICO-MILITARY MEASURES

(Model of general and complete disarmament as developed by READ)

	STAGE I: 1965–68	STAGE II: 1968–71	STAGE IIIA: 1971–74	STAGE IIIB: 1974–77
U.S. DEFENSE FORCES REDUCED	From 3.0 to 2.5 million	From 2.5 to 2.0 million	From 2.0 to 1.0 million	From 1.0 to 0.5 million
CUTOFFS IN NATIONAL PRODUCTION OF	"Soft" strategic delivery systems, e.g., bombers, liquid fuel rockets in unhardened bases, etc., tactical nuclear weapons	"Hard" strategic delivery systems; nuclear fuel	Conventional weapons, except spare parts and replacements	Unconventional weapons, e.g., chemical, biological, radiological warfare matériel, etc.; "dangerous" R&D—development of new weapon concepts, etc.
CUTBACKS IN NATIONAL INVENTORIES		50 per cent cut in "soft" strategic delivery vehicles and systems; one-half destroyed, one-half stockpiled for destruction in Stage IIIA	75 per cent cut in conventional weapons, of which one-third destroyed, one-third stockpiled for destruction in Stage IIIB, one-third transferred to IPF; remaining "soft" strategic delivery systems destroyed; all tactical nuclear weapons destroyed	All "hard" strategic delivery vehicles and systems except "reassurance reserve,"[a] e.g., 10 low yield Minuteman or Polaris missiles and delivery systems
BASES	Denuclearization of "soft" foreign bases	Denuclearization of "hard" foreign bases	Transfer to IDO police force (IPF) of foreign bases	Transfer to IDO deterrent force (IDF) of "hard" domestic bases; except "reassurance reserve,"[a] transfer to IPF of 50 per cent of nonnuclear domestic bases

	Stage 1	Stage 2	Stage 3	Stage 4
INSPECTION MEASURES	Test ban inspection; Inspection of missile launching pads; surprise attack inspection—all with bilateral or UN inspection	Transfer of national inspection functions (except secret intelligence) to IDO inspection force (IIF)		IDO research and development group (IRD) maintains inventory and inspection of national research and development
ARMS UTILIZATION AGREEMENTS ON	Nuclear test ban; restrictions on deployment of submarines, carriers, and forward flights of air wings; orbiting weapons	Missile testing; regional or zonal agreements	National withdrawal from tension boundaries	
INTERNATIONAL CONVENTIONS ACCEPTED ON	International Disarmament Organization (IDO); IDO inspection force (IIF)	IDO police force (IPF)	IDO deterrent force (IDF) IDO research and development group (IRD)	
INTERNATIONAL DISARMAMENT ORGANIZATION (IDO) OPERATIONS	IDO administration begins	IDO judiciary; IDO inspection force (IIF) begin	IDO police force (IPF) builds up to 0.5 million men, receives 25 per cent of national stocks of conventional weapons; stationing of IPF along tension boundaries	IPF raised to 1 million; IDO deterrent force (IDF) begins—rises to 0.5 million; receives all "hard" bases and delivery systems from national forces (except "reassurance reserve";a IDO research and development group (IRD) given a monopoly of "dangerous" R&D

a The "reassurance reserve" would be intended to increase willingness to accept GCD by making it unlikely that any attack could be made on the present nuclear powers without heavy sacrifices, but would leave the primary deterrent responsibility to IDO and would not enable any nation to destroy any other nation or to deter the IDO.

2. The United States would bear one-third the costs of the inspection, police, and strategic deterrent functions of an international disarmament organization, which would be given a monopoly of strategic weapons systems and defense research, and would be allowed to do enough inspection to provide a wide margin of assurance against evasion.

3. Cutoffs in weapons production would precede cutbacks in stocks of weapons, and would begin in the first stage.

4. "Soft," "unstable" weapons systems (such as bombers or liquid fuel rockets in unhardened bases), which are difficult to defend, and are useful primarily for first-strike or counterforce purposes, and are hence destabilizing, would have cutoffs before the more stable systems (such as "Minuteman" in reinforced bases and "Polaris").

5. A beginning on manpower cutbacks would be made immediately, and about a third would be cut back in the early stages.

6. The United States armed forces would be reduced to a size below that of 1939, in relation to population, but would retain a significant, if essentially defensive, capability which is too small to destroy another major nation or to deter law-enforcement actions of the international disarmament organization.[5]

7. Expenditures for inspection are included in national defense expenditures in the first stage, and begin to be included in the costs of the international disarmament organization only in the second stage. By 1965, satellite inspection systems should be sufficiently developed so that bilateral inspection systems and national espio-

---

tion period (as visualized by Melman in Chapter 3) seems highly unlikely to the present author. For this reason, the inspection task appears as larger, more difficult, and more expensive, and the estimated expenditures for this function in our model are considerably higher than those which Melman estimates are necessary for the type of disarmament process he is assuming

[5] The retention of a very few low-yield nuclear weapons by national forces of the existing nuclear powers is a highly controversial feature of this model. The proposal is included largely for psychological reasons, in the interest of improving the chance of acceptance of the disarmament program. It is, however, without any significant economic implications, since no new weapons production is implied. Thus, those who wish to drop this assumption may do so without affecting their response to our economic analysis.

nage operations would suffice for checking compliance on first-stage disarmament measures which involve production cutoffs in those arms that will probably be in excess supply and only minor reductions in defense forces. It is assumed that overkill capacity, by 1965, will be so large that the risk of manufacture of further stocks in contravention of the agreement would not be seriously destabilizing, particularly in view of the fact that they would shortly thereafter have to be destroyed.

THE EXPENDITURE MODEL OF DISARMAMENT

To translate this politico-military disarmament model into an *economic* model, it is necessary to estimate the changes in expenditures involved at each stage and in each category. Creating such a picture of the changes in defense expenditure, by date, and by type of defense purchase, is an essential step in estimating the total economic impact of disarmament and clarifying the adjustment problems it is likely to create.

The disarmament model shown below was first prepared in the READ program and later modified in details in discussion within the Consultant Panel on Economic Impacts of Disarmament to the United States Arms Control and Disarmament Agency (USACDA)—of which I was chairman.[6] The resultant expenditure model of disarmament shown in Table 2 has, of course, no official status, but should be understood as simply the result of private research and discussion.

This model should be viewed as essentially hypothetical and dependent on a particular set of assumptions. It is intended not as a literal forecast, but as a means of illustrating the kind of economic problems to which disarmament would give rise. Many of the essential data required for a true projection are lacking, while others are classified. With respect to certain novel programs

---

[6] Three members of the panel were also READ consultants and are contributors to this book—Marvin Hoffenberg, Murray Weidenbaum, and Richard Nelson. The report of the panel was published by the USACDA under the title *Economic Impacts of Disarmament,* U.S. Arms Control and Disarmament Agency, Economic Series I, Publication 2, January 1962.

(e.g., the cost of supranational inspection and enforcement systems) the range of even expert opinion is extremely wide because of disagreement as to what would be necessary and, also, as to how much it would cost. We have had, therefore, constantly to make simplifying assumptions, to utilize averages where expert opinion varied widely, and to adopt similar common-sense expedients for quantifying a future which is largely unknown. The margin of error in our estimating procedure is, however, probably not as large as those which would be implied by possible altera-

TABLE 2 – DISARMAMENT MODEL: EXPENDITURES

(Billions of 1960 dollars)

			U.S. EXPENDITURES FOR SECURITY AND ASSOCIATED PROGRAMS			
	1960	1965	STAGE I 1965–68	STAGE II 1968–71	STAGE IIIA 1971–74	STAGE IIIB 1974–77
U.S. DEFENSE						
Personnel	11.7	15.1	13.1	11.1	6.7	4.7
Operation and maintenance	10.2	12.6	8.9	6.0	3.9	2.1
Procurement (including R&D)	18.0	20.9	12.2	6.3	4.8	1.5
Aircraft	(6.9)	(6.0)	(2.0)	(0.5)	(0.5)	(0.5)
Missiles	(5.1)	(5.4)	(0.5)	(0.1)	(0.1)	(0.1)
Military space	(0.5)	(2.6)	(4.4)	(2.5)	(2.5)	(0.0)
Ships	(1.9)	(2.4)	(1.5)	(0.2)	(0.2)	(0.2)
Other	(3.6)	(4.5)	(3.8)	(3.0)	(1.5)	(0.7)
Construction	1.6	2.0	0.5	0.2	0.2	0.2
Military assistance program	1.6	2.4	2.0	1.5	0.0	0.0
Military AEC	2.1	1.4	0.5	0.2	0.0	0.0
Civil defense[a]	[b]	1.7	1.7	1.7	1.7	1.7
Total	45.2[c]	56.1	38.9	27.0	17.3	10.2
U.S. CONTRIBUTION TO INTERNATIONAL FUNCTIONS[d]						
Inspection				3.2	2.6	1.3
Police forces					1.8	2.7
Deterrent forces						2.6
Juridical & administrative				0.5	0.5	0.5
Total				3.7	4.9	7.1

TABLE 2 – Continued

	1960	1965	U.S. EXPENDITURES FOR SECURITY AND ASSOCIATED PROGRAMS			
			STAGE I 1965–68	STAGE II 1968–71	STAGE IIIA 1971–74	STAGE IIIB 1974–77
TOTAL U.S. EXPENDITURES ON SECURITY PROGRAMS	45.2	56.1	38.9	30.7	22.2	17.3
ASSOCIATED PROGRAMS						
NASAe	0.4	2.7	4.5	5.9	7.4	8.9
Civilian AECf	0.5	1.4	2.0	2.0	2.0	2.0
Total	0.9	4.1	6.5	7.9	9.4	10.9
GRAND TOTAL	46.1	60.2	45.4	38.6	31.6	28.2

AEC = Atomic Energy Commission.

SOURCE: Defense costs by categories in 1965 level of defense expenditures based on Bureau of the Budget projection in *Special Study* (January 1961); George Steiner, *National Defense and Southern California* 1961–1970, Los Angeles: Southern California Associates of the Committee for Economic Development, 1961—and confidential industry sources. Estimated defense reductions during disarmament based on politico-military assumptions of READ model of general and complete disarmament presented above, applied to estimated defense expenditures in 1965 by major vectors in accordance with the assumed pattern and timing of the disarmament program.

a Civil defense estimates are largely conjectural—based on maximum estimates of the Budget Bureau's *Special Study* (January 1961). Urban evacuation facilities, and decentralized shelters and food stores in the countryside might be viewed as insurance against a possible breakdown in the disarmament process in the early stages and as improving the credibility of the I.D.O. strategic deterrent. The projected impact of disarmament would, however, be unaltered if there were no civil defense program either before or during disarmament.

b Less than $50 million.

c Excluding Revolving Fund.

d The United States contribution to the international disarmament organization is assumed to cover one-third of total costs, but no charge is assumed for existing weapons or bases transferred to the IDO.

e The build-up of the Civilian Space Program before 1965 now appears to be more rapid than originally projected. It is not yet clear, however, whether this implies a more rapid rate of build-up between 1965 and 1977, which is the chief consideration with respect to its economic effects on the disarmament process illustrated in this model (See also note f).

f Including expenditures undertaken on behalf of NASA and sometimes included in published estimates of future space expenditures.

tions in the politico-military assumptions of the model. Our hope is merely that this model gives an essentially correct picture of the character of the economic problems which disarmament on these general assumptions, and at this pace, would create.

On the basis of Table 2, it appears that disarmament on the scale and at the tempo assumed in our model would involve a decline in United States defense expenditure of about $46 billion (in 1960 dollars) of which about $17 billion would occur in the first three years. If allowance is made for the offsets provided by the estimated United States contribution to the international disarmament organization and the planned expansion in civilian space and atomic energy programs, then the net decline would not be more than $32 billion in all, and not more than $5 billion a year even during the crucial introductory three-year period of maximum impact.

EMPLOYMENT MODEL OF DISARMAMENT

Along with the expenditure implications of the model, we may well be independently concerned about its employment characteristics. As a first step in translating the expenditure model into an employment model, we must estimate the manpower requirements, by industry, of each major vector of military end-use. Such an estimate has been prepared for 1965, showing estimated employment in selected industries directly and indirectly created by defense procurement of aircraft, missiles, ships, and other defense items, and by the military aid program, military operation and maintenance, and military construction.[7]

These estimates are based upon an input-output matrix prepared by Wassily W. Leontief and Marvin Hoffenberg for the READ program. The industries covered included those which in 1958 had fifty thousand or more employees directly or indirectly employed in filling military orders. These estimates should be viewed as only first approximations, in view of the limitations of the underlying data. The technical coefficients are based on 1947 data, adjusted in 1952, and further adjusted to take account of

[7] Detailed breakdown in mimeographed form available on request to the author.

some of the technological changes up to 1958. The effects on interindustry relations of the technological changes that have occurred since 1958, and particularly in the missile program, could not be included in the calculations. Moreover, the estimates are based on somewhat oversimplified assumptions about the parallels between changes in defense employment and in defense *expenditure,* although some effort has been made to correct for divergent productivity trends.

Working with these assumptions about the employment content of the defense program, it is possible to estimate the essential changes in employment which would occur in the implementation of a disarmament program such as has been described above. Table 3 presents an employment model, by major industry group, of general and complete disarmament, corresponding to the expenditure model shown in Table 2.

The employment model projects a total of defense-dependent employment of about 7.3 million persons by 1965. This includes over 3 million persons in industry, 3 million persons in the armed forces, and nearly 1.2 million civilian employees of defense agencies. The total projected decline in defense-dependent employment during disarmament is about 6.25 million—about 2.5 million from the armed forces, nearly 1 million civilian employees of defense agencies, and over 2.8 million from defense industry. Of the latter group, about 1.2 million would come from aircraft, missiles, ships, other vehicles and ordnance, and 0.33 million from electrical machinery. Substantial numbers in services, trade, transportation, and other industries would be affected even though they are not directly engaged in the production of military end-products.

It should be made very clear that the projected declines in defense employment are by no means equivalent to a prediction of increases in unemployment. The amounts of unemployment resulting from disarmament will be a function not only of the rate of release of manpower from defense activities, but also of the rate of build-up of demand for other goods and services, as well as of the success achieved in redeploying equipment and manpower to satisfy the new demand. Until we know the magnitude, type, and effectiveness of the adjustment program, we are not in

TABLE 3 – DISARMAMENT MODEL: EMPLOYMENT
(Thousands of persons)

INDUSTRY	DEFENSE-DEPENDENT EMPLOYMENT AS PER CENT OF TOTAL EMPLOYMENT	DEFENSE EMPLOY-MENT 1965	DECREASE IN DEFENSE EMPLOYMENT[a]				
			STAGE I 1965–68	STAGE II 1968–71	STAGE IIIA 1971–74	STAGE IIIB 1974–77	TOTAL
Chemicals	5.3	62.7	23.4	15.1	9.3	8.8	56.6
Fuel & power	7.3	85.8	28.7	20.2	13.4	11.2	73.5
(petroleum)	(10.4)	(51.7)	(15.9)	(11.8)	(9.3)	(6.6)	(43.6)
Primary metals	13.3	198.1	81.5	50.6	22.1	27.4	181.6
(iron & steel)	(9.8)	(90.5)	(35.5)	(23.5)	(11.0)	(11.7)	(81.7)
Fabricated metals	7.9	149.8	53.6	35.2	23.6	20.0	132.4
Nonelectrical machinery	5.2	91.8	29.9	22.2	18.1	12.3	82.5
Electrical machinery	20.9	376.4	126.5	85.3	68.2	61.5	341.5
(radio-communications)	(38.0)	(279.4)	(100.0)	(64.4)	(43.5)	(47.8)	(255.7)
Transportation equipment	38.5	1,302.2	504.7	375.6	145.9	173.1	1,199.3
(aircraft & parts)	(93.7)	(739.4)	(361.5)	(192.9)	(35.9)	(114.8)	(705.1)
(ships & boats)	(60.7)	(238.6)	(87.1)	(123.2)	(4.6)	(2.9)	(217.8)
(ordnance)	(100.0)	(290.6)	(45.3)	(51.8)	(96.8)	(51.6)	(245.5)
Instruments	20.1	66.8	30.5	17.2	4.5	10.9	63.1
Transportation	5.9	128.7	44.6	29.5	18.6	15.9	108.6
(RR & trucking)	(5.4)	(101.1)	(36.6)	(23.3)	(14.2)	(12.1)	(86.2)
Trade	1.4	159.5	60.4	36.3	24.0	16.2	136.9
Service, etc.	1.3	260.3	85.4	59.7	40.0	33.5	218.6
(business services)	(3.8)	(105.1)	(36.5)	(24.9)	(16.5)	(13.3)	(91.2)
(professional & service ind.)	(1.9)	(129.3)	(39.2)	(28.6)	(20.3)	(17.1)	(105.2)
Construction	2.1	81.8	37.2	7.5	0.0	0.0	44.7
Other industries[b]	2.4	228.8	84.8	52.7	31.4	26.4	195.3
Total	5.6	3,192.7	1,191.2	807.1	419.1	417.2	2,834.6

GOVERNMENT							
Armed forces	100.0	3,000.0	500.0	500.0	1,000.0	500.0	2,500.0
Civilian	11.2	1,171.0	327.0	270.0	179.0	178.0	954.0
Total	31.1c	4,171.0	827.0	770.0	1,179.0	678.0	3,454.0
TOTAL INDUSTRY AND GOVERNMENT	5.2	7,363.7	2,018.2	1,577.1	1,598.1	1,095.2	6,288.6

SOURCE: See note a.

a Reductions in employment directly or indirectly dependent on defense activity, implied by the reductions in defense expenditure shown in Table 2, as estimated on the basis of an input-output matrix prepared by Wassily Leontief and Marvin Hoffenberg for the READ program. This matrix is more detailed than that used in the Leontief-Hoffenberg material in Chapter 5, and provides information on the inputs supplied by each of fifty-seven industries to each of the following vectors of defense purchases: aircraft and missiles, ships, combat and support vehicles, ammunition, electronic and communication equipment, other major procurement, foreign military assistance, maintenance and operation, and new construction. "Indirect dependence" on defense expenditures is not here defined as including the multiplier effects of a decline in purchases or investments of those whose incomes are lowered as a result of the defense cuts, but covers only the implied decline in production of all those goods and services required to produce the defense end-products being cut out of the defense program. Note that this table allows only for the reductions in the United States defense program, and not for the offsets provided by the increase in United States contributions to IDO, or by the build-up in "associated programs."

b Food and kindred products, apparel and textile mill products, leather products, paper and allied products, rubber and rubber products, lumber and wood products, nonmetallic minerals and products, and miscellaneous manufacturing industries.

c Armed forces and civilian employees of defense agencies as a percentage of total employment in all government activities, including armed services and state and local government, estimated at 13 million in 1965.

a position to predict the amounts of unemployment to which disarmament may give rise.

An employment model of this sort may, nevertheless, provide some indication of the relative severity of the *redeployment* problem within the various industries. The redeployment index in Table 4 gives some indication of the extent to which the industry or sector would be likely to be affected by disarmament, the severity of its reconversion problem, or the number of jobs within the industry or sector which could be continued only by the creating of new demand to replace defense demand.

Table 4 suggests that redeployment burdens will be quite high in a few industries but rather small in most. Thus, in aircraft and ordnance, close to nine workers out of ten may be affected by disarmament; in ships and boats, more than one out of two; in radio communications, more than one out of three; in instruments, nearly one out of five; and in primary metals, about one out of eight. Even in these industries, however, the impact in the first three years would be substantially less severe, i.e., less than one out of two in aircraft, one out of five in ships and boats, one out of six in ordnance, and one out of seven in radio communications.

Substantial effects of the disarmament program are seen in the government sector. Over four-fifths of the armed forces will be demobilized, and nine-tenths of civilian employees of the defense departments. The cutbacks in both types of government defense employment would amount to over a quarter of all government employment at the federal, state, and local levels, though only up to 6 per cent in the first three years.

The over-all magnitude of the redeployment problem is here estimated at about eight per cent—being the total size of the cutback in estimated employment in defense industry, the armed forces, and the defense agencies as a percentage of the labor force. The comparable cutback in the first stage amounts to 2.5 per cent of the labor force. These are substantial figures, especially in view of the fact that around 97 per cent of the total effect is concentrated in those industries and sectors that are *directly* dependent on defense purchases (i.e., armed forces, civilian employment in defense agencies, transportation equipment and ordnance, electrical and nonelectrical machinery, and instruments).

TABLE 4 – INDEX OF DISARMAMENT REDEPLOYMENT BY SELECTED INDUSTRIES AND EMPLOYMENT SECTORS

| | CUTS IN DEFENSE EMPLOYMENT, AS PER CENT OF TOTAL EMPLOYMENT WITHIN THE INDUSTRY OR SECTOR[a] | |
	FULL PROGRAM 1965–77	FIRST STAGE ONLY 1965–67
INDUSTRY		
Chemicals	4.8	2.0
Fuel and power	6.3	2.4
Primary metals	12.2	5.5
Fabricated metals	7.0	2.8
Nonelectrical machinery	4.7	1.7
Radio-communications	34.7	13.6
Aircraft and parts	89.3	45.8
Ships and boats	55.4	22.2
Ordnance	84.6	15.6
Instruments	19.0	9.2
Transportation	5.0	2.0
Trade	1.2	0.5
Service, etc.	1.1	0.4
Construction	1.2	0.9
Total all industries	5.0	2.0
GOVERNMENT		
Armed forces	83.3	17.0
Civilians in defense agencies	92.8	35.2
Total government[b]	25.8	6.2
TOTAL INDUSTRY AND GOVERNMENT[c]	7.9	2.5

SOURCE: Table 3, plus 1965 labor force and employment estimates, prepared for READ by Mannie Kupinsky of the National Planning Association (available on request).

[a] Reductions in direct or indirect defense employment in the industry or sector by the end of specified period, as a percentage of estimated total 1965 employment in that industry or sector, including nondefense employment.

[b] Cuts in employment in the armed forces and the defense agencies as a percentage of total government employment, including state and local governments, and federal defense and nondefense employment (including armed forces). Total government employment is estimated at 13.4 million in 1965.

[c] Total cuts in defense-dependent employment in industry and government as a percentage of total 1965 labor force, estimated at 79.8 million.

It should be remembered, of course, that these redeployment estimates do not take account of the offsets supplied by the expansion in the civilian space and atomic energy programs, and from the United States contribution to international inspection, police, and deterrent functions. If their labor requirements per dollar of expenditure were roughly in line with those of the defense activities they replace (in fact, they will probably be lower), then they should offset about 30 per cent of the estimated cutbacks in defense employment. Net defense cuts after such offsets would then be only 5.5 per cent of the labor force and only 1.75 per cent of the labor force in the first three years. However, the shifts required for such offsets would often be at least as serious as interindustry shifts after the provision of deliberate compensatory offsets.

One important qualification must be mentioned. If the postulated defense cutbacks were not offset by expansion of private or public nondefense expenditures, their multiplier effects could create a far more severe impact than so far indicated. Thus, our measurement of impact and redeployment requirements is concerned with *direct* first-stage results, assuming multiplier effects are avoided by the provision of appropriate offsets. Discussion of multiplier effects and policies will be found in Chapters 6, 8, 10, and 15.

OCCUPATIONAL REDEPLOYMENT

Another aspect of great importance in judging the difficulties of disarmament transitions is the vocational and skill classifications of those released from defense-dependent employment. Some impressions on this score are provided by Table 5 on p. 45, on the occupational distribution of disarmament cuts. While these estimates are especially rough in view of our very limited knowledge of the distribution of skills and vocational abilities and experience, the table may, nevertheless, give a somewhat useful general impression of where the major problems will fall.

As there indicated, the four biggest vocational concentrations of defense-employment reductions will fall among craftsmen, foremen, and kindred workers (about 1.6 million), operatives and

TABLE 5 — ESTIMATED DECLINES IN DEFENSE-DEPENDENT
EMPLOYMENT DURING DISARMAMENT, BY OCCUPATIONAL
GROUPS, 1965–1977

(Thousands of persons)

	CIVILIAN[a]	ARMED FORCES	TOTAL[b]
Professional, technical, and kindred workers	606	250	856
Managers, officials, and proprietors	238	233	471
Subtotal	844	483	1,327
Clerical and kindred workers	705	450	1,155
Sales workers	53		53
Craftsmen, foremen, and kindred workers	841	728	1,569
Subtotal	1,599	1,178	2,777
Operatives and kindred workers	1,000	505	1,505
Service workers	178	265	443
Laborers	167	70	237
Subtotal	1,345	840	2,185
ALL OCCUPATIONS[b]	3,788	2,500	6,288

SOURCE: Total of employment declines, from Table 3. Civilian occupational distribution based on 1960 patterns shown in The Economic and Social Consequences of Disarmament, U.S. Arms Control and Disarmament Agency, 1962, Part II, Table 8, p. 44, Table 9, p. 45, Economic Series I, Publication 2. Armed Forces pattern based on estimates by Mannie Kupinsky of the National Planning Association, prepared for READ and based partly on estimates of Harold Wool, "The Armed Services as a Training Institution," Nation's Children, Volume 2: Development and Education, White House Conference on Children and Youth, 1960.

a In defense agencies and defense-dependent industries.

b Total not exactly equal to sum of parts because of rounding.

kindred workers (about the same number), clerical and kindred workers (around 1.2 million), and professional and technical workers (over 0.8 million). If we break the vocations down into three broad groups distinguished by levels of education, training, and income, we find a more nearly even distribution among the three categories than many would expect, with around 2.2 million in the lowest category, 2.8 million in the middle, and 1.3 million in the top (see subtotals in Table 5).

REGIONAL REDEPLOYMENT

It has not yet proved possible within the READ program to attempt a systematic study of the complex problems of the regional impact of disarmament and its redeployment implications. Two rough measures are, however, available of the extent to which various states would probably be affected. The first of these measures is the employment on major defense procurement as a percentage of industrial and of nonagricultural employment in the state. This provides a very rough indication of the probable difficulties of finding new jobs of comparable remuneration and skill requirements for workers likely to be released from major defense industries. The second criterion is the ratio of payments to the armed forces and to civilian employees by defense agencies (i.e., Department of Defense payrolls) in each state, as a percentage of total personal incomes in these states. This measure provides some indication of the extent to which the states concerned would feel the economic impact of a withdrawal or inactivation of the armed forces and defense facilities located within their borders.

While many of the states have an involvement in defense activities roughly proportional to the total size of their economies, in nearly half the states the relative involvement in defense activities is substantially higher. Table 6 lists those states with a dis-

TABLE 6 - STATES WITH ECONOMIES ESPECIALLY
VULNERABLE TO DISARMAMENT

	EMPLOYMENT IN MAJOR DEFENSE INDUSTRIES,[a] APRIL 1960, AS PER CENT OF		DEPT. OF DEFENSE PAYROLLS[b] AS PER CENT OF
	TOTAL MANUFACTURING EMPLOYMENT	TOTAL NONAGRICULTURAL EMPLOYMENT	PERSONAL INCOME, DEC. 31, 1960
Kansas	30.2[c]	6.2[c]	4.1
Washington	28.6[c]	8.6[c]	4.9
New Mexico	23.8[c]	1.7[c]	9.0
California	23.3	6.3	3.7
Connecticut	21.1	9.5	0.5
Arizona	20.6[c]	3.0[c]	4.2
Utah	20.4[c]	3.6[c]	6.7
Colorado	17.8	2.9	4.7
Florida	14.1	2.1	3.8

TABLE 6 – Continued

	EMPLOYMENT IN MAJOR DEFENSE INDUSTRIES,[a] APRIL 1960, AS PER CENT OF		DEPT. OF DEFENSE PAYROLLS[b] AS PER CENT OF
	TOTAL MANUFACTURING EMPLOYMENT	TOTAL NONAGRICULTURAL EMPLOYMENT	PERSONAL INCOME, DEC. 31, 1960
Maryland	12.2	3.5	5.2
Missouri	10.3	3.0	2.0
Texas	10.0	1.9	5.5
Massachusetts	9.5	3.5	2.3
Oklahoma	8.2[c]	1.2[c]	5.9
NATIONAL AVERAGE	7.3	2.2	2.9
Virginia	7.0	2.2	10.2
New Hampshire	5.0[c]	2.2[c]	7.4
Georgia	4.3[c]	1.4[c]	6.8
Alabama	3.9[c]	1.2[c]	6.1
Alaska	2.1[c]	0.2[c]	26.5
District of Columbia	1.5[c]	0.6[c]	10.8
South Carolina	1.1	0.4	7.6
Hawaii	0.4[c]	n.a.	18.2
Nevada	[d]	[d]	6.5

n.a. = not available.

SOURCES: Employment in defense industries and total covered employment in manufacturing from *Employment and Wages,* Department of Labor, Bureau of Employment Security, Second Quarter 1960, pp. 22, 30, 73, 74. Total nonagricultural employment from *Employment and Earnings,* Department of Labor, Bureau of Labor Statistics, June, 1961, p. 18. DOD payrolls from Department of Defense, Office of the Secretary of Defense, Directorate of Statistical Services. Personal income for 1960 from *Survey of Current Business,* Department of Commerce, August 1961, p. 13. Table originally prepared by READ, with assistance from Murray Weidenbaum.

a Ordnance, electronic components, aircraft and parts, shipbuilding and repairing. Not all employment in these industries (except ordnance) is on military production. Employment in these industries and total employment in manufacturing include only employment in firms covered by unemployment insurance, but in practice most of such employment is covered.

b Military pay and allowances and civilian Department of Defense wages and salaries.

c Incomplete because employment in defense industries excludes employment which, in one or more of the industries, was not given by the state, since that would disclose information about particular firms. For the whole country, the amount excluded from the state-by-state distribution amounted to 13,900 or 1.1 per cent of the total employment in major defense industries. For an individual state, of course, the exclusion might be much more important.

d Between zero and 1 per cent.

proportionately high economic involvement in defense activities as measured by industrial employment on major defense projects or by income generated by defense payrolls.

TABLE 7 – FIFTEEN COUNTIES MOST HEAVILY DEPENDENT ON DEFENSE PRIME CONTRACTS, 1960

COUNTY	PRIME CONTRACTS PER COUNTY (MILLIONS OF DOLLARS)	POPULATION (000)	PRIME CONTRACTS PER CAPITA DOLLARS
Box Elder, Utah	72.9	25	2,916
Fairfield, Conn.	228.7	97	2,357
Tioga, N.Y.	88.3	38	2,323
Ellmore, Idaho	39.1	17	2,300
Stephens, Texas	17.6	09	1,955
Newport News, Va.	220.6	114	1,935
Montgomery, Va.	54.6	33	1,654
Arapahoe, Colo.	178.9	113	1,583
Sedgwick, Kansas	488.0	343	1,422
Santa Clara, Calif.	775.9	642	1,208
Morris, N.J.	289.9	262	1,106
Coffee, Tenn.	31.0	29	1,068
Cobb, Va.	115.0	114	1,008
Burlington, N.J.	221.3	224	987
Grant, Wash.	43.8	46	953
TOTAL UNITED STATES	21,004.3	179,323	117

SOURCE: Data from Walter Isard and James Ganschow, *Awards of Prime Contracts by County, State and Metropolitan Area*, Philadelphia: University of Pennsylvania, 1962.

As there noted, Kansas, Washington, New Mexico, California, Connecticut, Arizona, and Utah have 20 to 30 per cent of their manufacturing employment in four major fields of defense procurement: ordnance, electronics, aircraft and missiles, and ship-building and repairing. Furthermore, Alaska, Hawaii, Washington, D.C., and Virginia have a tenth to a quarter of their incomes provided by defense agency payrolls. Clearly, these areas are likely to face readjustment problems of above-average difficulty.

A thoroughgoing analysis of these problems, however, would require a much more detailed survey of the location of defense activities in particular cities and subregions, together with advance indications of where the cuts would be most likely to come, and the alternative employment opportunities existing and likely to develop in those particular cities or subregions. In view of the complex network of subcontracting of defense procurement, it is extremely difficult to spot the location of defense production with any precision; and any survey limited to prime contracts and first-tier subcontracts may even be seriously misleading. Through the medium of subcontracting, a distribution of defense activities throughout the country occurs which is undoubtedly closer to the distribution of industrial and physical research capacity (especially in the newer industries and research fields) than would be indicated by the location of the recipients of prime contracts.

Nevertheless, a considerable regional concentration of defense-dependent economic activity is unmistakable, and this fact will unquestionably create a major set of readjustment problems in the event of disarmament.

At least a rough indication of which local areas have the most highly concentrated dependence on military prime contracts is afforded in Table 7. As is there made apparent, the counties which have the highest concentration of prime contracts per head are not invariably in states with the largest relative dependence on defense manufacturing. The counties listed would appear *a priori* to be subject to major readjustment problems in the event of disarmament.

3

The Cost of Inspection for Disarmament

Seymour Melman*

The purpose of inspection for disarmament is to give governments and populations mutual assurance of compliance with disarmament agreements. Such assurance is given mainly by establishing and operating inspection forces of such a nature as to make evasion of disarmament an enterprise of very doubtful workability. The result of such systems is to make it impossible for anyone to guarantee a successful evasion.

SOME PROBLEMS OF INSPECTION SYSTEMS

The arms race has produced the support of populations at large for the rules of secrecy and evasiveness that are conventional for military operations. The task of inspection for disarmament is to create a set of conditions under which any significant number of people who try to maintain the conditions of the arms race would be unable to calculate a successful evasion of disarmament on a scale to be militarily and politically meaningful.

One of the central conditions of the inspection problem is the

* SEYMOUR MELMAN is Associate Professor of Industrial and Management Engineering at Columbia University, editor of *Inspection for Disarmament,* and author of *The Peace Race* and other publications.

degree to which there is a change in the conventional dependence on military forces as final governors in international political bargaining. To the degree that military power continues as a primary arbiter in international dealings, one must expect evasion of disarmament agreements to be seriously considered and attempted. If, on the other hand, international relations, including competition among social systems, is developed along other lines—economic, for example—then it may be expected that attempts to evade disarmament agreements would be less probable. The design, the cost, and the workability of inspection of disarmament are substantially dependent, then, on the conditions that surround disarmament agreements. These circumstances must be added to the conditions of the disarmament process itself.

Inspection of partial disarmament is affected by conditions that are quite different from the ones to be expected when disarmament becomes rather extensive; thus, under partial disarmament, military establishments still exist and, it may be assumed, exercise the same sort of influence on national policy-making that is traditional to them. Accordingly, it may be expected that inspection for disarmament would have to tread a delicate path between two requirements: first, the necessary rigor of inspection to assure adequate probability of compliance with disarmament agreements; and second, precautions not to infringe unduly on the traditional prerogatives of armed forces, including secrecy in the deployment of weapons and personnel. From this standpoint, more extensive disarmament may be policed in a more straightforward way, with the inspectorate being given more extensive rights of access to places and to people than under partial disarmament.

The conduct of inspection is also affected by the condition of disarmament agreements: "Arms control" involves a very different set of problems from that encountered by a significantly diminishing level of military forces. Under arms control, the problem of inspection is essentially one of assuring each side that the major military forces in hand have not been extended beyond the boundaries of the agreement. In my opinion, this is a most difficult problem owing to the fact that military forces, by their very nature, include major elements of secrecy and evasiveness. Furthermore, the long indoctrination of military commanders is toward an effort to secure superiority in military strength. Since superiority is dependent upon a great number of factors—including the nature of weapons and their deployment in space and time—the problem of assuring compliance becomes an extremely difficult, if not unworkable, one. After all, there are many ways by which weapons can be modified. So long as major forces are in being and are given full sway in research, development, and procurement of weapons, then these possibilities are left wide open. Consider the problem: How can one define whether a given weapon is only a "replacement" for another one or a modification that constitutes a "new" weapon?

In contrast with arms control, a diminishing level of arms is a more workable inspection problem, especially when the disarmament process is carried out at high speed. The latter process is designed to cope with the classic problem of assuring "military parity on the way down" during a disarmament process owing to the problem of evaluating the military significance of particular weapons and of equating armed forces composed of varied weapons and fighting groups. One solution to the parity problem is essentially that of eliminating "the way down" as a condition of a disarmament process. By eliminating, I mean so shortening the period during which the disarming actually occurs that, for practical purposes, "the way down" ceases to be a problem. The technology that is involved here is that of disabling military forces on a large scale and with great speed. Thus, aircraft may be disabled by the removal of wheels and key control devices, missiles may be disabled by removing warheads and parts of essential guidance equipment, organizations of troops may be militarily disabled by assembling their communications equipment, piling up their arms, and segregating key officers so as to break the chains of command and remove major functional components from the organization. The use of methods of the sort suggested here as disabling devices is needed in order to give reasonable assurance that the forces or the weapons in question could hardly be used immediately thereafter for their designed purposes. Following a disabling process there would presumably be sufficient time for carrying out the complete dismantling of weapons and forces. These techniques are suggested here because they open up important capabilities for a reliable inspection function—as contrasted to the policy of security through armed forces that are either "stabilized" or reduced at a very slow rate.

PROBLEMS OF ERROR AND VIOLATION

Reliability in inspection systems and maximization of risk for evaders is therefore attained when disarmament is made extensive, when it is directed toward reduction of forces, and when that reduction is done at speed. The question remains, however, for the design of inspection systems: What can be the error that the disarming process could tolerate in order to give desired mutual assurance to the countries that are party to agreements? Error in an inspection system can result not only from deliberately evasive action, but also can arise from the normal behavior of military forces in being—since evasiveness and secrecy in many fields is an integral feature of the operation of these forces. Accordingly, the early stages of disarmament are bound to include problems of "violations," which must be dealt with in a way that is satisfactory to all sides. The primary criterion that may be considered for giving such assurance—whatever the "violation"—is this: It should not result in restricting the scope and the tempo of the ongoing disarming process itself. The latter is suggested because it is probable that an inspection system and the parties involved can sustain the risk of greater degrees of violation as the disarming process proceeds. I am implying here that the disarming process and the military safety of the nations involved become *less* vulnerable to violation as the disarming process reaches its terminal point. The point here is that small numbers of weapons and small military forces are capable of less effect—despite the proportional deviation that they imply from the agreed level of disarmament. For example, in order to carry out intercontinental military operations —including occupation of major territories—very large forces, numbering in the millions, are required. Therefore, this is clearly an implausible operation for a few thousand men.

The significance of violation of disarmament is also diminished by the establishment of international peace-keeping forces. From this standpoint, one of the important criteria in the design of a disarming process would be the designation of the stage at which the international police forces should at least equal the military capability of residual forces of any single major power.

The above discussion surely does not serve to exhaust the set of problems that are mentioned. The importance of this brief review, however, is to underscore that the required scope of an inspection process varies significantly according to the way the disarming process is carried out.

In the estimates that follow no attempt has been made to resolve this set of factors. Accordingly, estimates for the cost of inspection are prepared, not on the basis of rounded inspection systems, but rather on the basis of functional elements, it being understood that less cost will result from rapid and extensive disarming, while greater cost will be the effect of slow disarming, or of attempts to retain large national military forces.

ECONOMIC PROBLEMS OF DEFINING THE COST
OF INSPECTION SYSTEMS

Since the inspection system would be internationally operated with facilities and personnel in many countries, any estimating procedure for capital outlay involves variation in items like construction and transportation costs from country to country. While these vary considerably, no attempt could be made in this estimate to take these into account. Where construction costs are relevant, American costs have been used. This confers an upward bias on all of these estimates.

An international inspection organization will certainly be composed of various classes of personnel. In the present estimate, attention is focused on the technical or professional operating personnel. An attempt is made, however, to take into account service and maintenance organizations as well as general administrative staff for an international inspection organization. This is done by examining the published accounts of the United Nations organization and applying to the inspection organization the standards of salary payment and the ratios of professional to administrative and servicing staff as these obtain in the United Nations.

During the course of a disarmament process, it is more than likely that the requirements of an inspection organization will change appreciably. Thus, it is likely that the requirements for inspection could be gradually tapered off by mutual agreement after a few years of rather high-level activity. The estimates shown here are for such years of high-level activity and do not attempt to estimate the annual costs during periods of reduction in the inspection function.

Every attempt to gauge the money and manpower cost of an inspection operation surely includes errors of estimate. Such costs may be contrasted with the cost of operating the arms race. From this standpoint, it is clear that the inspection organization, even at maximum cost, is a modest activity, for whose operation the participating countries can well afford even the possibility of over-expenditure.

COST OF A NUCLEAR TEST BAN INSPECTION SYSTEM

One basis for estimating the cost of an international system to police an agreement against all nuclear tests is afforded by the system that was designed at the international meeting of scientists in Geneva, in 1958. Since then, however, various modifications have been suggested for such systems. These include additional instrumentation, unmanned seismographic and other stations in remote places, and variations in the methods of analysis of data to be gathered. Most of these proposed revisions have been in the direction of increasing the cost of the system. However, other proposals would be in the direction of reducing such a system cost. The latter include proposals for using existing networks of seismographic stations as part of the international inspection network.

Table 1 gives an estimate of the manpower requirement for such an international inspection system as prepared by the United States Air Force Technical Applications Center. A report of May 1961 obtained from the Office of the Secretary of Defense provides much underlying detail for the estimates of personnel that are shown here. For the Geneva control system proposed at that time, it postulates a system headquarters, ten regional offices, 170 land control posts and ten ship control posts, plus six aerial sampling bases.

The Advance Research Projects Agency of the United States Department of Defense has made available its estimate of capital

TABLE 1 – ESTIMATED TOTAL MANPOWER REQUIRE-MENTS FOR AN INTERNATIONAL NUCLEAR TEST BAN

	TOTAL	PROFESSIONAL	TECHNICAL	SUPPORT
Headquarters	1,727	713	509	505
Regional offices	1,130	420	460	250
Aerial control posts	786	96	168	522
Land control posts	14,576	3,200	8,112	3,264
Ship control posts	1,350	40	310	1,000
Communications relay	1,830	30	1,260	540
On-site inspection (50 teams)	650	350	250	50
Total	22,049	4,849	11,069	6,131

SOURCE: Reported as an appendix to a statement on the floor of the Senate by Senator Stuart Symington, June 12, 1961.

cost for each one of the "Geneva type" test ban monitoring stations. This estimate—$2.5 million per station, mainly for seismographs and allied instrumentation—is here tripled in order to account for 100 seismographs rather than the 31 suggested in the original Geneva outline. Thus, the capital outlay for a test ban detection system would be about $1.7 billion when allowance is included for data analysis and communications systems. The thorny nature of problems of estimation is indicated by the fact that the cost of constructing and equipping a station can increase by about 50 per cent when the work is to be done in areas remote from ordinary transport and communications systems. It is assumed here that communication of seismographic data would be by air courier rather than by telephone cable. The latter was ruled out in these estimates because of the very high cost of telephone cable construction—amounting to about $12,000 a mile in the United States. In my judgment, such a factor applied to a world-wide system would result in prohibitive costs, and therefore air delivery of data sheets was assumed as preferable.

HIGH-ALTITUDE MISSILE TESTING

One of the plausible early-stage agreements in a disarmament process is prohibition of unauthorized high-altitude missile testing. The purpose would be to curtail the development of the missile art for military purposes, and to concentrate all rocket research in the hands of authorized persons who pursue the art for its application to space exploration and allied purposes.

A useful technique for such an inspection system would be a network of radar machines so spaced around the surface of the earth as to intercept any object that penetrated above the earth's surface within a height of 125,000 to 500,000 feet. Samuel J. Rabinowitz, in a paper prepared in the Electronics Research Laboratory of Columbia University's School of Engineering, explains how such a network can be installed and operated.[1] The logic here is that this altitude range is well above the level of manned aircraft flight and below the altitude that must be reached by orbiting satellites. Accordingly, this altitude range selected for inspection is relatively "empty" and is, therefore, the more effectively inspectable.

Rabinowitz calls his plan an "alarm system" which:

can detect an unauthorized launching but may not be able to provide any detailed information about the type of vehicle detected or its trajectory. . . . Unauthorized testing will be detected when an alarm has been generated for which no previous notification to the control agency has been provided.

The problem of supplying the control agency with prior notification of legitimate penetrations of the surveillance region will not be onerous since the number of installations capable of legitimate launchings of rockets or satellites will probably remain in the low tens for the foreseeable future. Also, the number of such launchings per day will probably not exceed 10 to 20 during that time. Dying satellites which penetrate the surveillance volume from above on any given day will also be few in number and adequate warning of the imminent return of an Earth satellite should be available from the various national space agencies.

He has chosen the lowest usable operating frequency—450 megacycles per second—"consistent with a reasonable degree of in-

[1] Unpublished paper, "A Radar Alarm System for the Detection of Unauthorized Long Range Ballistic Missile Launchings," November 8, 1961. Rabinowitz is a senior research scientist in the Columbia School of Engineering.

vulnerability to a high false alarm rate due to aurora and meteor echoes."

According to the designer:

Each radar will cover about 635,000 square miles of territory. When we allow for siting problems, overlapping coverage, etc., the average coverage given by a single radar will probably be only 400,000 square miles. Since the total land area of the Earth is about 50,000,000 square miles and since, for reasons of lack of technical development in many areas of the Earth, less than half the Earth's area need be surveyed, at least initially, a total of 40 to 50 of these radars would be required in the alarm system.[2]

Estimates of the capital cost of a more extensive radar network of this sort are cited by courtesy of J. Salerno.[3] The initial cost of radar machines installed on land and ship sites may amount to about $10 billion. Annual operating costs of as much as $590 million are foreseen. There is probably an upward bias in these data, due to the high unit prices that were assumed for the radar machines. Nevertheless, there are problems of judgment involved here, and the matter cannot be resolved until the work is actually undertaken. The high capital cost of the radar net is owing to the location of numbers of stations on remote islands and on ships at sea. If certain of these came to be regarded as unnecessary, the capital cost of the system would be reduced appreciably.

It should be noted that this system would also monitor against outer-space testing of nuclear warheads, since any carrier rockets would be intercepted by the radar net. Thus, for the latter purpose the network would replace an expensive satellite system.

AERIAL INSPECTION

An international system of aerial reconnaissance would serve an international inspection organization by identifying and locating

[2] These quotations are from the paper cited above. This paper is filed in the Egleston (Engineering) Library of S. W. Mudd Building, Columbia University. Photo copies may be ordered at cost by addressing the librarian.
[3] See his "Cost of a Radar Network for a Missile Test Ban," in *Collected Papers of Summer Study on Arms Control of the American Academy of Arts and Sciences*, 1960, pp. 311 ff.

many possible sorts of prohibited activities under a disarming system. These include massing of troops and weapons, operations of military manufacturing and testing facilities, and construction of secret installations of various sorts.

Aerial inspection may often be carried out by alternative systems, the principal possibilities including manned aircraft and orbiting reconnaissance satellites. The operating characteristics of the latter are not yet known. Neither do we have reliable information concerning the cost of constructing and mounting such satellites in orbit. Accordingly, the present estimates are based upon aerial inspection with conventional aircraft. The operation would be carried out by a fleet of 75 planes of the Boeing 707 class, which, with appropriate photographic equipment, could be dispatched on long-ranging flights at appropriate altitudes, to carry out reconnaissance as directed from a control center. Such an air fleet could be maintained under contract with the commercial airlines that utilize similar planes.

The system is designed to cover the entire land surface of the earth and is based upon aerial reconnaissance in three classes of territory. The first class includes urban industrial areas and other areas that are heavily supplied with power. A second class of territory for inspection includes areas that are somewhat sparsely settled but include power facilities that provide opportunity for either manufacture or deployment of military matériel. The third class of reconnaissance territory includes no power networks or extensive transport systems. Activity would center primarily on the first zone, with inspection on a weekly basis; lesser attention would be given to the second zone; and only occasional sampling, to the third.

About fifty planes a day would be in actual operation, the remaining number being counted upon as a reserve for all contingencies, including time out for major maintenance. The cost of operating these planes is based on a figure of $150 per hour total operating cost as derived from data of major commercial airlines. Altogether, some 1,500 people would be required as professional operators of the system, and the initial outlay for installing such a system of aerial reconnaissance is estimated at about $420 million. These estimates are probably on the high side, because it is likely that an inspection system of this sort could make use of the large numbers of equivalent-capability aircraft that might be made available from the very large military pools rendered inactive by disarmament.

INDUSTRIAL PLANTS

The industrial plants that are vital for inspection under a disarming process are mainly those that produce military matériel as an important product. The main factories are those that produce fissionable materials for military purposes—such as the plants of the Atomic Energy Commission—or chemical or biological weapons; the whole range of factories that produce "conventional" types of military matériel; and the production centers for the newer weapons, such as missiles of all classes.

In the matter of conventional weapons the inspection problem is complicated by the fact that many of these implements can be produced within factories that do other sorts of work as well. Thus, many types of metal-working plants can produce military hardware. The situation is different for the manufacturer of fissionable materials and for the missile class of delivery systems. For these latter the production plants are highly specialized. It is also true, in the United States at least, that these factories are geographically concentrated. It is probable that the same condition exists elsewhere, since it is important to maintain close liaison among these plants in order to assure effective integration among the producers of many components.

Factories can be classified in terms of first, second, or third priority; and can be given frequency of attention accordingly. Classes of the first sort would include the major plants of the Atomic Energy Commission and the major plants that have specialized in the production of military matériel. In these cases it would be entirely reasonable to station resident inspectors so as to have some assurance that these facilities were not being operated. Nuclear reactors that are capable of producing substances convertible to weapons use are included here also. The second class would include those of subcontractors for the major military suppliers, with plants specializing in products part of whose use is military. The third class would include those which are competent to produce a variety of goods, including military, such as the range of metal-working establishments. A system of this sort operated in the United States would require the activity of about 2,700 professional personnel.[4]

MILITARY INSTALLATIONS

The units to be put under surveillance here are the installations that are operated by the armed forces themselves. Within the United States, the Army, Navy, and Air Force, and the Atomic Energy Commission together own 290,000 buildings.[5] An international inspectorate would classify these structures, again on a priority basis, giving top priority to weapons development and test centers, naval shipyards, and arsenals for the manufacture and storage of military equipment. A secondary classification would be given to facilities capable of being converted to these purposes. And the third class of military buildings would include the considerable number of warehouses, military barracks, and the like.

The inspection problem here is a remarkably complicated one under arms control or partial-reduction situations, for there the problem is one of controls against evasive or secretive activity by military forces in being that are highly trained in such methods. The inspection problem becomes a workable one only when entire defined sets of buildings are designated as inoperative and inactive. Under such conditions the inspection problem is simply one of making sure that the facilities are no longer used for military purposes. In many cases, this may be accomplished simply by closing down an area and posting a watchman.

The second and third classes of military structures can be inspected on a random sampling basis. Altogether, I estimate such

[4] For the method of estimation, see J. Wiesner, "Inspection for Disarmament," in *Arms Control*, ed. L. Henkin, Englewood Cliffs, N.J.: Prentice-Hall, 1961, Chap. 4.
[5] *Statistical Abstract of the United States, 1960*, Department of Commerce, p. 185.

an operation should involve a technical and professional staff of about 3,000 people.

MILITARY RESEARCH AND DEVELOPMENT

In a disarmament process, special attention must be given to military research and development establishments. These are crucial in developing technologies for weaponry, and also possess facilities for the production of small quantities of military matériel. The number of such facilities, for example in the United States, is unknown. Therefore I will assume, arbitrarily, that they number no more than two hundred.

These facilities are clearly of class 1 priority. Accordingly, the requirement under a disarming process would be either the closing and dismantling of certain facilities or their conversion to altogether different purposes. The closing of facilities would be the appropriate act for such units as ordnance testing stations, and conversion would be more relevant in the case of biological laboratories that are devoted to producing bacteriological warfare agents.

With an estimated two hundred installations of this sort in the United States, about three hundred people would be needed for the inspection function.

TECHNICAL PERSONNEL

One of the vital assets in the operation of military systems, either overt or clandestine, is a substantial staff of technically trained persons to design and produce weapons. A disarming process must accordingly include provision for making certain that the men once engaged in these activities are, in fact, now doing something else. For this purpose, a sampling system can be useful, based upon a record of military technical personnel. For some period of time, these people should be required to record their places of employment and residence with the inspection organization, which could, by appropriate sampling methods, keep tabs on this important group of men. Such a record system would also disclose whether these men have collected together in certain localities or enterprises, since that would serve as a warning signal to alert the inspectorate. I estimate that this function could be carried out by a staff of fifty people, if performed in the United States.

INSPECTION BY THE PEOPLE

One of the probable aspects of a far-flung inspection system would be the method of citizen supervision of disarmament, by which many gaps in the physical inspection systems could be covered. This method would make it obligatory for the citizens of each participating country to report violations of the international agreement to the inspection organization. The crucial activity here consists of arranging for information and admonition to the population from leaders, on a regular basis, to remind the people of their obligation to cooperate with the inspection organization and of the importance of doing so. Secondly, this function requires the operation of channels of access from the population to the inspectorate. Several methods have been suggested, including use of the postal system, which is monitored by test mail. A staff of people who are expert in public communications and opinion analysis, together with a plausible staff for the receipt and analysis of letters, is the requirement here. For these purposes, I estimate that a staff of 100 professionals would be needed for the United States.

ESTIMATES OF TOTAL COST

The cost estimates for world-wide inspection systems, which are summarized in Table 2, rest upon a set of assumptions, the most important of which are stated in the foregoing—that the nuclear test-ban system is the one designed by the international meeting of scientists at Geneva in 1958, that the manpower requirements are those prepared by the United States Air Force Technical Applications Center, that the disarming process will be spread over a period of time and therefore require substantial inspection installations which will function regularly for some period of years. Methods of arriving at the capital costs are explained above, for those functions in which the initial outlays called for are considerable. The annual operating expense estimates include allowance for professional service and administrative staffs, headquarters expense, and the annual cost of operating equipment such as planes and radar. Methods used in calculating these costs may call for further explanation.

TABLE 2 – ESTIMATED COSTS OF WORLD-WIDE INSPECTION FOR DISARMAMENT
(*Millions of dollars*)

METHOD OF INSPECTION	CAPITAL COST	COST OF ANNUAL OPERATION
Test ban	$ 1,700	$ 256
Radar net	10,010	590
Aerial inspection	420	77
Factories		238
Military installations		264
Military R&D		26
Military technologists		4
Budgets		26
Inspection by the people		8
Total	$12,130	$1,489

As indicated by the table, cost estimates for the inspection of factories, military installations, military research and development, military technologists, government budgets, and inspection by the people are based primarily upon the staff requirements, since capital outlay for equipment would probably be nominal. The exception to this might be the data-processing equipment that would be useful for surveillance over possible military production. Allowance for this has been made, in the annual-cost column, in terms of rental fees for such classes of equipment.

METHODS FOR ESTIMATING PERSONNEL NEEDS

For each inspection method, the personnel requirements have been based first upon the need for professional operating staff. Nonprofessional personnel for servicing administrative and maintenance operations have been estimated at 1.2 times the number of professionals. This is the ratio of administrative and service personnel to professional staff in the United Nations organization. For salary estimates, United Nations figures for comparable functions, both professional and nonprofessional, are applied. Finally, for each inspection method 30 per cent of the total salary estimate has been added in order to account for all manner of special equipment, such as computers, the costs of travel, and operation of headquarters.

For test ban monitoring, inspection against high-altitude missile testing, and aerial reconnaissance, world-wide estimates were made at the outset, while for the remaining types of inspection the costs of these operations were first calculated for the United States and then multiplied by three to obtain a world-wide estimate.

CONCLUDING COMMENT

The estimated total cost of inspection systems given here may well be high on the capital-cost side, since no allowance has been made for economies of quantity purchase of the relevant classes of equipment. I have also attempted to make generous allowances for personnel requirements, overhead, and headquarters operation. No allowance is made, either, for reduced operations as disarmament proceeds. Nevertheless, it is obvious that the cost of the inspection function at which we arrive, even with these generous estimates, is only a modest fraction—2 to 3 per cent (depending on speed of amortization of capital cost)—of the current annual expenditures for military purposes throughout the world.

4

Problems of Adjustment for Defense Industries

Murray L. Weidenbaum*

An analysis of the impact of disarmament on American industry necessarily begins with an examination of the military demand for goods and services prior to the nation's embarkation upon the disarmament program. Here we find the question of time rather crucial. There is no fixed military market basket which private industry regularly supplies.

This market basket is, in fact, undoubtedly subject to a more rapid rate of technological change than any other major sector of the American economy. Aside, then, from differences in levels of military spending, a general reduction in armaments would have a far different impact on American industries in 1962 than it would have had in 1952 or than it might have in 1972.

The first sections of this chapter consequently describe the present pattern of military demand, while subsequent sections point out the changes that have occurred in recent years and are likely to continue in the absence of disarmament, and indicate some of the adjustments which already have taken place as a result of these

*MURRAY L. WEIDENBAUM is Senior Economist at Stanford Research Institute. Until recently he was Corporate Economist for the Boeing Company and was formerly with the U.S. Bureau of the Budget.

changes. Finally, past diversification efforts of military suppliers are summarized, and the possibilities of new types of production by these companies are discussed.

PRESENT PATTERN OF MILITARY EXPENDITURES

Expenditures of the Department of Defense have risen from $19.8 billion in fiscal year 1951 to $43 billion in 1961, or by over 100 per cent, a growth rate far in excess of that of any other major area of the American economy. At the present time, Defense Department purchases of goods and services are equal to almost one-tenth of the gross national product. The proportion reached peaks of 48 per cent during World War II and 12 per cent during the Korean War, but was, of course, lower during the interwar period. The current level of military demand reflects the extended period of the cold war. An abrupt change in the nature of the external threat would probably cause another major shift in the proportion of the country's resources devoted to armaments.

Unlike sales to the private sectors of the economy, the scale and composition of military purchases are determined by the federal budget process rather than by market trends. The authorization of military spending results from the interaction of many competing demands and requirements not only of the various military services, but also of numerous nondefense programs and of taxpayer groups. The level is determined not only by the expected state of international affairs, but also by domestic political and economic conditions. The fiscal objective of a balanced budget or the economic objective of reducing government expenditures during an inflationary period may be important determinants of the total level of military outlays.

COMPOSITION OF MILITARY SPENDING

Military disbursements, as shown in Table 1, are classified by the Department of Defense into five categories: (1) military personnel costs, (2) operations and maintenance, (3) construction, (4) procurement, and (5) research and development. As much of the subsequent analysis will be based on these categories, some description may be in order.

TABLE 1 - DISTRIBUTION OF MILITARY EXPENDITURES,
FISCAL YEARS 1951 AND 1960
(*Billions of 1959 dollars and per cent of total*)

	1950-1951		1959-1960	
	AMOUNT	PER CENT	AMOUNT	PER CENT
OPERATING EXPENSES				
Military personnel costs	$ 9.3	38.4	$11.7	28.2
Operations and maintenance	8.6	35.4	10.2	24.4
Subtotal	17.9	73.8	21.9	52.6
CAPITAL OUTLAYS				
Plant (construction)	.6	2.4	1.7	4.0
Equipment				
Procurement	4.8	20.0	14.7	35.4
Research and development	.9	3.8	3.3	8.0
Subtotal	6.3	26.2	19.7	47.4
TOTAL	$24.2	100.0	$41.6	100.0

SOURCE: Reports of the Department of Defense.

The *military personnel* category covers pay, subsistence, trans-portation, and related outlays for the members of the armed forces. Expenditures in this category were 28 per cent of total military outlays in fiscal year 1960. As of June 30, 1960, the armed forces had on active duty 2.5 million men, 3 per cent of the nation's total labor force.

The *operations and maintenance* category covers the pay of civilian employees of the military establishment and consumption-type outlays. Purchases from private business are mainly petroleum products, spare parts, medical equipment, and office supplies. Operating expenditures of this nature were 24 per cent of total military expenditures in 1960. In contrast to the procurement category on p. 69, many of the military purchases here are standard commercial items or close variations. This latter category represents a limited market, but one of interest to nearly all elements of American industry. It is a relatively stable market, with a low rate of product obsolescence. It is dependent in good measure on the number of military and civilian personnel in the defense establishment.

Military construction projects cover air field, missile launching sites, Navy yards, and troop-training facilities. Expenditures in 1960 were 4 per cent of the military budget.

Procurement programs, consisting of the production and purchase of military weapons, accounted for 35 per cent of defense expenditures in 1960. Aircraft, missiles, and supporting electronics systems made up about three-fourths of total procurement. In the development of these new weapons, the explosive growth of science and technology dramatically demonstrates its effect. These military requirements demand continuous pushing of the frontiers of science.

The *research and development* category, covering the early stages of the weapon-creating cycle, amounted to 8 per cent of military expenditures in 1960. The bulk of these funds is devoted to aircraft and missile programs. About three-fourths of military R&D is allocated to the development of weapons systems with less than one-fourth to research. Of the portion for research, a modest amount—approximately $100 million in 1959—is allocated to basic research. Military research programs are concentrated, to the extent of over 80 per cent, in the field of the engineering sciences. Another 12 per cent goes to physics, chemistry, astronomy, and the other physical sciences, with the remaining 7 per cent divided among social, biological, and medical sciences and mathematics.

Because military research and development expenditures are of fairly recent origin and because they are growing so rapidly, a more detailed review of this category may be of interest.

MILITARY RESEARCH AND DEVELOPMENT

Industrial research and development, whether financed privately or with government money, has comprised approximately three-fourths of R&D expenditure in recent years (the other one-quarter being largely government), according to the National Science Foundation. The federal government has utilized extensively the R&D facilities of industrial firms to meet military requirements in such fields as aircraft, missiles, nuclear energy, and space exploration. Indeed, the major portion of the impressive growth in industrial R&D in recent years has been financed by the federal government, almost entirely through national security programs. Of the $4.4 billion obligated for industrial R&D by federal agencies in 1959, the Department of Defense accounted for $3.9 billion, or 88 per cent. The Atomic Energy Commission and the National Aeronautics and Space Administration, with a combined total in excess of $500 million, accounted for almost all of the remainder.

In the calendar years 1953–1959, federal expenditures for industrial R&D performance (not strictly comparable to the detail on an obligations basis cited above) increased almost fourfold, from $1.4 billion to $5.4 billion. During this seven-year period, R&D financed from company funds showed a smaller increase, in both absolute and relative terms—from $2.2 billion to $4.0 billion.

The breakdown of R&D expenditures by industry shows (Table

TABLE 2 – INDUSTRIAL R&D EXPENDITURE, BY INDUSTRY, FISCAL YEAR 1959

(Millions of dollars)

INDUSTRY	TOTAL R&D	FINANCED BY FEDERAL GOVERNMENT	PER CENT FINANCED BY FEDERAL GOVERNMENT
Aircraft and parts	$2,973	$2,544	85.6
Electrical equipment and communication	2,227	1,550	69.6
Chemicals and allied products	928	253	27.3
Machinery	910	382	42.0
Motor vehicles and other transportation equipment	863	249	28.8
Petroleum refining and extraction	260	16	6.2
Primary metals	137	14	10.2
Fabricated metal products	118	49	41.5
Rubber products	111	42	37.8
Stone, clay, and glass products	73	2	2.7
All other	838	320	38.2
Total	$9,438	$5,421	57.4

SOURCE: *Reviews of Data on Research and Development,* National Science Foundation, Number 24, December 1960, p. 7.

2) that in fiscal year 1959 the aircraft and parts and electrical equipment and communication industries together accounted for 55 per cent of the total of $9.4 billion. Significantly, in both these industries federal financing contributed a much higher portion of total R&D expenditures than in other industries. The aircraft industry received 86 per cent of its total $3 billion in R&D funds from the federal government; and the electrical equipment industry, almost 70 per cent of its $2.2 billion, while less than half of the R&D of other industries was financed by the government. These two industries, concerned so heavily with military aircraft, missiles, and space programs, received three-fourths of the total federal government expenditure on industrial R&D[1] Three other industries accounted for the bulk of the remaining one-fourth of federal industrial R&D funds—machinery, chemicals, and motor vehicles and other transportation equipment.

The R&D programs of several industries were financed almost entirely by company funds: stone, clay, and glass; petroleum refining and extraction; and primary metals themselves financed 90 per cent or more of the R&D; and the drug and medicine industry financed as much as 98 per cent of its research and development activities with its own resources.

The contrast between government-financed and internally-financed industrial R&D is in the fact that in the former, R&D is usually financed by the customer, prior to and independent of subsequent production. For a self-financed product, R&D is initially sponsored and financed by the producing firm itself and only subsequently is the firm reimbursed—in the selling price of the end item (and then only if the end item is successful).

[1] There may be a tendency to underestimate the government-financed portion of industrial R&D. In a letter to the writer, an official of the National Science Foundation has stated that, ". . . so far as we can ascertain, these data do not include company-initiated research and development indirectly borne by the Federal Government through 'overhead' charges on Federal contracts. In all instances where respondents have been asked about reporting practices on such 'overhead' charges, they have reported the company-initiated research and development as company-financed" (letter from Jacob Perlman, Head, Office of Special Studies, National Science Foundation, August 26, 1960).

Because of the large share of government financing of R&D in certain industries, much employment of scientists and engineers is indirectly dependent on the government. A survey by the Electronics Industries Association, in 1961, showed that 76 per cent of the 128,000 engineers and scientists employed by the United States electronics industry were supported by government funds.[2]

The two industries which receive the bulk of the military R&D funds—aircraft and electrical equipment manufacturing—also employed a large share, 25 per cent, of the 800,000 engineers and scientists in private industry as of January 1959. In some specialties the concentration was even greater, 46 per cent for mathematicians and 60 per cent for physicists. Of the engineers and scientists engaged primarily in research and development work—as contrasted to production, technical sales and servicing, administration, etc.—the aircraft and electrical industries accounted for 42 per cent.

The two industries also have the highest ratios of scientists and engineers to total employment, one out of nine in aircraft and one out of fourteen in electrical equipment.[3] Studies of the changing requirements of the military market indicate that the ratio of scientists and engineers in firms producing military weapons systems is likely to be increasing during the 1960's.

INDUSTRIAL DISTRIBUTION OF DEFENSE PRODUCTION

The great bulk of the aggregate prime military contracts over the ten-year period July 1, 1950–June 30, 1960 (90 per cent by value) were, of course, awarded to United States business firms for performance in the United States. Six per cent were to American and foreign firms for work performed outside of the continental United States, and 2 per cent each were to colleges and other nonprofit institutions and to in-house efforts by various military agencies.

[2] *Weekly Report,* Electronics Industries Association, June 12, 1961, Section AA.
[3] *Scientific and Technical Personnel in American Industry,* National Science Foundation, 1960, pp. 33–36.

Most of the contracts were awarded to large firms, with only 17 per cent going to firms classified as small business (fewer than 500 employees). However, a large portion of the work awarded to the larger firms is subcontracted to small business firms. A sample of the 100 companies receiving the largest volume of military prime contracts in fiscal year 1959 showed that they paid out 49.6 per cent of their receipts to their first-tier subcontractors and that 34.7 per cent of this amount went to small business firms.[4] In other words, about 17 per cent of their receipts were paid to small firms. Some of the amount subcontracted to big business was undoubtedly further subcontracted to small business firms.

Seventy-three per cent of the value of military prime contracts awarded in fiscal year 1960 went to 100 large companies. Within this amount, seven major industry groups accounted for over 90 per cent of the total—aircraft, electrical and electronics equipment, oil refining, construction, automobiles, rubber, and shipbuilding, in that order. Table 3 shows the details.

Sixty-five of the 100 companies were engaged directly in aircraft and missile work, or in electronics and research and development work directly related to aircraft and missile programs. Fifteen of the 100 were suppliers of aviation gasoline, jet propulsion fuels, and other petroleum products. Eight were builders of military base facilities in the United States or overseas. Four were shipbuilders, and the remaining eight include firms which supply ordnance, vehicles, and transportation or other services for the military establishment. Three of the 100 organizations were nonprofit institutions.

It should be noted that the distribution by industry is on a company and not on an establishment basis. Hence, the General Dynamics Corporation is listed under aircraft because most of its military contracts are for aeronautical production. However, about one-tenth of its military work is performed by the Electric Boat

---

[4] *100 Companies and 129 Subsidiary Corporations Listed According to Net Value of Military Prime Contract Awards,* Fiscal Year 1959, Office of the Secretary of Defense, p. 1.

TABLE 3 – INDUSTRIAL DISTRIBUTION OF MILITARY
CONTRACT AWARDS, FISCAL YEAR 1960

(Contracts received by the 100 largest military contractors in fiscal year
1959–1960)

INDUSTRY	VALUE OF CONTRACTS (MILLIONS OF DOLLARS)	PER CENT OF TOTAL
Aircraft and engines	$ 7,691.8	49.9
Electrical and electronic equipment	4,427.0	28.7
Electric equipment	1,559.1	10.1
Electronic components	1,143.7	7.4
Office and computing machines	711.1	4.6
Radio and television sets	546.3	3.5
Telephone communication	466.8	3.0
Oil refining	653.6	4.2
Heavy construction	483.2	3.1
Motor vehicles	436.2	2.7
Tires and tubes	411.3	2.7
Shipbuilding	246.8	1.6
Special industry machinery	125.3	0.8
Air transportation	122.6	0.8
Instruments	97.5	0.6
Miscellaneous chemicals	92.2	0.6
Engines and turbines	63.1	0.4
Steel works	62.2	0.4
Railroad equipment	39.5	0.3
Industrial chemicals	38.1	0.2
Farm machinery	25.6	0.2
Miscellaneous unclassified	394.4	2.8
Total	$15,410.4	100.0

SOURCE: Aerospace Industries Association, from Department of Defense data,
February 1961.

Division, the largest American producer of submarines. Defense
work is also carried on by its electronic and nuclear divisions. The
large share of defense work which is done by companies classified
as aircraft industry may reflect in part the diversity of their operations.

Similarly, although the bulk of the military contracts awarded
to the General Tire and Rubber Company is for work performed
by its subsidiary, Aerojet General Corporation, producer of rocket

engines, the entire company is classified in the rubber industry. (The latter company is an example of a firm primarily engaged in civilian production which has diversified to an important degree into the military market.)

FACTORS FOR CHANGE

Three major factors have influenced the level of military expenditures, especially the allocation among the major categories, and are likely to continue to do so in the future: (1) the successive shifts in emphasis from operations to procurement of increasingly expensive weapons, and from this to research and development; (2) the successive shifts within procurement and R&D from surface weapons to manned aircraft to missile and space systems; (3) the shift in the components of weapons systems from the fabrication of airframes and other metal products to electronics, chemical propulsion, and other complex "subsystems."

SHIFTS IN MILITARY EXPENDITURES TO PROCUREMENT AND R&D

A decade ago, 1951, about three-fourths of the military budget was devoted to operating costs such as pay of military and civilian personnel, maintenance activities, and office supplies. Only about one-fourth was devoted to capital-type outlays, such as procurement of weapons systems and other hard goods, research and development, and construction (see Table 1).

In 1960, operating expenses were only slightly in excess of one-half of total defense expenditures, and the other half was devoted mainly to procurement of military hard goods. The portion of the military budget devoted to R&D rose from around 4 per cent in 1951 to 8 per cent by 1960. (Part of the increase is simply due to the classification of some R&D expenditures as procurement in 1951.)

We project a slight further shift to capital outlays during the sixties, largely because of a further increase in the proportion devoted to research and development. As a harbinger of things to come, it is estimated that the research and development portion of the total cost of recent military weapons systems has risen from

20 per cent in the case of a long-range bomber to 60 per cent for an intercontinental ballistic missile. A weapons system may be proved out, but, before any mass production, suspended in favor of an even newer system offering somewhat better performance.

SHIFTS IN PROCUREMENT AND IN RESEARCH AND DEVELOPMENT

At the height of the Korean War in 1952 and 1953, the bulk of military procurement was in conventional land and sea weapons, such as combat vehicles, artillery, rifles, ammunition, and surface ships. By 1955 the share of aircraft had increased to a peak of over three-fifths of the total. Airplane production, in turn, has now begun to yield its position to missile and space programs; the latter are likely to be the major item in 1970. Within the missile and space category, a further shift is likely, from missiles to operational satellites and other space vehicles. Within the research and development category, which may be used as a "lead" indicator of future shifts in procurement, the astronautics area already has a growing share.

SHIFTS IN COST ELEMENTS

As a result of the changing composition of procurement, a growing percentage of military purchases from private industry is in electronics, propulsion, and other advanced, complex subsystems, rather than airframes or other fabricated structures. Even in the still large aircraft category, the emphasis on high-performance jet aircraft has accentuated this trend.

Air Force procurement now accounts for over two-thirds of total military procurement. Expenditures on airframe fabrication have declined from about three-fifths in 1954 to less than two-fifths in 1960, while the proportion for electronics approximately doubled during the same period. A continuation of this trend is likely.

The decline in importance of fabrication is emphasized by the steady fall in the number of pounds of airframe produced, from a peak of 148 million pounds in 1953 to 47 million pounds in 1959, a reduction of 68 per cent in six years. The decline has all been in military production; the amount of airframe produced for civilian planes actually rose during the same period, from 10 million in 1953 to 17 million in 1959.

RESULTING SHIFTS IN FIRMS AND EMPLOYMENT

These changes in the customer's requirements have had a concomitant effect on the companies supplying the military establishment. For example, during the period July 1950–June 1953, the time of peak procurement of Army ordnance equipment for the Korean War, General Motors, a major producer of tanks and trucks, was the number-one military contractor in volume of orders received. It had fallen to twentieth by 1960. A relatively new company, the General Dynamics Corporation—a product of successive mergers of Electric Boat Company, Consolidated Vultee Aircraft Corporation, Stromberg-Carlson and other firms—had risen to first place, primarily on its aircraft and missile work.

Within the aircraft industry, the fortunes of individual firms have risen and fallen. Grumman Aircraft Engineering Corporation, which was nineteenth on the list in 1960, did not appear at all as recently as 1956. Curtiss-Wright Corporation, the largest producer of aircraft in World War II (in terms of pounds of airframe manufactured) was down to 45th place in 1960. Moreover, its production did not include any complete aircraft, but was limited to engines and other components. The Martin Company, mainly on the strength of its shift from aircraft to missiles, rose from twenty-third largest holder of defense contracts in 1950–1953 to sixth in 1960.

Numerous changes occur each year in the composition of the list of major defense contractors. Twenty-one of the 100 firms on the 1959 list did not make the 1950 list. The diversified military supplier which achieved first place in 1959 dislodged a major aircraft company which was highest in 1958.

A striking, if not surprising, relationship is the close correspondence between "growth" industries and the industries which comprise the major military suppliers, reflecting, of course, the rapid increase in military demand and rapid technological changes in new weapons. Of the major manufacturing groups in the American economy, transportation equipment has shown the fastest increase, with a growth in income generated averaging 7.9 per cent a year during the period 1929–1957. The fastest-growing area within the transportation equipment group was "aircraft and parts," most of whose output was sold to the military establishment.

A close second among major manufacturing groups was electrical equipment, whose growth rate averaged 7.4 per cent a year. The electronics subgroups, the most rapidly expanding area within electrical manufacturing, currently sell over one-half of their output to the military.[5]

The basic changes which have been occurring in the composition of military procurement have altered significantly the type of manpower required by the firms producing for the defense market. A special Labor Department survey of aircraft and missile production found that while total employment in the two groups did not change much over the year from October 1958 to October 1959, there was significant change within the total: a substantial decline in employment on aircraft production in aircraft plants was offset by a rise in missile employment in both aircraft and nonaircraft plants.

The report also noted that anticipated shifts in military procurement will probably mean a heavier demand for engineers, scientists, and other highly trained workers. The emphasis will increasingly be on "the technically trained person with exceptional qualifications."[6]

For a typical producer of aircraft and missiles, the percentage of the work force represented by hourly production workers has declined from approximately two-thirds in 1954 to less than one-half at the present time. The estimates in Table 4 show that the decline should continue through the 1960's. In contrast, managerial, engineering, and scientific personnel are expected to rise from one-fifth to one-third of this work force during the same dec-

---

[5] M. L. Weidenbaum, "Some Economic Aspects of Military Procurement," *Current Economic Comment,* November 1960, p. 10.

[6] *Missiles and Aircraft, Recent Manpower Developments,* Department of Labor, Industry Manpower Survey No. 95, April 1960, p. 25.

TABLE 4 - CHANGING EMPLOYMENT REQUIREMENTS
OF A PRODUCER OF AIRCRAFT AND MISSILES

JOB CATEGORIES	PERCENTAGE DISTRIBUTION OF EMPLOYEES			
	1954	1959	1965	1970
Managerial	8	10	12	13
Technical	13	13	20	22
Semitechnical	3	8	9	10
Stenographic	2	3	3	3
Others	10	18	23	23
Industrial workers	64	48	33	29

SOURCE: Murray L. Weidenbaum, "The Impact of Military Procurement on American Industry," in J. A. Stockfisch (ed.), *Planning and Forecasting in the Defense Industries* (Belmont, Calif.: Wadsworth Publishing Company, 1962), p. 161.

ade. The rising importance of research and development costs compared to production costs is an obvious corollary.

Over the years there have also been significant shifts in the geographical distribution of military production. Of these developments, the growth of the West Coast industries during and following World War II has been the most striking. The decline of military orders to the automobile industry in the upper Middle West has been less dramatic, but significant. In the Korean War period, from 1950 to 1953, business firms in Michigan received 9.5 per cent of the total defense contracts awarded. The number of people employed exclusively in defense work totaled 220,000 in 1953. By 1960, the number working on defense projects in Michigan had fallen to 40,000, and the proportion of military prime contract awards going to firms in the state had fallen to less than 3 per cent.

HISTORICAL EXPERIENCE WITH DIVERSIFICATION

A summary of previous attempts of aircraft companies that are predominantly military suppliers to diversify into commercial markets may provide some insight into the possible ways industry might adjust to disarmament. The aircraft manufacturing industry, ever since it attained the production peaks of World War II, has been concerned with the problem of diversifying into new markets and new types of production in order to maintain and expand the scale of its operations. These attempts to diversify went through four different phases: (1) the immediate post-World War II burst of enthusiasm; (2) a settling down period; (3) a downgrading of efforts to diversify during the Korean War; and (4) a renewed interest, resulting initially from cutbacks in military procurement and subsequently from shifts within this procurement.

The efforts of the aircraft manufacturing companies to penetrate the civilian markets after World War II took a variety of forms and met with varying degrees of success and permanence. Many aircraft companies attempted to use their specialized know-how by concentrating on lines where their capabilities would be particularly useful, such as producing aluminum canoes and sport boats, which required their skills in fabricating aluminum products. Some of the "related" products were a bit far afield from their customary lines, including artificial hands, other prosthetic devices, and stainless steel (as well as aluminum) caskets.

A number of aircraft companies became subcontractors for established firms in civilian markets, building heater cases, parts for musical instruments, automobile parts, plumbing, and cabinets for radios. In some instances, aircraft firms joined with other companies to form new subsidiaries. More usually, aircraft companies—using their war-accumulated earnings and relying on tax provisions permitting the carryback of losses as offsets against previously paid taxes—acquired going concerns in other industries. Typical acquisitions included a producer of motion picture equipment; a manufacturer of precision parts in the automobile field; a designer of prefabricated houses; and a maker of motor buses, trolley coaches, and marine and industrial engines.

These early diversification efforts can be grouped into three major categories: (1) the temporary utilization of idle capacity and manpower to maintain a going organization and to tide it over until peacetime aircraft production would get under way; (2) the manufacture of items which it was hoped would win a permanent market, thus diversifying operations and lessening dependence on military orders; (3) the purchase of, or investment in, firms which would either broaden the base of operations, or merely earn a good profit.

The first category is not of particular relevance to the present study, as it involved only temporary diversification to satisfy temporary war-accumulated civilian demands. The third is also irrelevant, as these cases would not ordinarily involve the utilization of the physical resources—labor or plant and equipment—of the military producers.

The second category is the more relevant one; and, unfortunately, the experience here was not too promising. Most of the activities ultimately were abandoned as unsuccessful or marginal, or sold to firms traditionally oriented to industrial or consumer markets.

In general, the income from all three types of new venture was disappointing. They did not generate a significant fraction of sales attained during World War II, as illustrated by the experience of the major airframe companies during the postwar adjustment period 1946–1948, when sales declined to a tenth of their former peak and net losses totaled over $50 million (see Table 5).

Sales and profits remained low even after the immediate shock

TABLE 5 – NET SALES AND PROFITS OF TWELVE
MAJOR AIRFRAME COMPANIES, 1944–1959
(Millions of dollars)

	NET SALES	NET PROFIT
1944	$5,766	$ 59
1945	3,965	67
1946	519	−11
1947	545	−42
1948	843	2
1949	1,132	36
1950	1,388	63
1951	1,979	31
1952	3,731	82
1953	5,120	117
1954	4,927	183
1955	5,188	179
1956	5,637	156
1957	6,913	166
1958	7,079	138
1959	7,049	67

SOURCE: *Aerospace Facts and Figures,* 1960 Edition, Aerospace Industries Association, p. 86.

of postwar adjustment had worn off. While military orders continued, they were much below wartime levels. The production of civilian aircraft was much lower than had been envisioned in the early postwar forecasts. In addition, firms which had traditionally dominated civilian markets, but had temporarily converted to military production during the war, once again asserted their supremacy in many civilian areas. Traditional suppliers soon caught up with consumer demand. In the late 1940's a number of aircraft manufacturing companies terminated their leases on government-owned plants and abandoned postwar diversification ventures.

With the tremendous expansion of military orders for aircraft beginning in the latter half of 1950, the attention of the industry was increasingly re-focused on military production. This is not hard to understand. Priorities were readily available for military orders but were more difficult to obtain for civilian production. More basic, however, was the over-riding desire of the aircraft companies to build planes rather than canoes or coffins.

POST-KOREAN DIVERSIFICATION EFFORTS

At the end of the Korean War, there were, of course, cutbacks in military procurement. For reasons of necessity or just general desirability, aircraft firms began once again to give increased attention to nonmilitary and, to some extent, nonaircraft activities. These more recent efforts to diversify into civilian lines, taking account of some of the worst mistakes of the past, have generally relied on an extension of the company's technology into civilian, governmental, and industrial markets. Examples of diversification, aside from aircraft for the airline and executive markets, include industrial electronics, small gas turbine engines, nuclear reactors, wall panels for commercial building, heavy-duty land vehicles, and production for the civilian space program.

It is difficult to obtain data on the nonmilitary sales of the major military-supplying companies. On the basis of fairly representative data for the years 1952–1954, I concluded that the nongovernmental sales of the major aircraft companies during that period were almost entirely transport aircraft delivered to commercial airlines.[7] The more fragmentary data available for current periods yield a somewhat similar conclusion; however, sales of these commercial aircraft increased so that, according to a sample of major aircraft companies, nonmilitary sales rose from about 3 per cent of total sales in 1955 to almost one-fourth by 1960, the bulk of the increase being in sales of equipment to commercial airlines. Nonmilitary, nonaircraft deliveries of these companies represented less than 0.5 per cent of sales in 1955 and less than 3 per cent in 1960.

Some indication of the potential for adjustment on the part of major military suppliers can also be obtained by reference to the extent to which these companies have diversified within the military market. As recently as 1955, the overwhelming portion of the sales of the aircraft companies were major items of aeronautical equipment such as bombers, fighters, and transports. Currently, almost one-third of their military sales are components or subsystems of weapons systems, such as electronics and propulsion equipment for missiles. The bulk of this production of components is for systems on which the aircraft company is the prime contractor, such as electronic check-out equipment manufactured by Boeing for the Bomarc missile. However, over one-tenth of the military sales of these companies is now for components of systems and vehicles for which other companies are the prime contractors.

Analysis of the diversification experience of major military suppliers points up many difficulties. Military aircraft and electronics manufacturers have successfully made the transition to the design and production of missiles and space vehicles. However, their success in entering related commercial fields, such as industrial electronics, has been disappointing. In contrast, manufacturers of industrial electronic equipment have often penetrated the military electronics market quite successfully.

FUTURE POTENTIAL

This situation may point up the very specialized skills—and, hence, both strengths and weaknesses—of military suppliers as

[7] See M. L. Weidenbaum, "Product Diversification in the Aircraft Manufacturing Industry," *Analysts Journal*, May 1959, p. 4.

general industrial firms. On the one hand, they have unparalleled strength in scientific research and development. As pointed out above, the aircraft and electronics companies have a large proportion of the scientists and engineers in private industry. They are accustomed to designing and producing very complex systems of tremendous scope and magnitude, surpassing in terms of resource input the production of any comparable nondefense firms.

On the other hand, they have very rudimentary and limited marketing and distribution organizations, which are oriented to meeting military requirements rather than to consumer or industrial selling. Because of the nature of military needs, there is less emphasis on volume production at low costs. Rather, these firms are used to producing at low tolerance and high quality, under great pressure from the customer to develop even more advanced equipment. "Keeping up with Khrushchev" results in a different relationship between supplier and customer than "keeping up with the Joneses."

The bulk of the facilities used by these companies are assets built for the purpose and not merely converted to defense uses, as was the frequent case during World War II. Also, a major share of these assets is owned by the military establishment and only leased by the defense contractors.

It may be that the adjustments to disarmament by companies, such as aircraft manufacturers, heavily engaged in military production would be most fruitful in those areas of governmental and industrial demand which are relatively closely related to their past experiences and capabilities. Such areas of new or expanded activity may include the following: (1) transport aircraft and related equipment for commercial airlines; (2) smaller aircraft for business firms ("executive" aircraft) and for pleasure and other noncommercial purposes; (3) other forms of transportation, using adaptations of aerodynamic techniques, such as hydrofoil vessels and monorail systems; (4) basic and applied research, sponsored by civilian rather than military government agencies; (5) adaptation to commercial uses of many of the materials and processes developed to meet military requirements; (6) equipment for an expanded commercial space exploration program, including satellites, space vehicles, and supporting ground equipment; (7) utilization of the capability for designing and manufacturing large complex systems for comparable civilian work, such as integrated factories and regional development programs.

Some rough estimates are available on the diversification potential of one aspect of commercial space utilization—a global communications satellite operation. Assistant Secretary of the Army Richard S. Morse has estimated that the development and construction of a satellite communications system would represent an initial market of approximately $750 million and that the research and development cost would run about $200–$300 million and the investment cost about $500 million.

With wide-band widths, such a system would permit person-to-person dialing throughout the world. World-wide television facsimile programs would also be a possibility. The annual revenues from such a system by the late 1970's have been guessed at "several billion."[8]

Along these lines, a distinguished scientist in the civilian space program has stated that one of the lessons of history in the field of communication is that "an increase in capability has never gone unused."[9]

CONCLUDING OBSERVATIONS

Some of the likely effects on American industry that might result from a total elimination of the defense program in the 1960's, in the absence of compensating or offsetting programs are: (1) sharp curtailment of demand for the goods of some of the major growth areas of American industry, particularly the electrical and electronics and aerospace equipment manufacturers; (2) a major reduction in the level of research and development performed by American industry, possibly one-half or more; (3) a major decline in the employment of engineers and scientists, possibly up to one-

[8] *Hearings on Department of Defense Appropriations for 1962,* House Committee on Appropriations, 87th Cong., 1st Sess., 1961, p. 178.
[9] Homer J. Stewart, *"The Impact of Space Activities on Our General Economy,"* an address before the American Bar Association, August 25, 1959.

fourth of the current 300,000 employed by industry; (4) a very sizable decline in manufacturing volume and employment on the West Coast, the area most heavily dependent on military business.

Declines in military procurement and outlays for research and development of the magnitude indicated above could have a serious effect on the nation's rate of scientific progress and, consequently, on the rate of economic growth.

With a basically different business environment than in the immediate postwar period, and with an even greater concentration of defense work in extremely specialized facilities, it is likely that the adjustment to disarmament would be even more difficult than the reconversion following World War II. In general, the economic impact of disarmament is likely to be far deeper than indicated by the simple observation that military purchases are equal to only one-tenth of the gross national product.

Nevertheless, in the event of complete disarmament, it is my belief that the military-supplying firms would be willing to risk a substantial portion, if not all, of their capital in diversifying into other lines of business. In itself, this might provide an initial stimulus to the economy.

Frequently, major military suppliers have been successful when attempting to diversify *within* their general market areas but unsuccessful when they attempt to penetrate too far afield, such as in the consumer area. Hence, their potential for future diversification is rather limited, and research programs on economic conversion should examine closely the possibilities for utilizing in civilian projects the specialized knowledge and capacities which have been developed in the military production program.

PART II

Analysis of Disarmament Impacts on Production and Employment

5

Input-Output Analysis of Disarmament Impacts*

Wassily W. Leontief and Marvin Hoffenberg†

The federal government of the United States has been spending somewhat more than $40 billion per year on the maintenance of the military establishment and the procurement of arms. These outlays have absorbed about 10 per cent of the gross national product, and they have exceeded by several billion dollars the combined net annual investment in manufacturing, service industries, transportation, and agriculture. The negotiation of disarmament would eventually raise the possibility of a substantial cut in the military budget. Economists, market analysts, and the makers of fiscal policy in government and business have therefore begun to consider how the economy might otherwise employ the labor, the plant, and the

* This is a slightly abbreviated version of the article "The Economic Effects of Disarmament" in the April 1961 issue of *Scientific American*. Thanks are extended to *Scientific American* for permission to reprint.
† WASSILY W. LEONTIEF is the Henry Lee Professor of Economics at Harvard University where he has pioneered in the study of input-output analysis. He recently served on the international panel of experts which reported to the Secretary-General of the United Nations on the economic and social effects of disarmament. MARVIN HOFFENBERG, an economist with the Research Analysis Corporation, has previously worked with the Bureau of Labor Statistics, the Rand Corporation, and the Committee for Economic Development.

physical resources that now serve—directly and indirectly—the demands of the military establishment.

An increase in personal consumption, expansion of educational and medical services and facilities, acceleration of the rate of investment in domestic economic growth, enlargement of economic aid to underdeveloped countries—these are only a few of the many kinds of demand that would lay competing claims on the productive capacity made available by disarmament. There would be no problem if the goods that are listed in the typical procurement order from the United States Air Force missile base at Cape Canaveral also made up the shopping list of the average housewife. It would be merely a question of maintaining the total level of demand during the transition period. But swords do not serve readily as plowshares. In fact, the military shopping list is very different from the bills of goods presented by the various categories of civilian demand, and these in turn differ greatly from one another. So even if the total level of expenditures were maintained, the shift from military to nonmilitary budgets must be expected to increase the demand for the products of some industries and reduce the demand for the products of others. Furthermore, how the sales and employment figures of various industries will respond to the shifts depends upon the proportion in which each type of civilian demand, with its characteristic bill of goods, shares in the increase in total civilian demand.

The composition of the total civilian demand could possibly inhibit the over-all increase in nonmilitary expenditures and so hold the country's economic activity at a lower level, following a cut in the military budget. If most of the money saved were spent on highway construction, for example, a bottleneck would quickly develop in the supply of cement; meanwhile, the electronics industry, which contributes much to military output but relatively little (directly or indirectly) to road building, would remain idle. On the other hand, if funds were allocated to a more balanced pattern of demand, they would secure more nearly full employment of the available human and physical resources. In the long run, of course, any mismatch between the productive capacities of individual industries and the changed pattern of demand would be rectified by reallocation of capital and labor. But such adjustment, as is well known, is quite painful and could take many months or even several years. The loss of time would represent an irredeemable loss of real income to individual citizens and to the nation as a whole.

What is needed in order to anticipate and forestall such losses is a picture of the dependence of various industries on military demand, plus the bill of goods of each one of the more important kinds of private and public nonmilitary demand that are likely to increase when military demand is reduced. The present study is a pilot effort to develop this information and show how it can be applied to forecasting the consequences of the transfer of expenditures from military to civilian purchases. Our research was supported in part by the Research Program on Economic Adjustments to Disarmament of the Center for Research in Conflict Resolution at the University of Michigan. The study does not attempt to predict how much the various kinds of civilian purchase might expand, any more than it tries to predict the actual magnitude of military cuts. The figures in Tables 1 and 2 on pp. 94–97, however, make it possible to analyze the consequences of such shifts from military to civilian expenditures as can be predicted. They should be of considerable help in spelling out the concrete quantitative implications of the alternative fiscal measures that the government may have to take if and when disarmament becomes a fact.

These tables embody insights afforded by "input-output" analysis.[1] This technique is used today in many countries by governments and private businesses to chart the state of the national economy and to appraise the implications of specific economic actions that might affect its course. It anchors forecasting in the relatively fine stable structure of the economy and develops the important indirect relationships among the interdependent elements in the system.

In the highly integrated United States economy, for example, many industries deliver a large part or even all of their output not to final

---

[1] See Wassily W. Leontief, "Input-Output Economics," *Scientific American,* October 1951.

users but to other industries; in other words, a part or all of their output serves the needs of final users indirectly rather than directly. This does not make their dependence on the level and the structure of final demand any weaker, but it does make it more difficult to measure. In order to determine how much the demand for crude sulfur would diminish if the Army cut its purchases of trucks by $1 million, one must determine how much crude sulfur the chemical industry needs to make $1 million worth of sulfuric acid, how much sulfuric acid is used in the finishing of $1 million worth of steel sheet, and how much steel sheet goes into $1 million worth of trucks. This is only one of several such linked chains connecting the output of crude sulfur to the final sales of automobiles. The input-output table of a national economy incorporates just this kind of information. The table (more properly a deck of punched cards or a magnetic tape) of interindustry relationships shows how much of the product of every other industry each industry requires to make one unit of its output. It also shows the distribution of the output of each industry to every other industry and to the various categories of final demand.

As can be imagined, the preparation of such a table represents a major fact-finding and analytical task. The last complete, detailed input-output table of the United States was constructed for the year 1947. A trial check shows, however, that the structural relationships shown for that year still yield a reasonably good description of interindustry relationships in 1958. In the tables presented here, the description of the interindustry relations, that is, the input-output matrix itself, has been omitted in order to bring into relief the less obvious but crucially important structural relationships between the industries and the various kinds of demand they serve. In other words, our tables show the end product of analytical computations, not the raw statistical material that went into them. What would be the effect on employment of a 20 per cent, or $8 billion, cut in a $40 billion military budget if this cut were accompanied by an equal increase in nonmilitary expenditures? Taking the simple case of the transfer of the entire expenditure to one or another category of civilian demand, one need only multiply the figures in the chosen category in Table 1 by 80. Thus, on the unlikely assumption that the entire expenditure is moved into the "Government" column (which comprises all governmental demand except for military and construction activities of the government), as many as 329,000 jobs held in private business establishments would be eliminated, and this would be offset by the creation of 717,000 new jobs in other private industries. The equally unlikely shift of demand to "Exports (except military)" to foreign countries would cause far less strain as measured in turnover of the labor force (only 249,000 jobs would be lost and 342,000 new jobs created). As this result suggests, exports draw upon much the same industries as the military, though for different products. The column "Exports to India," which appears in Table 1, makes it possible to perform similar computations with the quite different bill of goods that would be involved in a substantial increase in economic aid to underdeveloped countries.

Table 2 shows the effects upon employment in the 58 industries that follow from a more reasonable assumption: the projected $8 billion cut in the military budget is here transferred *pro rata* to the various categories of civilian demand, leaving their relative magnitudes unchanged. As can be seen, a total of 253,815 jobs would be eliminated in 19 industries and a total of 541,855 new jobs would be created in the other 38 industries—a net gain of 288,040 jobs. For purposes of comparison, it may be observed that during the recession of 1957 and 1958, employment fell in 54 and expanded in only four of the 58 industries; the combined loss of jobs amounted at that time to 1,411,000 manyears and the gain to only 7,000.

The net increases in "Business Employment" indicated in the transfer of expenditures from military to civilian demand are important, for it is likely that disarmament would be accompanied by the release of large numbers of civilian and uniformed personnel of the Department of Defense. If the cuts in personnel were directly proportional to the cut in the budget, then each $100 million cut would be accompanied by the release of 1,977 civilian workers and 6,329 uniformed men. Not one of the net increases in total business employment computed in Table 1 and Table 2 would be adequate

TABLE 1 – EMPLOYMENT AFTER REALLOCATION OF $100 MILLION MILITARY PURCHASES

(1958 man years)

	EXPORTS (EXCEPT MILITARY)	EXPORTS TO INDIA (EXCEPT FOOD)	BUSINESS INVEST- MENT	PERSONAL CONSUMP- TION	PUBLIC SERVICES CONSTRUC- TION	MAINTE- NANCE CONSTRUC- TION	RESIDEN- TIAL CONSTRUC- TION	GOVERN- MENT (NON- MILI- TARY)
Aircraft and parts	−1,653.5	−1,554.7	−1,652.9	−1,703.8	−1,707.1	−1,707.1	−1,707.1	−1,705.0
Ordnance	−341.7	−341.7	−341.7	−341.7	−341.7	−341.7	−341.7	−341.7
Ships and boats	−275.1	−267.6	−271.0	−338.5	−349.1	−343.6	−343.0	−343.9
Radio	−408.3	−352.6	−238.9	−433.3	−497.3	−466.8	−497.3	−482.8
Aluminum	−7.6	−9.9	−4.0	−25.1	−21.7	−12.2	−20.4	−26.4
Instruments	−24.3	58.3	−9.1	−82.7	−55.5	−102.2	−101.7	−96.8
Apparel	−5.0	−23.1	−24.3	390.6	−27.1	−27.1	−27.1	−0.2
Copper	8.0	−7.9	12.0	−30.8	−19.2	−12.0	−12.0	−32.9
Plastics	51.8	14.4	−4.7	−17.1	−27.7	−19.3	−26.4	−34.6
Overseas transportation (water)	103.3	228.0	−9.7	−6.6	−9.7	−10.0	−10.2	−7.5
Other transportation	−33.8	−9.7	−64.3	73.7	−44.0	−66.9	−64.4	50.5
Electric light and power	−14.8	−2.1	−11.2	72.2	−21.8	−29.9	−23.9	23.1
Professional and services	−219.6	−189.9	−10.3	1,011.0	−185.1	−246.5	−26.1	8,555.7
Motors, generators	0.6	60.2	61.0	−67.2	−62.3	−66.5	−68.9	−76.2
Other nonferrous metals	4.4	18.8	16.9	−31.6	−25.3	−13.3	−22.7	−38.0
Metal stamping	1.9	55.4	18.9	−51.2	−66.8	−64.1	−68.5	−67.9
Machine tools	66.3	337.3	150.0	−37.3	−37.6	−43.0	−42.9	−39.6
Petroleum	1.4	63.2	−75.9	−4.5	3.7	−74.2	−91.5	−86.8
Power transmission equipment	24.5	77.5	31.3	−8.3	−3.6	−13.7	−14.2	−12.5
Engines and turbines	83.5	108.3	50.4	−10.8	−9.8	−13.7	−14.0	−6.7
Metal containers	16.3	11.0	−2.0	7.2	−5.6	−3.0	−6.2	−7.2
Electrical equipment (N.E.C.)	50.2	94.6	222.3	−9.1	−14.0	−8.3	−6.3	−17.5
Industrial machinery	116.6	162.6	531.9	−29.9	−33.2	−26.5	−25.3	−29.5
Leather and leather products	20.7	6.9	−2.6	80.0	−17.7	−16.5	−15.6	−7.6
Livestock, poultry	42.1	27.6	−14.1	113.8	−19.5	−12.1	−15.3	−1.2
Railway equipment	47.7	440.2	33.1	−5.8	−3.0	−6.0	−5.7	−3.2
Iron and steel forging	12.2	82.0	63.8	−56.8	36.7	−38.4	−38.5	−63.6
Cutlery, tools	25.9	28.8	56.5	−41.0	−7.8	−5.8	17.2	−54.1
Medical supplies	62.6	142.0	−9.0	23.5	−10.1	−8.8	−9.5	22.0

Iron and steel	115.3	152.2	329.7	−86.3	100.7	92.1	−8.7	−114.7
Organic chemicals	90.2	117.2	40.4	9.3	−8.7	3.8	−8.2	−4.4
Rubber and rubber products	66.0	116.6	28.2	20.4	14.8	−9.8	−7.1	−8.3
Plumbing fixtures	5.8	−4.1	20.1	1.6	−3.8	149.4	95.4	−9.6
Miscellaneous manufacturing industries	39.5	11.9	17.8	77.8	−11.0	−8.3	−9.3	27.2
Textile mill	421.0	497.1	−0.3	181.1	−24.5	−18.0	13.3	−19.9
Grain and feed crops	9.6	1.7	6.8	5.0	−1.0	0.1	0.1	−0.2
Paper and allied products	79.0	106.0	0.3	30.6	−5.7	14.4	13.7	−19.9
Inorganic chemicals	63.8	60.2	335.6	7.1	−4.4	2.5	−3.5	62.8
Fabricated metals	25.4	43.6	274.8	−14.6	212.3	165.3	91.2	−29.5
Nonmetallic minerals	49.8	144.0	50.0	−12.9	754.6	312.1	475.5	−36.6
Business services	200.0	389.7	231.6	465.2	197.4	−18.0	−3.7	14.1
Motor vehicles	125.9	247.5	347.0	78.8	7.3	−33.0	−31.4	5.3
Farm, building, mining machinery	198.6	242.0	13.0	−0.8	76.2	5.6	−2.8	27.7
Miscellaneous chemicals	84.0	198.5	328.9	28.9	7.6	104.2	13.6	−5.9
Lumber, wood products	33.9	71.9	99.6	49.2	34.2	328.1	991.6	−47.0
Pumps, compressors	96.6	204.5	3.1	15.2	13.9	10.3	15.3	−0.7
Electrical appliances	5.9	3.2	1,277.0	20.8	12.0	3.4	6.1	−1.5
Trade	737.9	1,577.5	3.9	2,351.6	294.0	974.9	1,046.2	−64.9
Tobacco, alcoholic beverages	50.3	40.4	240.8	55.4	−2.4	3.8	14.5	0.3
Railroads, trucking	373.5	983.4	25.5	129.0	401.4	135.4	258.6	18.7
Coal and coke	73.0	30.4	4.2	28.2	27.5	9.3	6.2	14.5
Gas utilities	2.9	6.0	39.0	42.4	5.6	1.3	2.5	1.3
Auto and other repairs	15.0	19.7	42.4	83.4	177.2	44.4	37.2	14.1
Banking, finance	138.9	79.7		714.6	82.3	27.2	73.3	30.2
Restaurants, hotels, amusements	218.4			856.3				97.6
Construction	−133.7	−133.7	1,957.1	−133.7	4,262.7	3,229.9	3,524.2	−133.7
Business employment: Increase	4,280.7	7,413.1	7,036.0	7,294.9	6,722.1	5,646.2	6,709.2	8,968.8
Decrease	−3,117.4	−2,897.0	−2,767.8	−3,610.4	−3,724.5	−3,910.9	−3,746.0	−4,113.9
Net change	1,163.3	4,516.1	4,268.2	3,684.5	2,997.6	1,735.3	2,963.2	4,854.9
Total employment: Increase	4,280.7	7,413.1	7,036.0	8,165.3	6,722.1	5,646.2	6,709.2	16,641.0
Decrease	−11,423.2	−11,202.8	−11,073.6	−11,916.2	−12,030.3	−12,216.7	−12,051.8	−10,443.0
Net change	−7,142.5	3,789.7	−4,037.6	−3,750.9	−5,308.2	−6,570.5	−5,342.6	6,198.0

NOTE: The columns in this table show the net change in employment in fifty-eight production sectors resulting from the transfer of $100 million of demand from the military to each of the nonmilitary demand categories. The figures at bottom show that the net increase in business employment would be offset in all but one demand category by release of uniformed and civilian personnel directly employed by Department of Defense.

TABLE 2 – EMPLOYMENT AFTER REALLOCATION OF $8 BILLION MILITARY PURCHASES TO OTHER DEMAND CATEGORIES

(*Thousands of 1958 man years*)

	CHANGE IN EMPLOY-MENT	PER CENT CHANGE IN EMPLOY-MENT
Ordnance	−27,336.0	−19.24
Aircraft and parts	−135,600.0	−17.90
Ships and boats	−26,320.8	−10.99
Radio	−33,036.8	−6.07
Aluminum	−1,707.2	−2.82
Instruments	−5,944.0	−2.42
Copper	−2,022.4	−2.36
Motors, generators	−4,086.4	−2.04
Iron and steel forging	−3,050.4	−1.31
Other nonferrous metals	−1,920.0	−1.31
Metal stamping	−3,526.4	−1.06
Plastics	−1,152.8	−0.70
Cutlery, tools	−1,924.0	−0.70
Insulated wire and cable	−1,035.2	−0.61
Machine tools	−1,055.2	−0.47
Petroleum	−1,988.8	−0.38
Power transmission equipment	−258.4	−0.29
Overseas transportation (water)	−139.2	−0.27
Iron and steel	−1,711.2	−0.26
Engines and turbines	38.4	0.04
Paper and allied products	1,945.6	0.36
Metal containers	344.0	0.44
Organic chemicals	800.8	0.46
Other transportation	3,064.8	0.60
Rubber and rubber products	1,592.0	0.63
Railroads, trucking	12,338.4	0.67
Electrical equipment (N.E.C.)	1,388.0	0.67
Electric light and power	3,609.6	0.73
Inorganic chemicals	1,048.0	0.74
Industrial machinery	2,915.2	0.74
Fabricated metals	3,062.4	0.78
Nonmetallic minerals	5,231.2	0.81
Coal and coke	2,186.4	0.92
Plumbing fixtures	1,073.6	0.93
Miscellaneous chemicals	2,328.0	0.94
Lumber, wood products	9,634.4	0.98
Business services	26,111.2	1.00
Motor vehicles	6,437.6	1.01
Leather and leather products	4,108.0	1.15
Medical supplies	1,694.4	1.17

TABLE 2 – Continued

		CHANGE IN EMPLOY- MENT	PER CENT CHANGE IN EMPLOY- MENT
Miscellaneous manufacturing industries		4,548.0	1.21
Textile mill		11,252.0	1.24
Pumps, compressors		2,124.8	1.26
Construction		36,086.4	1.36
Livestock, poultry		5,940.8	1.40
Grain and feed crops		297.6	1.40
Electrical appliances		1,187.2	1.44
Farm, building, mining machinery		3,953.6	1.44
Professional and services		108,730.4	1.46
Gas utilities		2,317.6	1.47
Trade		144,533.6	1.51
Auto and other repairs		5,402.4	1.51
Food products		14,848.0	1.53
Apparel		20,199.2	1.61
Banking, finance		39,332.0	1.66
Tobacco, alcoholic beverages		3,225.6	1.69
Restaurants, hotels, amusements		46,824.8	1.81
Railway equipment		99.2	1.95
Business employment:	Increase	541,855.2	1.42
	Decrease	−253,815.2	−6.85
	Net change	288,040.0	0.69
Total employment:	Increase	639,376.5	1.41
	Decrease	−760,135.2	−11.99
	Net change	−120,758.7	−0.22

NOTE: The figures here reflect the changes in employment by the fifty-eight production sectors that would follow from a 20 per cent, or $8 billion, cut in military
expenditure and reallocation of this demand proportionally to other demand categories. The totals show a net increase of 288,040 job openings under "Business employment" but a net deficit of 120,759 job openings under "Total employment,"
resulting from release of personnel by the military.

to absorb entirely this addition to the rolls of job seekers. The
tables provide the means, however, for trying out sets of assumptions different from the simple ones demonstrated here.

The analytical methods employed in this study can obviously be
used to answer many further questions. How would the industrial
impact of disarmament be felt in various parts of the country?
What would be the magnitude—and the effect on other industries

—of the short-run production bottlenecks that could prevent some industries from supplying the additional output called for by changes in the composition of demand? How would the creation of the additional productive capacities required to meet such increased demand affect the level of output in industries supplying the requisite capital goods?

In making use of the material presented here, and in formulating additional questions, it is most important to keep in mind the fact that military expenditures constitute only one factor affecting the state of the United States economy. Since a substantial portion of the economic resources now serving military needs could be used to increase private or public investment, the question of the economic implications of disarmament necessarily leads to the more general problem of economic development and growth. In so far as foreign trade, and in particular foreign aid, enter into the picture, the effects of reduced military expenditures would have to be traced beyond the borders of our own national economy. This means that the present study does not pretend to answer all the questions, and suggests the nature of the fact-finding labor that is required if major economic changes are to be subjected to concrete, quantitative analysis.

6

Econometric Analysis of Disarmament Impacts

Daniel B. Suits*

The purpose of this chapter is to explore the orders of magnitude involved in the economic adjustment to disarmament by use of a set of multipliers derived from an econometric model of the United States economy.

The discussion is divided into five parts. Part I is devoted to a short definition of the adjustment problem. The econometric model used in the measurement was compiled by the Research Seminar in Quantitative Economics at the University of Michigan, and has proved highly successful both as an analytical device and as a tool of economic forecasting. The model and its application have been described elsewhere,[1] but for the benefit of readers unfamiliar with econometric models, Part II of this chapter is devoted to a general description of their nature and use. Part III contains the multipliers derived from the econometric model, and explains and illustrates their use in estimating the economic impact of governmental actions. In Part IV the multipliers are put to work in estimating the magnitude of the adjustment problem. The calculations are

* DANIEL B. SUITS is Professor of Economics at the University of Michigan and Director of the Research Seminar on Quantitative Economics.
[1] Daniel B. Suits, "Forecasting and Analysis with an Econometric Model," *American Economic Review*, March 1962, pp. 104–132.

based on a programmed reduction in defense expenditure of $32 billion, scheduled over a twelve-year period; alternative combinations of offsets are considered. The results are evaluated in the concluding part. It will be shown that while the magnitude of the problem appears large at first sight, use of even the most obvious offsets reduces the order of magnitude far below that of a mild postwar recession.

1. THE ADJUSTMENT PROBLEM

Millions of men and women are employed today in building, maintaining, and developing weapons; learning how to use these weapons; and standing by, prepared to use these weapons. Others are engaged in producing, maintaining, improving, and expanding the auxiliary services required for the support and operation of modern weapons. Still others are engaged in manufacturing materials for weapons production, supply, and supporting activities. These activities not only occupy the time and skill of millions of people, they also require large amounts of oil, copper, iron ore, timber, and other precious natural resources almost beyond listing.

Economically, disarmament means that manpower and natural resources no longer demanded for these activities become available to society for other purposes. With the termination of the defense program the millions of people and billions of dollars in resources must be shifted to other uses. It is clear that such a large-scale reorientation of activity will require a series of major readjustments in the economy. The purpose of this study is to estimate the general size of this economic adjustment, and to compare it to other adjustments that we have already experienced. Since the impact varies with the magnitude and steepness of the arms reduction, it is necessary to make working assumptions with respect to the character of the disarmament program.

An economic adjustment program for disarmament consists of a set of governmental actions that determine the use to be made of the resources released. The number of alternative actions that can be pursued for this purpose is myriad, and many of the individual possibilities differ from one another in subtle ways. In this analysis we will limit ourselves to the study of a few broad alternatives in general adjustment policy.

1. *Tax reduction.* The most obvious governmental action to consider—and one that will be adopted to some extent as part of any disarmament program—is to reduce taxes. This restores income to the consumer or private investor to buy the kinds of goods and services he wants. Of course, the exact impact of tax reduction will depend on which taxes are reduced and by how much. To fix a general order of magnitude, this study is limited to reduction in the personal income tax in the form of a general lowering of the tax schedule, but with no important change in marginal rates.

2. *Expanded expenditure on other government services.* A second obvious action to consider—and, again, one that will doubtless be part of any program—is to increase expenditure on other government services. Once more, there is a wide range of impacts, depending on whether the additional expenditure is for roads, schools, parks, reforestation, post office buildings, or flood control. But these differences are of second-order magnitude compared to the global estimates we are trying to make. Therefore, we will distinguish only two types of government expenditure:

    a. Purchases from private business

    b. Hiring additional government employees

3. *Transfer payments.* The third action we will study is expansion of government transfer payments, such as social security retirement benefits and unemployment compensation, with or without equivalent expansion in social security contributions or taxes.

4. *Reduction in armaments expenditure.* Finally, it is necessary to explore the implications of the action of disarmament itself. This consists of a programmed reduction of armaments production and of armed services personnel. The response of the economy to the action of disarmament establishes the amount of resources made available for other uses, and which adjustment policies aim to reabsorb. These responses are estimated from an econometric model of the United States economy, and their proper evaluation depends on some familiarity with the use of such models.

II. THE ECONOMY AND THE
ECONOMETRIC MODEL

An economic system is a set of institutions for the production, distribution, and consumption of goods and services. In a democratic, individual-centered society these institutions respond primarily to the desires of millions of households as expressed by the distribution of their purchases in the market place. Thus, when households receive additional income, it is their free disposition of it, coupled with the competition of business firms to serve them, that determines whether more automobiles, more shirts, or more food will be produced, and how much or many of each.

The number of factors influencing the behavior of any given family is vast. What a particular family does with its own income depends on the constellation of prices of all kinds of goods; on the grade, quality, and style of things available to buy; on the region; the time of year; the education, experience, and background of the family; on what the neighbors are doing—or will think and say—and on the millions of things that make one family different from another. But while it is impossible to predict what any given family will do in a specified situation, the stability of habits is such that, taking a large number of families, and one year with another, a systematic average pattern of behavior emerges. Thus, while some individual families will spend more and some less, the average response is stable and predictable: On the average, families spend two-thirds of any increase in disposable income.

Due to the stability of average consumer behavior, it can be approximated by a simple mathematical equation. The behavior of business firms and the operation of other economic institutions can be similarly treated. Thus, the application of appropriate statistical procedures enables us to derive a set of equations that approximates the behavior of the actual economic system. Such a set of equations is called an econometric model.

Once a model has been compiled it can be used to trace out the economic impacts of government actions. For example, a $1 billion reduction in income taxes has the direct effect of adding $1 billion to the disposable income of consumers. In response to this, consumers as a whole will increase their purchases of goods and services by $0.67 billion. The new sales increase business profits and stimulate production; they probably also result in additions to plant and equipment and in a larger inventory of stocks. The resulting increase in employment and wages induces a second round of expenditure, to be followed by a third, and so on.

The econometric model enables us to calculate, at least approximately, the total effect of the chain of events set in motion by any specified government action, and to estimate the impact on production, employment, profits, income, wages, government revenues, and other economic magnitudes.

III. MULTIPLIER RESPONSES TO SELECTED GOVERNMENT ACTIONS

Table 1 shows the response of the United States economy to a selection of government actions, as calculated from a thirty-two-equation model of the United States economy.[2] Each line in the table corresponds to a particular economic magnitude and shows the response to be expected from a change of $1 billion in the indicated government activity. All responses are measured from the level that would have been attained in the absence of the action. We see from the first column of the table that an increase of $1 billion in government purchases from private firms raises the gross national product by $1.304 billion, of which $0.295 billion is consumption expenditure resulting from responses by income receivers.

It transcends our purpose to describe exactly how these multipliers were obtained from a system of thirty-two equations, but it is easy to demonstrate that they are of the correct order of magnitude: An additional $1 billion of sales to government raises corporate profits, at the margin, by about $600 million, and wages by about $400 million. The corporate profits tax takes half of the additional profit, leaving $300 million after taxes. Because of the stability of dividend policy, however, only about a third of this

2 Illustration of the derivation of multipliers from the model will be found in the article cited in note 1, especially pp. 122–127.

TABLE 1 – MULTIPLIERS FOR SELECTED ACTIVITIES

(Billions of dollars)

	GOVERNMENT PURCHASES +$1.0	GOVERNMENT EMPLOYMENT[a] +$1.0	FEDERAL INCOME TAX LEVEL +$1.0	FEDERAL INCOME TAX YIELD +$1.0	SOCIAL SECURITY TRANSACTIONS +$1.0	PRIVATE INVESTMENT IN PLANT AND EQUIPMENT +$1.0
Gross national product	1.304	1.903	−1.119	−1.798	0.825	1.690
Consumption expenditure	0.295	0.738	−0.915	−1.470	0.674	0.382
Unemployment insurance benefits	−0.160	−0.390	0.091	0.146	−0.069	−0.137
Tax receipts						
Federal	0.458	0.220	0.622	1.000	0.274	0.586
State and Local	0.030	0.034	−0.045	−0.072	0.033	0.058
Social Insurance	0.030	0.051	−0.024	−0.039	0.018	0.038
EMPLOYMENT (millions of persons)	0.089	0.322	−0.076	−0.122	0.056	0.115

a Additional government wage expenditure of $1.0 billion to hire 260,000 employees.

is passed on in the form of dividends. Thus, only half of the initial billion is received as personal income. The personal income tax removes something more than a fifth of this, leaving disposable income of about $400 million, of which about two-thirds, or $267 million, is re-spent by consumers. This marginal propensity to re-spend about one-fourth of an initial increment of GNP implies a multiplier of $\dfrac{1.00}{1.00 - 0.25}$ = 1.33, in close agreement with the tabulated figure.

The additional federal tax receipts ($300 million from the corporate profits tax and $100 million from the personal income tax) amounts to about 40 per cent of the initial expenditure, in keeping with the tabulated figure of $0.458 billion.

This figure is especially interesting from the fiscal standpoint. Note that it means that nearly half of the government outlay is recovered in higher tax yields. By virtue of this recoupment, an addition of $1 billion to federal expenditure adds only $1.000 − $0.458 = $0.542 billion to the federal deficit, with no alteration in tax rates. Moreover, the additions to state and local tax revenues and to social insurance receipts constitute further recoupment from the standpoint of government as a whole, although it does not appear in the federal accounts. In addition, increased employment (89,000 people) reduces unemployment insurance benefits by $160 million, to act as another form of recoupment. All told, about $624 million is recovered out of each additional billion of expenditure.

The second column of Table 1 shows the response of the economy to employment of additional government personnel. The effect of this action depends both on the number of persons hired and on the total amount of wages paid. The tabulated figures are derived from a wage expenditure of $1 billion to hire 260,000 new employees. This corresponds to average annual earnings of federal military personnel in 1960. Due to the fact that the direct payment of wages initially bypasses the corporate profits tax and the sluggish dividend response, the GNP multiplier effect of additional personnel is considerably higher than that of government purchases.

In keeping with this fact, the impact on consumption is correspondingly greater, and the federal tax recoupment smaller. The sizable increase in employment and the reduction in unemployment insurance benefits reflect the direct effect of hiring the 260,000 people.

The effects of alteration in the federal personal income tax are given in two columns. The first corresponds to a change in the tax law that would raise the yield of the tax by $1.0 billion at the level of incomes existing *before* the economy adjusts to the change. The repressive effect of the tax increase itself, however, results in a fall in income; and tax revenues actually realized are only $622 million, as shown. The second tax column shows the consequences of a tax increase sufficient to yield $1 billion of new revenue *after* the economy has adapted to the new tax level. Since the economic implications of tax reductions are exactly the opposite of tax increases, these are obtained by simply reversing the signs of the tax multipliers.

The column headed "Social Security Transfers" shows the effect of an increase of $1 billion in social security payments. These transfers add directly to disposable income and stimulate consumption expenditure. This, in turn, reduces unemployment, and generates a small recoupment in reduced unemployment benefits.

The final column of the table shows the impact of $1 billion of new private investment in plant and equipment. This is, of course, a private rather than a government action—though it may be induced in response to certain government action, e.g., accelerated depreciation allowances—and is inserted for purposes of comparison.

To estimate the effect of a complete government program, the various components of such a program are classified under the headings of Table 1. The amounts of expenditure increase or decrease implied by each component are then multiplied by the appropriate multiplier and the results summed to give the total impact of the program. For example, given a program consisting of an increase in government purchases from private firms of $2 billion and additional government wages of $3 billion, the effect on gross national product would be:

$2 \times 1.304 + 3 \times 1.903 = \$8.317$ billion.

Federal tax recoupment would be

$2 \times .458 + 3 \times .220 = \$1.576$ billion.

The program would increase total employment by

$2 \times .089 + 3 \times .322 = 1.144$ million.

Moreover, in the absence of tax legislation, the expenditure of $5 billion would increase the federal deficit by $5.000 − $1.576 = $3.424 billion.

IV. ADJUSTMENT TO DISARMAMENT

The disarmament program to be studied is the model of general and complete disarmament proposed by READ.[3] This envisages a programmed net reduction of defense outlays from a projected annual peak level of $60.2 billion in 1965 to a level of $28.2 billion in 1977 after allowances for expansion in contributions to a world peace authority and for certain defense-associated programs in civilian space and atomic energy programs. The details of the reductions are shown in Chapter 2. For our purposes, the program consists of a net reduction of expenditure of $32 billion, divided between $10.4 billion in wages and salaries and $21.6 billion in purchases from private industry. Applying the multipliers of Table 1 to these components we get the full economic implications of the program before any offsets are applied.

As shown in the first column of Table 2, with no alternative markets provided for released resources, the decline in gross national product is 50 per cent larger than the expenditure cutback. So far from obtaining any share of the potential benefits of disarmament, consumers would find their own spending power reduced, and yearly consumption expenditure would be cut back by $14 billion, even after the $8 billion rise in annual unemployment benefits, accompanying the 5 million decline in employment. Tax receipts, particularly those of the federal government, would decline drastically, but by much less than the expenditure reduction, leaving the federal government with a $20 billion annual surplus.

[3] *Economic Impacts of Disarmament,* U.S. Arms Control and Disarmament Agency, Economic Series I, Publication 2, January 1962.

TABLE 2 - DISARMAMENT IMPACT UNDER ALTERNATIVE OFFSET PROGRAMS[a]

(*Billions of dollars*)

	IMPACT IN ABSENCE OF OFFSETS	TAX REDUCTION PROGRAM[b]		TAX REDUCTION PLUS STATE AID[c]	
		OFFSETS	NET IMPACT AFTER OFFSETS	OFFSETS	NET IMPACT AFTER OFFSETS
Gross national product	−47.9	36.6	−11.3	39.7	−8.2
Consumption expenditure	−14.1	29.6	15.5	24.6	10.5
Government expenditure	−32.0	0.3	−31.7	10.0	−22.0
Unemployment insurance benefits	7.6	−3.0	4.6	−4.7	2.9
TAX RECEIPTS					
Federal	−12.2	−19.9	−32.1	−9.8	−22.0
State and local	−1.1	1.4	0.3	1.1	0.0
Social insurance	−1.2	0.8	−0.4	0.9	−0.3
GOVERNMENT SURPLUS (+) OR DEFICIT (−)					
Federal	+19.8	−19.9	+0.1	−19.8	0.0
State and local	−1.1	+1.1	+0.0	+1.1	0.0
Social insurance	−8.8	+5.5	−3.5	+5.6	−3.2
EMPLOYMENT (millions of persons)	−5.2	2.5	−2.7	3.7	−1.5

[a] Assuming general and complete disarmament on the READ model, involving cuts of $21.6 billion in defense purchases from the private sector and $10.4 billion in expenditures on defense personnel.

[b] Under this plan, federal taxes would be reduced by $20 billion and state and local government expenditures would be increased by $300 million.

[c] Under this plan, personal taxes would be reduced by $13.2 billion; state and local governments would receive, and spend, an additional $10 billion of state aid from the federal government.

It is, of course, unrealistic to suppose that any government would deliberately choose an adjustment program that imposes additional burdens on the economy instead of a sharing of benefits. Nevertheless, the calculations provide more than a straw target. In the first place it is an essential beginning to the calculation of offsets. Secondly, Table 2 establishes a limit to the problems to be encountered in the economics of disarmament, marking the worst that can reasonably be expected.[4] Before calculating offsets it is useful to evaluate the worst.

There are several yardsticks by which to measure the impact shown in Table 2. While a change in GNP of $48 billion is large in absolute terms, it is less imposing in relation to normal cyclical variations. During recovery from the recession of 1960, the GNP rose from $501 billion in the first quarter of 1961 to reach $549 billion by the first quarter of 1962. This was a cyclical swing of $48 billion concentrated in exactly one year; the adjustment of Table 2 is a reverse swing of equal magnitude, but spread over twelve years instead of twelve months! This is an average decline of $4 billion per year; between 1957 and 1958, the real GNP (in 1961 dollars) fell by $7 billion, nearly double this rate.

The additional unemployment of 5.2 million to be created by disarmament in the absence of offsets can likewise be compared with recent experience. During the recession of 1958 the level of unemployment rose from 2.5 million in September 1957 to 5.8 million in June 1958, a cyclical increase of 3.3 million in a period of nine months. The increase contemplated in Table 2 is only 60 per cent larger and, again, is spread over a period of twelve years. The average increase in unemployment would amount to less than 0.5 million per year. This can be compared with current annual increases in the labor force of 1 to 1.5 million per year. In other words, the problem of adjustment to disarmament, at its worst, is only a half or a third that of the annual problem of absorption of a growing labor force.

Turning now to more positive offset programs, let us consider two alternative programs, which would avoid the projected $20 billion federal budget surplus that would arise in the absence of offset programs. The first of these, which may be entitled the Tax Reduction Program, envisages a $20 billion reduction in federal personal income taxes—along with a minor $300 hundred million

---

[4] One important qualification should be made to this statement. Only a minor allowance has been made for the disturbing impact of the program on private investment. However, even if the government *literally* terminated the armaments program without even tax cuts, the impact could hardly be double that shown in the first column of Table 2.

increase in state and local expenditures. The second alternative, which may be designated the Tax Reduction and State Aid Program, envisages personal income tax reductions of only $13.2 billion and a transfer payment of $10 billion to state and local governments, permitting increases in their expenditures.

The straight tax reduction alternative, envisaged in the second column of Table 2, involves passing the federal surplus on to the consumer by an effective reduction of $20 billion in the personal income tax. This action converts the small deficit in state and local accounts into a surplus of $0.3 billion, and it is assumed that this too is spent at the state and local level. As a net result, about half of the $32 billion reduction in defense expenditure would be transferred into additional consumption, with an attendant reduction in the level of unemployment. The net decline of $11 billion in the GNP would then be of the order of magnitude of the drop that can occur from one quarter to the next in a mild postwar recession. Again, spread over a twelve-year period, the rate of decline would be less than $1 billion per year.

The implied increase in unemployment of 2.7 million would be smaller than the rise in unemployment in a mild postwar cyclical swing. Indeed, it is only 50 per cent larger than a single year's growth in the labor force, and over the twelve years would amount to only a 200,000 annual increase.

In the alternative possible program of offsets, shown in the third column of Table 2, the resources released by disarmament are divided between the private consumer, in the form of income tax reduction, and state and local government services, in the form of a $10 billion state aid program, expenditure of which is assumed to be equally divided between purchases from firms and hiring of additional personnel. As would be expected, this program stimulates consumption somewhat less and employment somewhat more than the preceding, and the rise in unemployment would be only about a quarter as serious as in the absence of offsets.

V. CONCLUSIONS

The interested reader will doubtless want to experiment with other combinations of offsetting activities, but there is no need to multiply examples here. The general order of magnitudes associated with any program are already clear. As would be expected, absolute figures are large. In fact, it is evident that an abrupt, politically irresponsible termination of the defense program would unquestionably precipitate a serious economic crisis. But a program of general and complete disarmament on the READ model, scheduled over a twelve-year period, combined with only the most elementary offsets in the form of tax reduction and transfer expenditure creates an adjustment problem of a lower order of magnitude than that posed year in and year out by the growth of the labor force and increasing productivity. In fact, the impact of disarmament represents a slight—almost unnoticeable—intensification of the problem of adjustment to economic growth in general.

This is not to say that an adequate economic adjustment to disarmament can be made entirely without friction. It does mean that the problems to be encountered are qualitatively the same, and quantitatively much smaller than the problems of daily adjustment in a growing economy. The health of the economy depends on how well we manage these persistent problems; the adjustment to disarmament is little more than a detail of that larger adjustment.

7

Impact of Disarmament on Research and Development

Richard R. Nelson*

WHY ARE WE CONCERNED?

It is not just a coincidence that the 1950's, which were marked by the largest peacetime military budgets in American history, were also marked by a striking rise in the percentage of our economic resources allocated to scientific research and development. Indeed, there are tight links between these two phenomena, running both ways.

Somewhere in the neighborhood of 15 per cent of our defense outlays are for Research and Development (henceforth denoted R&D), and somewhere between 50 per cent and 60 per cent of our total R&D expenditures is financed by defense agencies.[1] Although these measures are crude, it is clear that our defense expenditure has had a very major impact on the magnitude and allocation of our R&D effort.

---

* RICHARD R. NELSON is on the staff of the Council of Economic Advisers. He was previously at the Carnegie Institute of Technology and the Rand Corporation.

[1] In this chapter defense R&D is defined to include the programs of the Department of Defense and the military programs of the Atomic Energy Commission. National Aeronautics and Space Administration work is not included.

112

Looking at the matter the other way around, our post-World War II history of no major central war between the two big power blocs and, at the same time, extremely high levels of peacetime military expenditure must be attributed, in large part, to R&D. Modern science has created a world in which both the potential devastation to an aggressor against a well-prepared adversary, and the costs required to be well prepared, are unprecedented. It is modern science which lies behind both the balance and the delicateness of the delicate balance of terror.

It is clear that significant arms reduction would have a major impact on the size and allocation of our R&D effort. Why should this be of concern? There are two conceptually distinct reasons. One is the familiar problem of adjustment and frictional unemployment. The second is rather special, and related to the nature and role of R&D in a basically free-enterprise economy. Research and development is an activity yielding a large crop of external economies. A significant cutback in R&D could retard the rate of technological progress in our economy. This point will be elaborated, and qualified later.

MEASURING THE R&D IMPACT OF DEFENSE

Anyone who thinks it an easy matter to separate military from non-military R&D should try it. For example, the civilian jet passenger plane in widest use is an adaptation of an aircraft designed for the Air Force. Civilian uses of electronic equipment developed for military purposes are already numerous and important. On the other hand, much of our military equipment incorporates hosts of devices, materials, processes, designs, and concepts not originally conceived or developed for military purposes. In research, it is difficult to think of many areas of physics or mathematics where the results of really significant breakthroughs would not affect both civilian and military technology; and nowadays many areas of genetics, medicine, and even geology may have important military applications.[2]

The fact that many research areas and many development proj-

[2] See, for example, H. Striner, R. Sherman and L. Karadbil, *Defense Spending and the U.S. Economy*, ORO, Baltimore, Md.: Johns Hopkins, 1959.

ects may have both military and civilian applications leads to several difficult problems in attempting to assess the impact of our defense effort on R&D. One problem relates to the fact that defense support of research often is a substitute for, not an addition to, nondefense support. A good deal of the space research financed by the Department of Defense (DOD) would probably be picked up by NASA if the DOD stopped its support, and similarly if NASA closed down, a good part of its work would almost certainly be financed by the DOD. Much of the work undertaken in private industrial laboratories, say, on semiconductor devices, would be financed by the companies themselves if DOD support was withdrawn, and the DOD might well provide more funds if the companies cut back on their own financing. The same holds, both ways, with respect to a considerable amount of research undertaken at the universities and other nonprofit centers.[3]

Even if we ignore the "substitution" problem, defense spending on R&D may be a very inaccurate measure of the impact of our defense effort on R&D. To see some of the problems, consider the impact of, say, a $4 billion defense contract with a major aircraft company for the design, development, and procurement of a new ballistic missile. Assume that $1 billion of the contract are especially labeled R&D, and thus appear on the National Science Foundation (NSF) accounts for "defense" R&D. Much of the work on the contract will be subcontracted out, and though much of this subcontracting work may involve considerable research and development on components, R&D work done by subcontractors may or may not be accounted under the $1 billion figure. Generally, some of it is, and some of it is not. It is, if the prime contractor allots part of the R&D contract to subcontractors. But when the prime contractor has an option to shop around to find the best components, and possible subcontractors compete with each other to provide the best component design, or prototype, the R&D work is done on the potential subcontractor's own financing. When a firm

---

[3] The history of the synthetic rubber industry testifies to the importance of this substitution effect (see Robert Solo "Research and Development in the Synthetic Rubber Industry," *Quarterly Journal of Economics*, 1954).

gains the subcontract, the terms of the formal contract are for delivery of hardware. The R&D expense is covered in the contract sum, but in the DOD's books this is hardware outlay, and in the NSF's books this is privately financed R&D. With the materials, sub-sub-components, and other inputs to the weapon system well down at the base of the assembly pyramid the story is similar. And to get all of the R&D associated with the $4 billion weapons-system contract, we must trace our way back through the entire input-output matrix, attempting to estimate the induced R&D outlays of the firms supplying the subcontractors, the firms supplying these firms, and so on.

How much R&D then is related to the $1 billion defense R&D outlay? Clearly, the figure is significantly greater than $1 billion. But to say more than this we must make quite detailed calculations. And if we are to estimate the "net" impact of the contract, we must take account of the uses to which the resources allocated to defense R&D would have been put had the defense contract not been let. Thus, we must postulate the alternative composition of final demand, and trace through the R&D implications. The resulting figure should then be subtracted from the figures obtained from the R&D induced by the weapons-system contract.

Further, it seems clear that the defense effort has had a significant impact on the net demand for scientists and engineers. To the extent that the net defense impact on R&D (as sketched above) has been positive, our defense effort has raised the demand for scientists and engineers, and has thereby stimulated an increase in the output of these people by our educational institutions. The impact of a changing defense budget on the structure of education and incentives for careers is important, but in the calculations which will follow it will be ignored.

A SIMPLE LINEAR MODEL

For present purposes we are interested in the impact of certain specified reductions in the national military effort on R&D. The model presented here is extremely naïve, but it helps to shed some light on the problem. For convenience, we shall take as reference a 50 per cent cutback in defense spending, spread over a number of years. But all our results will be in terms of *any* cutback in defense spending. In the formal analysis it will be assumed that defense R&D is cut back proportionately with over-all defense spending.[4]

The model rests on the following assumptions: Defense expenditures on R&D just about cover all of the outlay on R&D induced by our defense effort; all other R&D is induced by nondefense final demand. The ratio of defense R&D to defense final demand can be treated as a constant, as can the ratio of nondefense R&D to nondefense final demand. On such assumptions, we can use these constants to estimate what might happen to R&D expenditures when demand shifts from defense to nondefense. We shall assume that appropriate fiscal and monetary policy assures that all declines in defense final demand are compensated for by equal dollar increases in civilian final demand.

In 1960, about $14 billion of our economy's resources were spent on R&D. The Department of Defense and the military part of the Atomic Energy Commission supported somewhere around $7 billion of this work.[5] Total 1960 defense expenditure was about $45 billion, including some of the AEC's work, and thus defense R&D was between 15 and 16 per cent of defense final demand. Since gross national product for 1960 was about $500 billion, nondefense R&D represented about 1.5 per cent of nondefense final demand. If these ratios stay constant, a dollar reduction in military final demand would result in a fourteen cent reduction in total R&D. Thus, cutting the military budget in half and increasing civilian demand to compensate would result in a reduction in total R&D outlay of about $3.2 billion, or about 23 per cent. It appears,

[4] The assumption is highly unrealistic, but it is not clear in what direction it is unrealistic. From the point of view of achieving a stable agreement, it might be of the utmost importance that military R&D be stopped. From the point of view of a nation participating in an arms control agreement, it is of the utmost importance that other nations do not increase their relative technical sophistication and reach a situation where they can build up a superior force rapidly. The disarmament authority itself might well conduct considerable R&D on detection.
[5] The NSF calculates that the total government contribution was about $9 billion. It is estimated that between 75 and 80 per cent of this is military.

then, that on these assumptions the proportional drop in total R&D expenditure in the economy would be about half as great as the proportional cutback in military expenditure, or, to put it another way, the elasticity is approximately 0.46.

This estimate of the expenditure impact significantly overstates the impact of disarmament on employment of scientists and engineers. There are two reasons for this. First, expenditure on R&D covers considerably more than the salaries of scientists and engineers. A large percentage (more than half) of the expense is for materials and equipment and for the salaries of technical assistants and administrative personnel. In military R&D, because of the heavy emphasis on systems development, which involves heavy hardware outlays, the percentage of total R&D outlay attributable to salaries of scientists and engineers is significantly smaller than in nonmilitary R&D. It is estimated that the defense R&D dollar hires only three-quarters the number of R&D scientists and engineers as does the nondefense R&D dollar.

Second, the preceding calculations have treated only R&D scientists and engineers, and only about one-third of our scientists and engineers are engaged in R&D (on a full-time-equivalent basis). About two-thirds of their time is spent on problems of production control and planning, administration, sales, and teaching. Further, in the defense industries, R&D scientists and engineers comprise a much larger share of the total number than in nondefense industries. It is estimated that approximately 50 per cent of the engineers and scientists in defense work are in R&D, while in nondefense work the figure is only 25 per cent.

Taking into account both the greater R&D outlay per scientist and engineer in military R&D work, and the smaller ratio of total scientists and engineers to R&D scientists and engineers in military work, it can be determined that the preceding calculations overstate, by approximately a factor of two, the impact of a compensated decline in defense spending on the employment of scientists and engineers. While a 50 per cent decline in defense spending would lead to a 23 per cent cutback in R&D spending, it would lead to only a 12 per cent cutback in employment of scientists and engineers.

The preceding calculations did not take into account the significant difference in R&D for different industries of the civilian economy. Clearly, if civilian demand expands in such a way as to call forth a high level of output in the electrical equipment industry, for example, this would lead to a larger total national R&D effort than if civilian demand increased principally for, say, agricultural products. It is, therefore, useful to explore the effects of different compositions of increases in nonmilitary demand.

Leontief and Hoffenberg have estimated,[6] by input-output techniques, the increased sales levels of the various industries which would be induced by a $1 million increase in investment, consumption, military spending, and other final-demand categories. Although the Leontief-Hoffenberg industry breakdown does not exactly match the industry breakdown by the NSF, I have tried to link the two. My rough calculations indicate that $1.00 of consumption final demand generates 0.5 cents of R&D expenditure; $1.00 of investment final demand, about 3.5 cents of R&D spending; with the other Leontief-Hoffenberg nonmilitary final demand categories falling between these two categories in their R&D impact.

If we calculate the elasticity of R&D expenditures with respect to defense expenditure, using the above ratios and assuming that defense R&D is cut back proportionately with defense expenditure, we find that if investment final demand fills the gap, the elasticity is about 0.4 and if consumption final demand fills the gap, the elasticity is nearly 0.5. The difference is not much to get excited about. If we assume that civilian final demand will switch more toward electronics, then the elasticities are somewhat reduced. But it seems clear that it will take very major changes in the composition of nonmilitary final demand for the elasticity to drop to around 0.3, assuming constant R&D-to-sales ratios, and assuming military R&D to fall proportionately with military final demand.

The reason for the rather surprising lack of sensitivity is obvious. The amount of R&D generated per dollar of defense final demand

[6] Wassily W. Leontief and Marvin Hoffenberg, "The Economic Effects of Disarmament," *Scientific American*, April 1961. See also Chapter 5.

is so large relative to the amount generated by any other category of final demand that differences in the other categories have but a small effect on the computed elasticity.

A MORE DETAILED VIEW

The figures ground out by these rough calculations suggest, first, that if R&D-sales ratios do not change very much, a cutback in defense expenditure compensated by an increase in nondefense final demand will lead to a proportional reduction in R&D outlay somewhat less than half as great. Second, if the ratio of scientists and engineers to total sales does not change in the different industries, a given proportional cutback in defense spending will result in a proportional cutback in employment of scientists and engineers about one-quarter as great.

It is worthwhile to look beneath the aggregative figures to try to get some feel for the sector-by-sector impact of arms reduction. Let us first look at the organizations and industries which would be most affected.

In 1960–1961, of the R&D total of $14 billion, $10.5 billion, or 75 per cent, was performed by industry; the federal government performed $2.1 billion, or 15 per cent; and universities and other nonprofit institutions performed $1.4 billion, or 10 per cent.

The Department of Defense financed about 75 per cent of the work done in government facilities, slightly more than 50 per cent of the work performed by industry, and about 25 per cent of the work performed by colleges and universities and other nonprofit institutions. If one-half of the expenditure of the AEC is included, the figure for the universities and other nonprofit organizations rises to about 35 per cent. Thus, defense cutbacks would seem likely to fall with greatest proportional impact on government-owned facilities, with next greatest on industry, and least upon universities and other nonprofit centers.

Examination of the type of R&D performed by these organizations suggests a similar conclusion. It is likely that basic research projects financed by the DOD would not be cut back as much as R&D tied to weapons. And where defense spending for basic research is cut back, these projects would become prime candidates for nondefense support. About 3 per cent of DOD-supported work in industry is basic research; 10 per cent of the work in government laboratories and about 40 per cent of the work in colleges and universities financed by the DOD is classified as basic research.[7] Thus, both because the DOD finances a relatively small share of R&D at the universities, and because much of that work is basic research which is unlikely to be cut back drastically, the impact of disarmament on R&D at the universities should not be particularly great. It also should be noted that about one-third of defense-related work conducted by the universities is done in special centers set up for that purpose.

A large proportion of DOD-financed work carried on by industry is closely tied to specific weapon systems, and thus is apt to be very sensitive to arms reduction. Somewhere around 85 per cent of it is development work. However, the impact of disarmament on industry R&D is likely to be concentrated in a few industries. Of the DOD's industrial R&D spending, more than 50 per cent goes to the aircraft and parts industry, and about 20 per cent to the electronics industry. Looked at in another way, the Department of Defense supports better than half of the R&D done in three industries—aircraft, 85 per cent; electrical equipment, about 60 per cent; and communications, about 50 per cent—while in such industries as food, chemicals, petroleum, and primary metals, it provides less than 10 per cent of the funds.

The fact that military R&D has a different "mix" than nonmilitary R&D suggests that disarmament would affect the various scientific and technical professions very differently. Unfortunately, the scientific and technical manpower data are much too aggregate to provide support for this conjecture. The data[8] show that the aircraft and parts industry and the electrical equipment industry do

---

[7] It should be noted that the DOD supports a much smaller fraction of basic research than total R&D. Indeed, the DOD supports only about 15 per cent of the total basic research done in the United States. If AEC support is added, the figure comes to about 25 per cent. For this reason, as well as those stated above, the impact of disarmament is likely to be much less on basic research than on other kinds of R&D.

[8] *Scientific and Technical Personnel in American Industry,* National Science Foundation, 1960.

not employ a disproportionately large share of engineers.[9] But the data do not break down the types of engineers, and it is clear that these industries employ a much larger share of aeronautical and electronic engineers. The data do show that these two industries employ a greater than proportional share of the physicists and mathematicians in industry.[10] But these groups are likely to have little difficulty in finding employment elsewhere. While the manpower data do not clearly suggest that there may be serious problems of shifting defense R&D personnel to nondefense jobs, it must be stressed that the reason may well be that the data are inadequate, not that there will be no problem.

THE WORKINGS OF THE MARKET

The previous analysis was based on given, and assumed constant, R&D-to-sales ratios. But before it is assumed that the figures calculated by the model provide a rough measure of the job for public policy instruments, we should examine how the market mechanism is likely to contribute to the solution to the problem. In particular, how might R&D-to-sales ratios change in response to an excess supply of scientists and engineers?

The determinants of R&D spending have been under increasing study by economists. There is mounting evidence that the level of R&D spending can be reasonably well explained by a model which assumes that firm managers act as if they have a target R&D-to-sales ratio, and that they try to reduce any discrepancy between this target ratio (or rule of thumb) and the actual R&D-to-sales ratio. The widespread (but far from universal) existence of a target R&D-to-sales ratio has been uncovered by NSF interviews; Norton Seeber has collected considerable evidence on this point, and Edwin Mansfield has tested such a model statistically and found it quite reliable.[11]

[9] They hire 27 per cent of engineers in industry and 25 per cent of total scientists and engineers.
[10] Sixty per cent and 49 per cent, respectively.
[11] Seeber's work is as yet unpublished. Mansfield's results are published in *The Rate and Direction of Inventive Activity: Economic and Social Factors,* Princeton, N.J.: Princeton University Press for National Bureau of Economic Research, 1962.

The use of a model assuming adjustment of a variable toward a target or rule-of-thumb value is in increasing use in economic analysis. The analogous rule of thumb for investment behavior is the capital-output ratio (the rule of thumb which lies behind acceleration models); for pricing behavior, it is the percentage markup over cost. To the extent that such targets exist, or that firms behave as if they existed, "behavioral" models based on these targets can be useful predictive tools.

But over relatively long periods of time, particularly when prices and technologies are changing, it seems likely that short-run rules of thumb also change. On the average, the rules of thumb (the R&D-to-sales ratio, the price markup, the inventory-sales ratio) should change so as to move closer toward that which is optimal. For present purposes, optimal and expected, profit maximizing, will be considered as synonymous.

The optimal expenditure on R&D obviously requires that the discounted future returns from increasing the quantity of resources applied to R&D equals the cost of these additional resources. The effect of decreases in R&D costs upon the optimal quantity of R&D resources depends on the shape of the marginal efficiency curve. If, for example, this curve is of unitary elasticity (is a rectangular hyperbola), then a 1 per cent decline in R&D unit costs will lead to a 1 per cent increase in the optimal quantity of resources applied to R&D.

It can be shown that the unitary elasticity assumption is consistent with the observation that, for firms that spend anything at all on R&D, the R&D-sales ratio is not systematically related to firm size.[12] Perhaps, therefore, the unitary elasticity assumption is suggestive of the orders of magnitude involved. Earlier in this chapter, it was suggested that a 50 per cent cutback in military expenditures would lead to approximately a 23 per cent cutback in R&D spending, holding R&D unit costs constant. The preceding analysis suggests that a 23 per cent reduction in R&D unit costs would enable the market itself to take up the slack. To restore R&D

[12] See Jacob Schmookler, "Bigness, Fewness, and Research," *Journal of Political Economy,* December 1959.

employment would require a cost reduction of less than 20 per cent.[13]

The costs of R&D, however, include much more than the salaries of scientists and engineers. In fact, the salaries of scientists and engineers comprise only a little more than a quarter of total R&D costs in American industry. In 1957, R&D cost per scientist or engineer averaged $34,000. During the same year, the average payroll cost per R&D scientist or engineer was $8,900.[14] Part of the difference is attributable to the payroll costs of supporting personnel. Total payroll costs of scientists and engineers and supporting personnel comprised about half of total R&D costs in American industry in 1957. For the military industries (aircraft and electrical equipment) the figure is about 45 per cent; for other industries, about 55 per cent.[15] For American industry as a whole there were about 1.8 supporting personnel (technicians, draftsmen, management) per R&D scientist and engineer. For the military industries the figure is about 2.2; and for the civilian industries, about 1.5.[16] The remaining 50 per cent of R&D cost is accounted for by materials and overhead.

The fact that wages and salaries of scientists and engineers make up only a little over one-quarter of R&D costs makes it difficult to estimate the elasticity of R&D employment of scientists and engineers with respect to a cut in wage and salary levels. The crucial factor is the elasticity of substitution between scientists and engineers and other R&D factors of production.

At one extreme, if R&D factor proportions are relatively fixed, in order to achieve an X per cent increase in employment of scientists and engineers, the market will require a fall in the salaries of significantly more than X per cent, unless the costs of other R&D inputs are reduced also. However, if R&D factor proportions are

[13] The reduction in R&D employment calculated by the model falls between the reduction in R&D spending and the reduction in total employment of scientists and engineers.
[14] *Funds for Research and Development in Industry*, National Science Foundation, 1957, 1960.
[15] *Ibid.*
[16] *Scientists and Engineers in American Industry—1956*, National Science Foundation, 1959.

relatively flexible, then the stickiness of other factor prices may actually help the employment situation for scientists and engineers. To gain an X per cent increase in employment will require a less than X per cent decline in salaries. Unfortunately, there exists almost no data from which either the elasticity of substitutions or the likely market response of the cost of the other factors can be estimated.

The dynamics of the adjustment mechanism, however, are likely to be relatively favorable. The target R&D-to-sales ratios are likely to be adjusted upwards in response to a slack market for scientists and engineers. The recent work of R. Cyert and J. March[17] suggests that the decision rules established by a firm are likely to be relatively stable if this generates results which are satisfactory. However, if the results are less than satisfactory, the organization or individual tends to re-examine the decision rules and search for improvement. For the purpose of this analysis, satisfactory profits will be defined as the rate of return that capital and management could be earning elsewhere over the long run.

Obviously, the profits of a firm depend on the nearness of its target R&D-to-sales ratio to the optimum ratio. Thus, when a firm spends more on R&D it can either help or hurt its own profit position, depending on whether it is moving closer to or further away from the optimal position. However, let us assume that as other firms increase their R&D spending, a firm which does not increase its own spending will experience a decline in its market share. And the fall in its market share could be reflected in smaller profits.

Thus, if disarmament leads to an increase in the optimal R&D-sales ratio, then as soon as a few firms act to increase their spending, this will put pressure on other firms to reevaluate their own R&D decisions. And firms under profit pressure may well be able to determine their appropriate R&D response by imitating the more successful firms, the firms which increased their R&D spending earlier. As Sidney Winter has pointed out in an unpublished paper, the economic system tends to enforce good decision rules not only by killing off inefficient firms, but by providing models for them to

[17] "A Behavioral Theory of the Firm," in preparation.

imitate to become more efficient.[18] Norton Seeber and the National Science Foundation have found considerable evidence that firms in an industry pay a considerable amount of attention to the R&D policies of the more successful firms.

PROBLEMS OF PUBLIC POLICY

What does the preceding analysis imply with respect to appropriate public policies? Let us look first at the employment problem, then at the welfare problem.

Employment: Although scientists and engineers will probably be harder hit by arms reduction than any other occupational group (save military people), it is not likely that unemployment of scientists and engineers will be more than a very short-run problem. R&D is one of the fastest growing activities in our economy, despite some retardation in the last few years; and the employment of scientists and engineers is growing at a faster rate than employment of almost any other occupational group. In recent years, R&D has been growing at a yearly rate of over 10 per cent, while GNP has been growing at about 3.5 per cent (in money terms). Employment of scientists and engineers has been growing at a yearly rate of about 6 per cent, while over-all employment has been growing at less than 1.5 per cent. The earlier calculations assumed a given and constant ratio of civilian R&D to civilian demand. In fact, this ratio has been growing rapidly over the past ten years. It can be shown that if the ratio of civilian R&D to civilian final demand does not decrease its rate of growth dramatically, then a phased disarmament program might not reduce total R&D spending or employment at all, but rather would (temporarily) retard its rate of growth. If the response of R&D employment to changes in salaries is reasonably great, and scientists are reasonably mobile, this suggests that the impact of arms reduction on employment of scientists and engineers is likely to be more a temporary retardation of rate of growth of salaries than significant unemployment.

[18] Winter's unpublished paper, "Economic National Select Theory of the Firm," points out some important ways in ... tion" may mislead.

However, in a situation where demand has shifted greatly, the federal government can play a very helpful role in oiling the adjustment mechanism. Programs might be developed to help scientists and engineers previously engaged in defense work tailor their training to the problems of civilian industry. Quite possibly something should be done to reduce the cost of moving, since there is likely to be a significant shift in the geographical composition of demand. Making moving expenses fully tax deductible seems a reasonable step. Perhaps the government should go further, and develop tax credit schemes to facilitate mobility.

If more action is deemed necessary, then a step up in the peacetime space program is ideally suited for the job. The industries involved, the locations, the skills, are almost a perfect match for those which will be hit hardest by arms reduction. Whether an increase in the space program is justified on the basis of other criteria is another question.

Welfare: As has been stated earlier, our concern about a cutback in R&D resulting from a reduction in defense spending transcends our concern with maintaining full employment. We tend to think (rightly) of R&D as an activity yielding a bountiful crop of external economies, as an activity to which the market will allocate too small a fraction of our resources in the absence of public action. If we take this point of view, our defense effort is yielding us a bonus by causing a larger R&D effort than we would have in the absence of our defense programs, and one of the real costs of arms reduction might be the shifting of resources away from R&D.

However, much of the discussion of the economic impact of our defense and space R&D efforts has tended to ignore the fact that the overwhelming percentage of defense R&D dollars is spent on work aimed at creating a specific new component or system for the military. Certainly, this kind of R&D contributes far less to the dvance of civilian technology than R&D concerned more directly h civilian problems.

e civilian economy obviously does gain some by-product ad from the R&D financed by defense agencies. But military easingly is exploring areas far away from those of clear the civilian economy. While it is difficult to measure the degree of civilian relevance of defense R&D programs, clearly research on mildew-resistant fabrics for military use is much more likely to have civilian application than research on nose cones. A very large percentage of the civilian applications of military R&D listed in the ORO study mentioned earlier are of the mildew-resistant-cloth type, and this type of R&D probably is a much smaller percentage of total military work today than before the missile age.

Indeed, the case can be made that in recent years the growth of military and space R&D has significantly retarded the growth of civilian R&D. Between 1954 and 1961, while the number of total scientists and engineers in R&D in industry grew at approximately a 10 per cent annual rate, the number financed by private industry out of its own funds and, presumably, involved principally on civilian programs, grew at only one-third that rate. There is considerable feeling among R&D directors that the growth of defense R&D, by bidding up salaries and by taking the cream of the new science and engineering graduates, has tended to reduce significantly the quantity and quality of R&D undertaken in civilian-oriented laboratories.

In any case, a significant increase in R&D resources could be used with large benefit to society. In many of the civilian industries very little R&D is presently directed toward improving products and processes. While in the aircraft and parts industry and the communications and other electrical equipment industry (the industries accounting for more than 80 per cent of government research funds spent in industry) R&D spending exceeds 10 per cent of sales, for all other industries taken together the figure does not exceed 3 per cent. Increased R&D spending undoubtedly would yield high returns in many of these industries. The civilian economy would benefit especially from increased long-range research and experimentation with advanced technological possibilities of the sort that the research teams presently employed by defense industries have conducted so successfully. The freeing of these highly trained research resources for application to civilian technology would hold great promise for increasing the welfare of the American people.

In addition to the nonmilitary domestic uses for R&D resources that would be freed by disarmament, these resources could be used to complement an expanded foreign aid program. Research and development might be focused on such problems as development of simple teaching machines and related communications equipment, techniques for overcoming aridity, efficient and low-cost transportation systems, cheap and reliable power sources, and other equipment and processes specially tailored to the resource and labor availabilities of the less developed economies.

A disarmament program would provide an unmatched opportunity to review public policies toward nonmilitary R&D. For the first time in years we would be faced with a slack market for scientists and engineers. There are urgent needs for more research and development in areas where private incentives and financial capabilities are weak. Government support might be given to enlarged research programs in such fields as urban transportation and housing. Policies to encourage more basic research might be considered. The freeing of R&D resources could be one of the most important economic benefits of disarmament. Because the uses of the R&D resources which would be freed by disarmament are so important and so many, the economic benefits of disarmament would dwarf the problem.

PART III

Analysis of Disarmament Adjustments

8

Monetary and Fiscal Adjustments to Disarmament

Warren Smith*

THE DIMENSIONS OF THE PROBLEM

The kind of disarmament program we are talking about would involve a reduction of defense and related expenditures from a peak of about $62 billion in 1965 to around $29 billion in 1977, a decline of some $33 billion spread over a period of twelve years, with a disproportionately heavy rate of decline, of around $5 billion per year, for the first three years.[1] On the basis of projections by the Council of Economic Advisers,[2] we may set potential GNP (valued at 1960 prices) at about $630 billion in 1965, and $950 billion in 1977. Thus, the total proposed reduction of $33 billion in military spending over the twelve-year period 1965 to 1977 would amount to only slightly more than 4 per cent of our potential

* WARREN SMITH, Professor of Economics in the University of Michigan, is currently on leave and serving on the staff of the President's Council of Economic Advisers. He is author of "Debt Management in the United States," a study paper prepared for the Joint Economic Committee.

[1] See Chapter 2.
[2] "The American Economy in 1961: Problems and Policies," Statement of the Council of Economic Advisers in *January 1961 Economic Report of the President and the Economic Situation and Outlook,* Hearings before the Joint Economic Committee, 87th Cong., 1st Sess.

average annual GNP of approximately $780 billion during this period.

It seems apparent that if we are successful in maintaining a climate of healthy economic growth and if we adopt intelligent policies to facilitate the process of economic adjustment, we should experience no great difficulty in absorbing reductions in defense spending of this magnitude.

MONETARY-FISCAL POLICIES

The basic purpose of fiscal and monetary policy is to achieve the level of aggregate monetary demand most consistent with economic stability.[3] The view has increasingly come to be accepted that there are many combinations of tax, expenditure, and monetary policies which will achieve any specified level of aggregate demand under given circumstances. That is, within limits, different policy measures are substitutes as far as the control of aggregate demand is concerned. However, the particular combination of measures, or "policy mix," adopted may have important implications as far as the allocation of resources among the broad categories of consumption, private investment, and the provision of government services is concerned.

In designing a program of fiscal and monetary measures to compensate for the deflationary effects of disarmament, I believe it is essential to view the problem as one of selecting a policy mix which will maintain a desirable level of aggregate demand while, at the same time, influencing in an appropriate way the reallocation of our resources. The fiscal and monetary tools at our disposal are, however, not all equally effective. In view of the heavy emphasis

[3] In an economy characterized—as ours appears to have been in the last few years—by price rigidities and cost pressures on the price level, the selection of the appropriate level of aggregate demand involves many difficulties and requires the making of basic value judgments concerning the importance to be attached to the two important—and partially inconsistent —criteria of economic stability, the prevention of changes in the value of money, and the maintenance of high levels of employment and reasonably full utilization of economic resources. Although I believe this problem is a serious one, I can see little reason to suppose that a program of disarmament such as we are considering would accentuate the problem.

that has been placed on monetary policy as an economic regulator in the last few years, it seems especially important that we recognize the limitations of policies designed to influence aggregate demand through manipulation of money, financial assets, interest rates, and credit availability.

DEBT RETIREMENT AND MONETARY EXPANSION AS OFFSETS TO REDUCED EXPENDITURES

In the eyes of legislators, government officials, and the general public, the fiscal problem posed by a reduction in defense spending may appear in the form of a question: What disposition should the government make of the budget surplus which would result from a cut in defense spending? Should it retire part of the public debt? Or reduce taxes? Or increase nondefense spending? Or engage in some combination of these actions?

There is perhaps no idea that enjoys greater popularity than the notion that the public debt should be paid off at the first opportunity. There is evidence that a sizable segment of the general public holds this view and would favor the use of at least a portion of any surplus resulting from reduced defense spending to retire debt.[4] In view of these attitudes, it is important to consider the wisdom and feasibility of such a policy.

The effects produced by a cut in government purchases of goods and services and use of a resulting budget surplus for debt retirement are rather complex. In the first place, the cut in spending is directly and strongly deflationary, because it constitutes an outright reduction in final demand for goods and services. The results of the debt retirement are, in general, inflationary, but depend somewhat on what types of investors hold the debt that is retired.

When it cuts expenditures while maintaining tax collections at the original level, the Treasury reduces the publicly-held money supply, since it fails to put back into circulation the dollars that are paid over to it by taxpayers. If it uses the dollars to retire debt held by nonbank investors, however, it restores the money supply to its

[4] See Emile Benoit, "The Propensity to Reduce the National Debt out of Defense Savings," *American Economic Review*, May 1961, pp. 455–456.

original level.[5] But the money which was originally taken from taxpayers on income account with no *quid pro quo*—thereby reducing taxpayers' net worth—is turned back to investors on asset account through an exchange of money for securities. With a reduced supply of bonds and the same supply of money as originally, bond prices will be somewhat higher and interest rates lower. Finally, the operation leaves the public with a smaller amount of wealth in the form of net claims against the government than it had to begin with. Since most of the available evidence suggests that neither the interest rate nor the wealth effects on income-generating expenditures are very strong, the results of the whole operation are: (1) *a strongly deflationary income effect,* (2) *a weakly inflationary interest-rate* effect, and (3) *a weakly deflationary wealth effect.* The net result is almost surely powerfully deflationary.[6]

If the debt that is retired is owned by commercial banks, the income effect is, of course, exactly the same as in the above case, while the interest rate and wealth effects are essentially the same, although there are differences in detail. When the funds accumulated by the Treasury are used to retire bank-held debt, the banks find themselves with the same reserves as they originally held, but their earnings assets and deposits are reduced by equal amounts. Under normal circumstances, they will expand credit by making

[5] If the Treasury deposits the tax proceeds that it does not spend in its accounts at Federal Reserve banks, the reserves of member banks are reduced when the taxes are collected and then restored to their original level when the funds are used for debt retirement. On the other hand, to the extent that the tax collections are held on deposit in commercial banks pending their use for debt retirement, aggregate member bank reserves are not affected.
[6] For simplicity of exposition, it has been implicitly assumed in the foregoing discussion that the budget was balanced initially, and that the reduction in expenditures created a surplus which was used for debt retirement. However, the same forces would be at work if the Treasury had a budget surplus to begin with which was increased by the reduction in expenditure, or if it was operating at a deficit initially and if the deficit was reduced by the cut in expenditures. In these cases, both the supply of bonds and the public's holdings of net claims against the government would be reduced relative to what they would have been if the Treasury had not reduced expenditures, so that interest rate and wealth effects similar to those referred to above would be present.

loans to or buying securities from the public until their earnings assets and the money supply have been restored approximately to the original level. In order to acquire debt from the public, the banks will reduce interest rates or relax credit standards. When the process is completed, the public will hold the same amount of money as originally but its indebtedness to the banks will be increased and/or its holdings of government securities will be reduced as a result of sales of such securities to the banks. Thus, the public's net claims will have been reduced by the amount of debt retired in essentially the same way as occurred in the case in which the debt retired by the Treasury was held by nonbanks. Again, there is a strongly deflationary income effect, a weakly inflationary interest rate effect, and a weakly deflationary wealth effect; and the total operation is unmistakably deflationary.

The third possibility, which is somewhat different from the first two, occurs if the debt that is retired by the Treasury is held by the Federal Reserve System. Again, there is the same deflationary income effect, as was explained above, and net claims held by the public are again reduced, this time because in the first instance the public is left with the same amount of government securities as originally and the same amount of indebtedness to the banks, but its money holdings are reduced by the amount of the cut in government spending. In this case, however, the interest rate effect, instead of being weakly inflationary, is fairly strongly deflationary. This is because the use of funds collected from the public to retire debt held by the Federal Reserve not only reduces the money supply but also reduces bank reserves by an equal amount. This reduces excess bank reserves and (unless, of course, it is offset by some other action) forces the banks into a multiple contraction of earnings assets and deposits, which pushes up interest rates and tightens credit conditions. In this case, then, there is a strongly deflationary income effect, a fairly strongly deflationary interest rate effect, and a weakly deflationary wealth effect; and the entire process is even more strongly deflationary than in the first two cases.

Actually the reason for the difference between the last case (retirement of Federal Reserve-held debt) and the first two cases (retirement of debt held by the nonbank public or by commercial banks) is that, when viewed in the proper perspective, there is no debt retirement in the last case, since the debt held by the Federal Reserve does not influence spending decisions, and since virtually all of any incremental payments of interest to the Federal Reserve are turned back to the Treasury at the end of the year in the form of voluntary payments of interest on Federal Reserve notes, it is therefore best not to regard Treasury securities held by the Federal Reserve as part of the public debt. Thus, the "retirement" of debt held by the Federal Reserve is a formality, and the result of such retirement is the same as though the Treasury had impounded the budget surplus and placed it on deposit with the Federal Reserve. Accordingly, when we speak of debt retirement, we shall mean the retirement of debt held by the nonbank public or the commercial banks.

A MODEL FOR ANALYZING DEBT RETIREMENT

The chief positive economic argument that has been advanced in favor of a policy of surplus budgeting and debt retirement is that the budget surplus represents an addition to national saving and that the use of the surplus for debt retirement puts additional funds into the capital market, thereby lowering interest rates and stimulating private investment. Thus, such a policy, by the stimulus it provides to private investment, is said to be conducive to a more rapid pace of economic growth. While there is an element of truth in this argument, the above discussion of the mechanics of debt retirement suggests that the stimulus to investment would not be sufficient to overcome the deflationary effects of the reduction in government expenditures. Some of the proponents of debt retirement recognize this and suggest that a policy of debt retirement may need to be supplemented by an expansive monetary policy (or, perhaps, other measures) to provide a further stimulus to investment.[7]

---

[7] The possible need to supplement debt retirement by other measures to stimulate investment is recognized, for example, by the Commission on Money and Credit, *Money and Credit: Their Influence on Jobs, Prices, and Growth,* Englewood Cliffs, N.J.: Prentice-Hall, 1961, especially Chaps. 5 and 9.

In view of the interest in and support for a policy of debt retirement that has often been expressed, it seems worthwhile to supplement the somewhat mechanical description of the process of debt retirement given above by a more formal analysis.[8]

The argument for a policy of retiring debt out of budget surpluses in order to stimulate investment and accelerate growth would be strongest in what may be termed the *classical case,* in which liquidity preference is inelastic with respect to the interest rate, that is, where a cut in government expenditures has no effect on income. In this case, when government expenditures are reduced and the resulting surplus funds are thrown into the capital market through debt retirement, the fall in the interest rate does not cause the public to hold more money but rather increases investment and/or reduces saving (i.e., increases consumption) by as much as government expenditures decline, thus leaving income constant. The way in which the increase in private expenditures is divided between investment and consumption depends upon the interest elasticities of investment and saving; if saving is completely interest-inelastic, the increase in investment is equal to the fall in government expenditures, and the growth-accelerating effect is maximized.

The complete antithesis of the classical case is what may be called the "ultra-Keynesian" case. Here, either spending is completely inelastic with respect to the interest rate, or liquidity preference is completely elastic with respect to the interest rate. Under these circumstances, the debt retirement itself has no inflationary effect, either because all of the money injected into the economy is absorbed into idle balances without reducing the interest rate, or because such a decline in the interest rate as occurs does not cause any increase in expenditures. Consequently, the entire effect of the operation is the deflationary effect produced by the cut in government expenditures, as reflected in the ordinary Keynesian multiplier.

Obviously the "truth" lies somewhere between the classical and

[8] The details of the analysis, based on a static equilibrium model of an essentially Keynesian variety, are available to interested readers in mimeographed form, upon application to the author.

ultra-Keynesian extremes. As far as I know, none of the numerous studies of the determinants of aggregate personal saving that have been made in recent years have turned up any indications that interest rates have any appreciable effect on saving. Studies based on sample interview surveys at the Survey Research Center of the University of Michigan suggest that although the form in which household savings are held may be influenced by relative yields on different types of assets, interest rates do not have any appreciable effect on the aggregate saving rate.[9] Since consumer borrowing for the purpose of purchasing durable goods other than houses is treated as negative personal saving in the national income accounts, it would be possible for rising interest rates to increase saving by discouraging the use of consumer credit. However, there is very little evidence that consumer borrowing is, in practice, noticeably sensitive to interest rates and general credit conditions.[10] Nor does there seem to be any evidence that interest rates exert an appreciable effect on business saving.[11]

The great majority of the numerous studies of the determinants of business investment that have been made in recent years have failed to find a significant interest rate effect.[12] There are rather cogent theoretical reasons for expecting investment to be rather insensitive to interest rates, and prevailing business practices (notably the preference for internal financing) and institutional arrangements relating to the financing of investment apparently serve to insulate investment still further from the effects of interest rates.[13] However, the evidence is not entirely negative; a few recent studies

[9] See George Katona, *The Powerful Consumer*, New York: McGraw-Hill, 1960, pp. 222–223.
[10] For a discussion of this matter, see *Staff Report on Employment, Growth and Price Levels*, prepared for consideration by the Joint Economic Committee, December 1959, 86th Cong., 1st Sess., pp. 385–390.
[11] See John Lintner, "The Determinants of Corporate Savings," in W. W. Heller, F. M. Boddy, and C. L. Nelson (eds.), *Savings in the Modern Economy*, Minneapolis: University of Minnesota Press, 1953, pp. 230–255.
[12] For a useful summary of research in this field, see J. R. Meyer and Edwin Kuh, *The Investment Decision*, Cambridge, Mass.: Harvard University Press, 1957, pp. 23–35. The findings with respect to interest rates are summarized on pp. 25–26.
[13] For a discussion of these matters, see *Staff Report on Employment, Growth, and Price Levels, op. cit.*, pp. 368–381.

have turned up bits of evidence suggesting some interest elasticity.[14] Residential construction, which is included in gross private domestic investment in our national income accounts, has undoubtedly been affected significantly by changes in interest rates and credit conditions in recent years.[15] It seems quite clear, however, that the effects produced in this sector have been due, in part, to institutional peculiarities in the field of mortgage finance and do not represent an interest elasticity in the usual sense. As a result of the legal ceilings applicable to FHA-insured and VA-guaranteed mortgages, increases in market interest rates have attracted funds into corporate and state and local government securities, thereby draining funds away from the mortgage market and causing residential construction to decline, while declining market interest rates have had the opposite effect.[16] It is often argued that if interest rates on

[14] Using quarterly data on manufacturers' fixed investment for the period from mid-1948 to mid-1955, Franz Gehrels and Suzanne Wiggins ("Interest Rates and Manufacturers' Fixed Investment," *American Economic Review*, March 1957, pp. 79–92) found that interest rates exerted a significant effect on such investment but with a lag of one year. Yehuda Grunfeld ("The Determinants of Corporate Investment," in A. C. Harberger (ed.), *The Demand for Durable Goods*, Chicago: University of Chicago Press, 1960, pp. 211–266) in a study of plant and equipment investment by eight large firms, using annual data for the period 1935–1954, has found interest elasticities for various companies ranging up to −2.1 and averaging somewhere in the neighborhood of −0.5. He first finds that investment is well explained by the stock of plant and equipment and the market value of the firm's securities, both taken as of the end of the previous year. He then uses the capitalization formula to break down the value of the firm into two components—Moody's Aaa corporate bond yield and an implicit estimate of expected profits (adjusted for borrower's risk)—and introduces these two variables in place of the value of the firm. Finally, T. C. Liu ("A Quarterly Model of the U.S. Economy, 1947–59," paper delivered at a meeting of the Econometric Society in St. Louis, Mo., on December 30, 1960) has used an investment function employing an exponentially distributed lag in his quarterly econometric model and has found a significant interest elasticity of investment.

[15] For a discussion of the recent tendency for residential construction to behave in a countercyclical fashion, see J. M. Guttentag, "The Short Cycle in Residential Construction," *American Economic Review*, June 1961, pp. 275–298. In my opinion, Guttentag underrates the role played by the interest rate ceilings on FHA-insured and VA-guaranteed mortgages in producing this countercyclical pattern.

[16] See S. B. Klaman, "The Availability of Residential Mortgage Credit," J. J. O'Leary, "The Effects of Monetary Policies on the Residential Mortgage Market," and W. L. Smith, "The Impact of Monetary Policy on Residential

mortgages were free to fluctuate, housing would still be sensitive to their fluctuations due to the fact that interest cost is such a large element in the cost of a house financed by a long-term mortgage of the type that is now commonplace. However, there is no evidence bearing on this point, since we have had no experience with freely fluctuating mortgage interest rates under present-day conditions.[17]

Since, under our present institutional arrangements, residential construction is affected by the interest rate and since there is some slight evidence of an interest effect on business investment, I shall take the interest elasticity of private investment (including residential construction) to be −0.5. Admittedly, this is little more than a guess, but I doubt very much that it underestimates the sensitivity of investment to interest rates.

In addition to private investment, interest rates and credit conditions may also influence, to some extent, debt-financed public investment by state and local government units. While the effects of interest rates in this sector have been the subject of considerable discussion and it seems to be generally agreed that such effects exist, there has been no satisfactory study, to my knowledge, indicating their magnitude; and I would judge that although significant, the effects are rather small.[18] According to the report of the Commission on Money and Credit, "estimates of the percentage of

---

Construction, 1948–58," in *Study of Mortgage Credit* (Senate Subcommittee on Housing, Committee on Banking and Currency, 85th Cong., 2nd Sess.), 1958, pp. 189–208, 235–243, and 244–264, respectively.

[17] A study by R. F. Muth ("The Demand for Non-Farm Housing," in Harberger, *op. cit.*, pp. 29–96), covering the period 1915–1941 (with war years omitted), indicates an interest elasticity of demand for new housing construction of about −0.8. Aside from failing to take adequate account of demographic variables (such as household formation), this study is of doubtful value as applied to the postwar period due to the great changes that have taken place in mortgage financing since the 1930's, such as the greatly increased use of amortized mortgages and of government-backed mortgages under the FHA and VA programs.

[18] For further discussion, see *Staff Report on Employment, Growth, and Price Levels, op. cit.*, pp. 381–385; F. E. Morris, "Impact of Monetary Policy on State and Local Governments: An Empirical Study," *Journal of Finance*, May 1960, pp. 232–249.

state and local construction expenditures shifted from the later phases of a boom to the following recession as a result of rising interest rates and tight credit range from 2 to 5 percent."[19] During the 1955–1957 period of credit restraint, the average interest rate on state and local government obligations rose from 2.49 per cent in June 1955 to 3.89 per cent in September 1957, a relative increase of 56 per cent. If we accept the upper limit of the range suggested by the Commission and accept the final year of the period 1955–1957 as the "later phases of the boom," we might estimate that the 56 per cent rise in the interest rate caused the postponement of 5 per cent of a year's expenditures, giving a rough estimate of the elasticity of $-(5/56)$, or a little less than -0.1.

Including state and local government construction expenditures, with appropriate weight attached, along with business investment and residential construction, we obtain a crude estimate of the overall interest elasticity of investment of -0.45. Recent studies of the demand for money seem to indicate that the interest elasticity of liquidity preference increases as interest rates decline, ranging between approximately -0.5 and -0.7, and averaging about -0.6 for the normal ranges of interest rates.[20]

---

[19] *Op. cit.*, p. 51. The nature and source of the evidence referred to are not revealed.

[20] These estimates are based upon a study by C. F. Christ ("Interest Rates and 'Portfolio Selection' among Liquid Assets," paper presented at a meeting of the Econometric Society, St. Louis, Mo., December 30, 1960). Christ's analysis is patterned after that of H. A. Latane, "Cash Balances and the Interest Rate—A Pragmatic Approach," *Review of Economics and Statistics,* November 1954, pp. 456–460. See also Latane's later article "Income Velocity and Interest Rates: A Pragmatic Approach," *Review of Economics and Statistics,* November 1960, pp. 445–449. Another recent study (Martin Bronfenbrenner and Thomas Mayer, "Liquidity Functions in the American Economy," *Econometrica,* October 1960, pp. 810–834), in which constant elasticity functions are used and the stock of national wealth is introduced as a variable, produces elasticity estimates ranging between $-.09$ and -1.10 for different formulations of the demand-for-money function. In some of the formulations, however, a dubious and artificial distinction between active and idle balances is employed; in all of the formulations which use total money balances as the dependent variable and introduce income as a variable, the elasticities of demand for money with respect to the stock of wealth turn out to be negative, a result which seems quite implausible. Another study which places great emphasis on the wealth effect (H. F.

According to the traditional view, the demand for money for transactions purposes changes proportionately with income. Some recent theoretical studies of the demand for transactions balances suggest the possibility that there are economies of scale in the use of cash balances; for certain simple transactions patterns these studies indicate that transactions balances should vary with the square root of income.[21] Nevertheless, we shall use an income elasticity of demand for money of unity in our calculations.

Using the admittedly crude estimate of −0.45 for the interest elasticity of investment, and −016 for the interest elasticity of liquidity preference, and unity for the income elasticity of liquidity preference, and assuming that the marginal propensity to pay taxes out of GNP is 0.33 and that the marginal propensity to spend out of after-tax gross income is 0.9, our analysis yields an estimate of 1.92 for the static multiplier applicable to a change in government expenditures with the money supply held constant.[22]

Lydall, "Income, Assets, and the Demand for Money," *Review of Economics and Statistics,* February 1958, pp. 1–14) produces an estimate of −2.72 for the elasticity of personal demand for bank deposits in Britain in 1954. However, this study uses a "trick method" of deducing the elasticity, which probably overstates it substantially and, in any case, does not appear to be very reliable.

21 See W. J. Baumol, "The Transactions Demand for Cash: An Inventory Theoretic Approach," *Quarterly Journal of Economics,* November 1952, pp. 545–556; and James Tobin, "The Interest Elasticity of the Transactions Demand for Cash," *Review of Economics and Statistics,* August 1956, pp. 241–247. As a result of these theoretical considerations as well as observation of the efforts that have been made by businesses to economize cash balances (see C. E. Silberman, "The Big Corporate Lenders," *Fortune,* August 1956, pp. 111–114), there has recently been a tendency to de-emphasize the Keynesian speculative motive and to emphasize instead the transactions motive as the source of the interest elasticity of demand for money.

22 Recent studies of the short-run dynamics of income change have placed the value of the multiplier for periods in the neighborhood of a year, applicable to situation of declining income and neglecting monetary effects, at about 1.5, when induced inventory adjustments are excluded, and about 2.5 when they are included (see, for example, the model, based on quarterly data, presented in J. S. Duesenberry, Otto Eckstein, and Gary Fromm, "A Simulation of the United States Economy in Recession," *Econometrica,* October 1960, pp. 749–809). Similar results have been obtained, with a model using annual data, in the Research Seminar in Quantitative Economics at the University of Michigan. Many quantitative estimates have indicated

Since, with the above assumptions, the "ordinary" multiplier without monetary reaction is about 2.5, the presence of the "monetary factor" reduces the size of the multiplier from 2.50 to 1.92, a reduction of about 23 per cent. A $5 billion reduction of government expenditures would reduce equilibrium income by about $12.5 billion if the resulting funds were not used to retire debt (or if the effects of debt retirement were completely immobilized by unfavorable elasticities), while a $5 billion cut in expenditures accompanied by an equal amount of debt retirement under the conditions assumed above would reduce income by $9.6 billion. The reduction in expenditures by itself would reduce income by $12.5 billion, but use of the funds for debt retirement would have a stimulating effect, amounting to $2.9 billion (or 23 per cent of the $12.5 billion decline in income), thus reducing the net decline to $9.6 billion.

MONETARY EXPANSION TO SUPPLEMENT DEBT RETIREMENT

The Federal Reserve may be properly viewed as engaged in debt retirement when it purchases government securities in the open market, as it thereby reduces the *publicly-held* debt. It is more appropriate to regard the national debt as including only the publicly-held debt, rather than, as traditionally, the gross public debt, including United States government obligations held in government investment accounts and by the Federal Reserve. In fact, from a purely technical standpoint, the Federal Reserve has considerably greater debt retirement powers than does the Treasury. The Treasury cannot retire debt except by using funds accumulated as a result of present or past cash budget surpluses—that is, it can use only funds derived from a current excess of tax receipts over expenditures or by reducing the level of its balances held in Federal Reserve or private commercial or savings banks; of course, these balances must have been built up in the first

---

that, with our present tax system, a change in GNP tends to change the budget deficit or surplus in the opposite direction and by an amount equal to one-third to two-fifths of the change in GNP. Thus, while the static multiplier presented above leaves much to be desired, it is broadly consistent with the available empirical evidence.

place as a result of earlier excesses of tax receipts over expenditures. Since the Treasury normally carries only such cash balances as it needs for operating purposes, in practice under normal circumstances its debt retirement potential is pretty much limited to current cash budget surpluses. The Federal Reserve, on the other hand, is technically in a position to retire debt almost without limit by simply creating the funds needed for the purpose.[23]

Moreover, debt retirement by the Treasury has a less expansionary effect than debt retirement by the Federal Reserve, since, Treasury debt retirement merely restores to the economy money which was originally taken away in taxes, whereas Federal Reserve purchases of securities increase the supply of bank reserves and may result in the creation of new money through the process of bank credit expansion to the extent of some six to seven times the amount of securities purchased. A Treasury budget surplus that is used to retire debt also produces, as pointed out above, a reduction in the net stock of claims held by the public, thereby producing a slightly deflationary—but cumulative—wealth effect, whereas Federal Reserve purchases of securities have no effects on the stock of net claims held by the public.

Treasury debt retirement is also subject to a serious administrative disadvantage as compared with Federal Reserve operations. If the Treasury wishes to retire debt, it must plan its tax and expenditure policies well in advance in order to have the desired budget surplus. If, as is almost certain to be the case under the circumstances we are considering, the combined effects of the reduction in spending and the retirement of debt are undesirably

---

[23] The only significant limitation on the Federal Reserve's debt retirement powers is that imposed by the requirement that the system must maintain a 25 per cent reserve in the form of gold certificates against its notes and deposits. Since the 25 per cent requirement implies a 4-to-1 ratio of note and deposit liabilities to reserves, the system would, in mid-1961, have been able to buy about $23.2 billion of securities in the open market before exhausting its excess reserves. There has recently been considerable support for repeal of the reserves requirements of the Federal Reserve banks on the ground that by freeing the gold certificate reserves held by the system, it would strengthen the balance-of-payments position of the United States (see *Money and Credit: Their Influence on Jobs, Prices, and Growth*, p. 234).

deflationary, it is extremely difficult to rearrange the Treasury's tax and expenditure policies to correct the mistake. The Federal Reserve, however, since its administrative machinery is highly flexible and its operations are in no way tied to the budget, can change the scale and even the direction of its operations from day to day as the circumstances require.

The question to which we shall address ourselves now is: How large an increase in the money supply will be necessary to compensate for the deflationary effects resulting from a reduction in government expenditures and use of the resulting budget surplus to retire debt?

Under the assumptions we have been making concerning the interest elasticities of investment and liquidity preference and with a money supply of $144.5 billion (as at the end of 1960), we estimate that a cut in defense expenditures of $5 billion a year, with the resulting surplus used to retire debt, would require an increase of about $12 billion in the money supply in order to prevent equilibrium income from declining.

The amount of open market operations necessary to produce this required change in the money supply would be about $2 billion. The total amount of debt retirement needed to offset a reduction of $5 billion in expenditures would therefore be, under the given assumptions, about $7 billion—$5 billion by the Treasury, using the budget surplus, and $2 billion more by the Federal Reserve, through open market operations.[24]

The above analysis brings out the fact that the deflationary effect of a reduction in government spending can, in principle, be offset by the use of the proceeds of the expenditure cut to retire debt, supplemented by additional measures (such as open market purchases by the Federal Reserve) to ease credit and to lower interest rates. However, our calculations—admittedly rather crude

[24] It should be noted that the Federal Reserve could bring about the necessary increase in the money supply and bank credit by lowering member bank reserve requirements rather than by open market operations if it chose to do so. For a discussion of the merits of open market operations versus reserve requirement changes as a means of controlling the money supply (see W. L. Smith, "Reserve Requirements in the American Monetary System," study prepared for the Commission on Money and Credit, to be published).

—suggest that very vigorous monetary measures would be required to supplement debt retirement in order to offset the deflationary effects of reduced spending and maintain the initial level of aggregate demand.

Actually, it seems likely that, if anything, we have overestimated the potency of monetary measures. The evidence that income-generating expenditures (except for residential construction) possess any appreciable interest elasticity is exceedingly limited, and our estimate of −0.45 for this elasticity may well be too high. Moreover, recent work on the institutional aspects of our monetary and financial system[25] seems to suggest that the existence of large stocks of close money substitutes (such as Treasury bills, time deposits, etc.), together with skillful manipulation by financial institutions, have greatly facilitated the activation and de-activation of cash balances in response to interest rate changes, thereby increasing the interest elasticity of liquidity preference. Accordingly, it seems quite possible that our estimate of −0.6 for such liquidity preference elasticity is too small (in absolute value). And, even if our estimates are roughly correct "on the average," it seems quite likely that as interest rates decline, we might be faced with declining interest elasticity of expenditures and increasing interest elasticity of liquidity preference and, thus, experience a progressive weakening of the monetary effect.[26]

[25] For a summary, see *Staff Report on Employment, Growth, and Price Levels, op. cit.,* pp. 344–362.
[26] For an argument that the interest sensitivity of investment is likely to be lower at high interest rates, see A. H. Hansen, *Business Cycles and National Income,* New York: McGraw-Hill, 1951, pp. 133–138. To the extent that the stimulus to investment resulting from debt retirement and monetary expansion requires reductions in the long-term rate of interest, a speculative preference for liquidity in the form of short-term securities might prove to be an obstacle, since the existence of conventional views concerning the "normal" level of interest rates may interfere with the process of bringing down the long-term rate. That is, if investors feel that the decline in the long-term rate will be temporary, they may retreat into the short term market, thus reducing the demand for bonds and serving to check the fall in the long-term rate. Such a reaction probably accounts for the sluggish response of the long-term rate to conditions of easy money in the 1930's. Even though, in this version, it is the demand for liquidity in the form of short-term securities, rather than the demand for money, that is interest-

PROBLEMS OF TIMING

In addition to the limited effectiveness of monetary measures, whether they take the form of debt retirement by the Treasury or increases in the money supply through Federal Reserve action, there are serious difficulties involved in timing such measures so as to counteract effectively the deflationary impact of reductions in government spending. There seem to be quite lengthy lags between the time when action is taken to ease credit conditions and the time when such effects as these actions produce are felt by the economy. In part, these are financial lags—that is, lags between the time when action is taken to expand the money supply and ease credit and the time when interest rates and credit conditions exhibit the desired response.[27] In addition, there are lags between the time when interest rates and credit conditions respond and the time when income-generating expenditures are affected, and further lags between the response of expenditures and the impact on production, employment, and income.[28]

This suggests that even if the ultimate effects produced by debt retirement and monetary expansion were of sufficient magnitude to provide an adequate offset to reduced defense expenditures, there would be difficulties in employing such a policy, because it

---

elastic, the existence of such a situation may necessitate a large increase in the money supply to bring about the necessary change in the long-term rate, thereby producing an effect similar to a highly elastic liquidity preference in the orthodox Keynesian sense. On the structure of interest rates, see F. A. Lutz, "The Structure of Interest Rates," *Quarterly Journal of Economics,* November 1940, pp. 36–63, reprinted in William Fellner and B. F. Haley (eds.), *Readings in the Theory of Income Distribution,* Philadelphia: Blakiston, 1946, pp. 449–529; R. A. Musgrave, *The Theory of Public Finance,* New York: McGraw-Hill, 1959, Chap. XXIV; and W. L. Smith, *Debt Management in the United States,* Study Paper No. 19, Joint Economic Committee, 86th Cong., 1st Sess., 1960, Chap. IV.

[27] For a discussion of the lags in the reaction of financial markets, see W. L. Smith, "On the Effectiveness of Monetary Policy," *American Economic Review,* September 1956, pp. 588–606. This article discusses the lags in the context of a restrictive policy to deal with inflation; for a policy of credit easing designed to induce expansion, the lags are probably even longer.

[28] See Thomas Mayer, "The Inflexibility of Monetary Policy," *Review of Economics and Statistics,* November 1958, pp. 358–374.

would be necessary to institute measures to ease credit before expenditures were reduced, since the monetary lags are substantially longer than those associated with reduction in government expenditures.[29]

This problem is further accentuated by the fact that the deflationary effects of reductions in defense spending are likely to be set in motion before expenditures are actually reduced and before the expected budget surplus is realized. Reductions in defense orders are almost certain to induce inventory adjustments and changes in production schedules which will have substantial deflationary effects even before expenditures are reduced.[30] Moreover, the institution of an extensive disarmament program is likely to have a rather immediate deflationary impact through its "announcement effects" on business and consumer expectations. If no offsetting action is taken until such time as expenditures actually decline, the deflationary effects of the reduction in defense orders, together with the announcement effects, may precipitate a decline in production, income, and employment, thus bringing about a decline in tax collections and an increase in transfer expenditures due to the operation of the automatic stabilizers. Thus, instead of an immediate budget surplus available for debt retirement, the Treasury might even find itself faced with a budget deficit, which it would have to finance by additional borrowing in the early stages of a disarmament program. At the very least, these effects are likely to delay the appearance of a budget surplus

[29] In his paper, "The Supply of Money and Changes in Prices and Output," in *The Relationship of Prices to Economic Stability and Growth,* compendium of papers submitted by panelists appearing before the Joint Economic Committee, 85th Cong., 2nd Sess., 1958, pp. 241–256, Milton Freidman estimated that the lag between increases in the rate of change of the money supply and upturns in economic activity has ranged between five and twenty-one months, and has averaged twelve months for nineteen business cycles covering the period from 1879 to 1954.

[30] This is pointed out in Benoit, *op. cit.,* p. 457. On the effects of changes in government orders on economic activity, see M. L. Weidenbaum, *Government Spending: Process and Measurement,* Seattle, Washington, Boeing Airplane Co., 1958, and "The Timing of the Economic Impact of Government Spending," *National Tax Journal,* March 1959, pp. 79–85; also *Staff Report on Employment, Growth, and Price Levels, op. cit.,* pp. 213–215.

available for debt retirement and to complicate considerably the problems of timing the initiation of the necessary compensatory action.

GROWTH OF PUBLIC AND PRIVATE DEBT

Another argument against a policy emphasizing debt retirement as an offset to reductions in defense expenditures is based on an alleged historical tendency for the ratio of total outstanding public and private debt to GNP to remain relatively constant over long periods of time. From this observation, the inference is drawn that total debt must grow more or less in pace with GNP and that if the stock of government debt declines as a result of a succession of budget surpluses that are used for debt retirement, it will be necessary for private debt to grow that much faster, thereby creating a danger that the burden of interest and amortization payments on private debt will impinge on the volume of available purchasing power and will endanger prosperity.[31]

An examination of the data on public and private debt compiled by the Department of Commerce does perhaps lend some credence to the idea that the ratio of aggregate net debt to GNP has shown a measure of stability; nevertheless, this interpretation needs to be carefully qualified.[32] It happens that the debt-to-GNP ratio was the same (1.70) in 1959 as in 1923; however, during the four decades since 1920—leaving out the abnormal years of the Great Depression and World War II—it has ranged from

[31] See Benoit, *op. cit.*, p. 459. The stability of the total-debt-to-GNP ratio was pointed out by P. W. McCracken ("The Debt Problem and Economic Growth," *Michigan Business Review*, November 1956, pp. 11—15), although he did not draw any clear inference as to the desirability of debt retirement. It may be noted that the same problem could be present, although to a lesser degree, even under conditions of deficit financing if the deficits were not large enough to keep the public debt growing in pace with GNP.

[32] My calculations are based on data published in various issues of the *Survey of Current Business*. For a discussion of the concepts employed, see E. T. Bonnell, "Public and Private Debt in 1949," *Survey of Current Business*, Department of Commerce, October 1950, pp. 9—15. I have adjusted the Commerce series for total debt and federal government debt by deducting the amount of government securities held by the Federal Reserve System.

1.53 in 1951 and 1952 to 1.88 in 1928.[33] In any case, however, it is apparent that the composition of the debt has been anything but stable. The federal debt rose relative to GNP during the 1930's and during World War II as a result of deficit financing during the depression and the war. Since the end of the war, the ratio has been declining, not because the absolute amount of debt outstanding has declined sharply, but because it has remained more or less constant while GNP has risen. However, the ratio (0.45) of federal debt to GNP in 1959 was still approximately double the average ratio (0.23) that prevailed during the 1920's. Except for the decade of the 1930's, the ratio of state and local government debt to GNP has not shown a great deal of variation. The ratio of private debt (including both corporate and individual and noncorporate debt) to GNP rose during the 1930's, declined sharply during World War II, and has been rising since. However, in 1959 it was 1.13, which was about 20 per cent lower than the average ratio (1.43) which prevailed in the 1920's. I can see no reason to suppose that a rise in the ratios of private debt to GNP to the levels prevailing in the 1920's or perhaps even higher should be a source of concern. We have no knowledge which permits us to say at what point an increasing ratio of private debt to income is likely to exert a dangerously depressive effect on the current propensity to spend.[34] One fact that should be borne in mind is

---

[33] There is obviously a question as to what is the proper standard to use in judging whether the ratio is "stable."

[34] An analysis of the growth of consumer credit by Alain Enthoven ("The Growth of Installment Credit and the Future of Prosperity," *American Economic Review*, December 1957, pp. 613—629) shows the need for sophistication in the interpretation of relationships between debt and income. Enthoven uses a life-cycle model, in which each year a new group of consumer borrowers in the early stages of household formation enters the market and another (and smaller) group leaves the market (i.e., pays off its debt). He demonstrates that a continuous geometric rate of growth of the *absolute annual increments* to outstanding debt is not an unreasonable possibility. With this model, if we start from a condition in which the ratio of debt to income is very small (as was the case at the end of World War II), the ratio will increase rapidly at first but the rate of increase in the ratio will gradually slow down, and the ratio itself will eventually approach a constant. Apart from cyclical fluctuations, the trend in the growth of consumer credit since the end of World War II seems to be consistent with such a model.

that the debt of one economic unit is necessarily an asset held by some other unit, so that growth of debt necessarily implies a parallel growth of financial assets. Taking account of both sides of the balance sheet, during the decade 1950–1959 the financial position of consumers in the aggregate has improved, despite a tremendous increase in consumer debt, because financial asset holdings of consumers increased even more rapidly than consumer debt.[35]

While it seems quite likely that rapid cyclical expansions and contractions in certain types of indebtedness (such as consumer credit) have served to intensify cyclical fluctuations, I can see no evidence to suggest that the economy is incapable of adjusting to various patterns of secular growth or decline in the stock of government securities. Accordingly, I can see no reason to accept this particular argument against debt retirement as a valid one.[36]

Although the analysis presented above is rather crude, at least in its quantitative aspects, I believe it strongly suggests that a policy of using a portion of the proceeds resulting from reduced defense spending to retire publicly held debt would produce dangerously deflationary tendencies. It is not even clear that if debt retirement was supplemented by vigorous monetary expansion, it

[35] According to Federal Reserve flow-of-funds data, total financial asset holdings of the consumer and nonprofit organizations sector increased from $365.1 billion in 1945 to $935.0 billion in 1960, a rise of $569.9 billion; during the same period the total indebtedness of the sector increased from $27.1 billion to $209.3 billion, an increase of $182.2 billion. That is, the increase in debt was less than one-third of the growth in financial asset holdings. Thus, despite the fact that this was a period in which mortgage indebtedness and consumer credit each increased nearly tenfold (from $14.3 billion to $135.3 billion and from $5.7 billion to $56.0 billion, respectively), thereby causing considerable concern in some quarters regarding the solvency of consumers, it would appear that the financial position of households in the aggregate improved substantially. (Data are from *Federal Reserve Bulletin*, August 1959, p. 1057, and August 1961, p. 995.)

[36] It may be noted that in order to hold the ratio of federal debt to GNP constant at the 1959 level of 0.45 if the GNP should rise 3.5 per cent above the level of $550 billion, the federal debt would have to be increased by $8.7 billion in a year. And the increases would have to grow larger year by year to preserve the ratio if the GNP should grow at a constant percentage rate. Barring a war or other national emergency, it seems wholly unrealistic to expect such increases; indeed, it appears that the ratio is almost certain to decline.

would be capable of offsetting the deflationary effects of reduced expenditures. This suggests that the basic adjustments to correct for reduced defense spending would need to be made through fiscal policy, either by increasing nondefense spending, or by reducing taxes, or by some combination of these policies.[37]

A SUGGESTED APPROACH TO ECONOMIC POLICY FOR DISARMAMENT

The basic problem of formulating fiscal and monetary policies to offset the economic effects of a disarmament program is simply an extension of the situation regularly facing those responsible for the formulation of policy. At the present time, our potential national output is increasing at a rate of nearly $20 billion per year, and the task of monetary and fiscal policy is to keep aggregate demand growing at a pace just sufficient to absorb the additional supplies of goods and services becoming available. With a disarmament program of the scope we are considering, the problem in 1965 would be to keep aggregate demand growing at a rate of about $28 to $35 billion per year, despite declining defense expenditures.

There are many different policy "packages" which will yield any desired level of aggregate demand, but the different packages have different effects on the allocation of resources, as between private consumption, private investment, and the production of additional services in the public sector.

The necessary coordination of policy formulation is more difficult to achieve in the United States than it is in countries which have a parliamentary system of government. It is necessary for the President to present his proposed annual budget in January for the fiscal year beginning six months later. Thus, it is extremely difficult to tell at the time the budget is presented what the state of the economy will be when this budget goes into effect half a

---

[37] Since the multiplier effects applicable to reductions in taxes or increases in transfer payments are generally smaller than the multiplier effects attaching to increased expenditures on goods and services, it appears that to the extent that reduced defense spending was to be offset by tax reductions or increases in transfer payments, it would be necessary for the budget to move, on a marginal basis, in the direction of a deficit rather than a surplus.

year later. Further difficulties arise out of the fact that the President's budget is little more than a proposal which is quite certain to be changed—perhaps rather substantially—as a result of Congressional action. Moreover, the President's proposals concerning government expenditures are considered piecemeal by the Congress, and his proposals with respect to taxation are considered separately from his proposals concerning expenditures.

In spite of these serious difficulties, I believe that under our political and economic institutions, the annual budget must and will form the basis of our fiscal stabilization program and that it should be formulated on the basis of the best forecasts that can be made, including estimates of the economic effects that are likely to be produced by changes in taxes and government expenditures.[38]

The budget proposal should contain an explicit statement concerning the expected impact of the budget—including both the tax and expenditure proposals—on the economy, thereby encouraging the Congress to consider the budget as a whole.

THE NEED FOR FLEXIBILITY

Errors will inevitably be made in the formulation of basic fiscal policy as embodied in the annual budget. Such errors may arise out of failure to estimate correctly the effects produced by fiscal adjustments, inability to forecast accurately the state of the economy at the time such policies go into effect, and failure on the part of the Congress to adopt the budget suggested by the President.

The effects of monetary policy are too weak to make it safe to entrust to it any portion of the basic burden of adjustment, but it does have a considerable advantage over discretionary fiscal policy in flexibility and adaptability. Accordingly, it would appear that the proper role for monetary policy is that of assisting in the process of correcting the errors that inevitably occur in the formulation of basic fiscal policy.

The interest rate ceilings on FHA-insured and VA-guaranteed mortgages have produced some rather peculiar effects on the allocation of mortgage credit, and it might be desirable to eliminate

[38] See Chapter 6.

them. However, if this were done, the ceilings should probably be replaced by specific selective controls over the downpayments and maturities of government-supported mortgages in order to preserve our ability to control expenditures on residential construction, since this has proved to be a useful instrument of stabilization policy. It might also be desirable to restore to the Federal Reserve the authority to employ selective controls in the field of consumer credit.[39]

Automatic fiscal stabilizers also have a role to play. Our present stabilizers are of the type that have been referred to by A. W. Phillips as "proportional correctives"—that is, the magnitude of their offsetting effect on aggregate demand is approximately proportional to the amount by which income deviates from high-level equilibrium. Such stabilizers are incapable, in themselves, of reversing fluctuations in economic activity and restoring equilibrium at high levels of economic activity, but they do serve the useful purpose of damping fluctuations by reducing the size of the multiplier and weakening the tendency for changes in the level of activity to become cumulative.[40]

One of the fiscal problems that seems likely to arise with disarmament concerns the effects of heavy defense cuts on the functioning of automatic stabilization. Such stabilization can be said to depend on (1) *the size of the government sector* of the economy, as reflected in the ratio of taxes to income; and (2) *the progressivity of the tax system,* as reflected in sensitivities of the bases of the various taxes to income, the sensitivities of the various taxes to their bases, and the proportions in which the various taxes are "mixed" to form the tax system. If reduced defense expenditures are accompanied by reduced taxes and a smaller government

[39] The Commission on Money and Credit has recommended that the interest rate ceilings on FHA-insured and VA-guaranteed mortgages be eliminated and that the terms of such mortgages be varied in a countercyclical fashion. On the issue of consumer credit controls, the commission was divided and did not take a position (see *Money and Credit: Their Influence on Jobs, Prices, and Growth,* pp. 73–75).

[40] A. W. Phillips, "Stabilization Policy in a Closed Economy," *Economic Journal,* June 1954, pp. 290–323; and "Stabilization Policy and the Time-Forms of Lagged Responses," *Economic Journal,* June 1957, pp. 265–277.

sector, it will be necessary to increase the progressivity of the tax system by appropriate adjustments if the effectiveness of the automatic stabilizers is not to be reduced. With a substantial reduction in the level of taxes, it would be quite difficult to make sufficient adjustments to prevent a decline in the amount of built-in stability.

Monetary policy and automatic fiscal stabilizers are likely to prove to be inadequate for the purpose of offsetting the destabilizing effects of errors in the formulation of annual budgets. In order to provide an additional instrument for this purpose, I believe it would be highly desirable for Congress to grant the President authority to make temporary adjustments in personal income tax rates. This authority should be hedged by sufficient checks to preserve basic Congressional control over tax policy but should be sufficiently flexible to permit the President to make limited changes in tax rates on short notice in order to deal with economic instability.[41]

CONCLUDING COMMENTS

I have argued at some length in this paper that it would be dangerous to rely on debt retirement and monetary policy to accomplish any substantial portion of the economic readjustments that would be required by a program of disarmament. Instead, I believe it would be desirable to attempt to accomplish as much as possible of the realignment of demand through the medium of basic changes in government expenditures and taxes as embodied in the annual budget developed by the President and acted on by Congress. The task of correcting errors resulting from the various imperfections in the budgetary process, could be left to discretionary monetary policy, together with automatic fiscal stabilizers and temporary discretionary adjustments in personal income taxes by the President under a delegation of authority by the Congress.

Despite the fact that I would not favor placing very much of

[41] The Commission on Money and Credit has recently recommended that the Congress delegate to the President limited authority to make countercylical changes in the first-bracket rate of the personal income tax (see *Money and Credit: Their Influence on Jobs, Prices, and Growth*, pp. 133–137.

the burden of economic adjustments on monetary policy, I do believe that it is important that the actions of the monetary authorities be effectively integrated into the process of policy formulation in order to ensure that the fiscal and monetary policies are not working at cross purposes. To this end, it is important that continuing thought be given to possible means of improving the administrative arrangements within the Federal Reserve System and of providing for full coordination of all of our economic policies affecting the level of employment and the rate of economic growth.[42]

[42] The Commission on Money and Credit has recommended that the Board of Governors be reduced from seven to five members, that all of the major credit control powers exercised by the Federal Reserve System be placed in the hands of the Board, and that the term of the chairman of the board be changed to coincide with the term of the President of the United States (*ibid.*, pp. 85—90). The commission also proposed the formation of an unofficial advisory board within the executive branch to assist the President in discharging his responsibilities in the field of national economic policy (*ibid.*, pp. 274—277).

9

Impact of Disarmament on the Financial Structure of the United States

*Robert Kavesh and Judith Mackey**

Within the READ framework, this chapter explores the impact which disarmament and alternative methods of adjustment to it might have on the financial structure of the United States, assuming the maintenance of full employment.

The assumption may appear to some as avoiding the main problem, but we do not consider that this is necessarily so. Essentially our approach shows what pattern of ownership of securities would be compatible with full employment under given circumstances of cutbacks in defense expenditure, and with particular adjustment policies adopted to offset such cutbacks. The study of the internal inconsistencies and strains in the projected pattern of security ownership should enable economic and financial analysts to throw some light on the effectiveness of particular adjustment policies contemplated, and on the problems they would

* ROBERT A. KAVESH is Professor of Economics and Finance at the Graduate School of Business Administration of New York University, consultant to various banks, and Secretary-Treasurer of the American Finance Corporation. He was on the research staff of the Commission on Money and Credit. JUDITH MACKEY is a Vice President of Townsend-Greenspan Company, Inc., and an economic consultant and writer.

encounter. While this chapter has not carried this line of analysis very far, it has at least arranged the material and made the projections in ways which would facilitate such analysis. In this sense, the present study should be viewed as a preliminary piece of research preparatory to later work.

In exploring the financial implications of alternative fiscal policy adjustments, we have had recourse to five separate models—of which the first two are of particular importance for exploring the range of alternatives and are included in Table 1, pp. 170–171. These models are as follows:

1. The tax-cut model
2. The debt-cut model
3. The federal spending offset model
4. The combination model
5. A nondisarmament or "judgment" model
   as a basis for comparison

The chief assumptions of the five models are as follows:

1. *Tax cut*—Defense outlays will be offset precisely by cuts in federal taxes, with no change in the level of federal debt and no increase in federal expenditures.

2. *Cut in federal debt*—Defense outlays will be offset precisely by a reduction in the federal debt, with no cuts in federal taxes and no increase in federal expenditures.

3. *Increase in other federal spending*—Defense outlays will be offset precisely by an increase in federal spending for nonmilitary goods and services, with no change in the federal debt and no cuts in federal taxes.

4. *Combination of the three approaches*—The funds released by disarmament will be redistributed among the foregoing alternatives in some relatively balanced manner.

5. *Judgment model*—In order to place the disarmament models in a more meaningful perspective, a nondisarmament or "judgment" model has also been developed, based on a somewhat slower defense buildup in military outlays prior to 1965 than that assumed in the READ projections, with no downtrend thereafter. It, too, is a full-employment model.

The GNP projections with which we start are based upon the familiar type of projecting technique utilizing manhour and productivity trends. Projections were made in constant 1959 dollars with growth rates averaging 4 per cent a year from 1959 to 1965, and 4½ per cent thereafter. The full employment total in 1975 is $938 billion in all adjustment models. However, as will be expected, some important differences appear in the components of GNP under the alternative adjustment models, even though the full-employment GNP totals are identical. For example, in the tax-cut model, personal consumption is $654 billion, compared with $643 billion in the debt-reduction model. In the debt-reduction model, on the other hand, business fixed investment reaches the total of $106 billion, compared with the tax-cut model, where it reaches only $99 billion. In the federal spending model, non-defense expenditures are projected to reach nearly $40 billion, compared to the mere $10 billion anticipated under the debt-reduction or tax-cut models.

There was less variation with respect to the other GNP components because of the overriding elements of uniformity introduced by the full-employment assumption.[1]

THE FINANCIAL STRUCTURE OF THE ECONOMY

The central content of our research in this area has been the projection of a distribution of financial securities consistent with each of the major models of disarmament adjustment. The primary linkage and basis of projection have been found in the Gurley-Shaw concept of primary securities.

Primary securities represent the legal confirmation of the transfer of loan or equity funds to their final users. In short, they are "all debt and equity obligations of nonfinancial economic units."[2]

---

[1] The details of these GNP projections, as well as the detailed breakdown of the distribution of securities under alternative assumptions, are available in mimeographed form, on request, from the authors.

[2] John J. Gurley, *Liquidity and Financial Institutions in the Postwar Period*, Study Papers No. 14, prepared in connection with the study of employment, growth and price levels, Joint Economic Committee, 86th Cong., 1st Sess., January 25, 1960, p. 25.

They include United States government securities, corporate bonds and stocks, mortgages, consumer debt, bank loans other than consumer loans, trade credit, and policy loans by life insurance companies.

The total volume of outstanding primary securities historically has had a very close relationship to GNP, particularly in periods of high economic activity. At such times, the ratio of total outstanding primary securities to GNP has tended to average 2.5.

This ratio, however, cannot be treated as an absolute. Certain economic situations tend to produce a higher volume of primary securities relative to GNP, while other conditions help dampen the relative increase in primary securities. In this study, the tax-cut model demonstrates a greater reliance on primary securities than does the nondisarmament (judgment) model; the debt-cut model illustrates a narrower recourse to primary securities.

Thus, the amounts and kinds of outstanding primary securities, and the holdings of them by various participants in the capital market, were estimated on the basis of historical full-employment relationships as modified by the specific theoretical requirements of each model.

TAX-CUT ADJUSTMENT MODEL

The tax-cut model assumes that the annual declines in armament expenditures would be matched precisely by cuts in federal taxes, and that there would be a shift in the balance of GNP from the public to the private sectors. Clearly, the *type* of reduction would be highly relevant in determining the impact that this tax cut would have.

The assumption in this model is that by 1975 the corporate tax would have been reduced to roughly 40 per cent, while the rate on personal taxes would range in accordance with income brackets from a minimum of 15 per cent to a maximum of 65 per cent.

A tax-cut program of this size and type would release a large amount of funds for additional private spending. Its actual utilization would depend upon the nature of the reaction by consumers and businessmen to the situation. The literature on the consumption function can provide support for any major thesis concerning the behavior of consumers. The difficulties created by the lack of an accepted theoretical approach are compounded in this case by the uniqueness of the situation we are envisaging. The kinds and amounts of tax cuts projected by the model are completely un-precedented. Consequently, it was necessary to rely heavily on intuitive insights as to the probable effects on spending and saving under the extraordinary conditions implicit in the model.

We suspect that the general reaction to the tax cuts would be one of caution at first. In view of the length and severity of the cold war, some skepticism regarding the feasibility of disarmament would be understandable; and consumers might, therefore, look upon the reductions in the early years as precarious and tentative. Slowness in raising living standards substantially, despite the higher disposable income available as a result of the tax cuts, would con-stitute a reasonable enough response to such an exceptional set of circumstances.

As a result, the savings rate probably would rise for several years after 1965. Later, as disarmament progressed, people would tend to have fewer reservations about the program; they would have more confidence in its permanence. The tax-cut schedule, therefore, would become a more reliable factor in their calcula-tions. Adjustment to the higher level of disposable income would bring the savings rate back down to a more balanced relationship with income.

These assumptions have been incorporated into the economic and financial projections provided for the tax-cut model. The high level of savings in the early period places strong pressure on sav-ings institutions to move savings out into investments, with conse-quent downward pressures on interest rates. The cheaper cost and greater availability of credit would induce some additional borrow-ing by states and localities, by home owners (or prospective home owners) and by purchasers of equities.

In subsequent years, people would become more willing to rely upon the expectation of further tax cuts; they would incor-porate these attitudes into a higher level of spending and direct investment. One manifestation would be freer spending on con-sumer goods and services. The greater profitability of business, first as a result of the tax cut and later in consequence of the higher volume of consumer spending, would lead to a greater investment in equities. The resultant upswing in equity prices would make these securities even more attractive. This would bring a larger volume of funds into the stock market, generating a strong bull market.

Initially, people would have tremendous resources open to them because of their large backlogs of accumulated savings. In addition, they would be encouraged to supplement their savings with loan funds. The encouragement would derive from the relatively low cost of borrowed money, their confidence in their ability to repay debt out of funds released by future tax cuts, the heightened atmosphere that good times were prevailing and awareness of the profitable investment opportunities which seem to accompany the early stages of a bull market.

The expectation of continued declines in the tax burden would be partially negated in time. In the final years of the program the actual tax cuts would be quite small. However, this would not dampen the economy immediately, since the bull market probably would be in full swing by then. In such an environment, people are willing to undertake additional debt in order to take advantage of the quick profits which are associated with speculative-inflationary periods. This would push interest rates up sharply, particularly on short-term funds.

By 1975 the speculative elements should have assumed much greater dominance. The fiscal and monetary authorities would be faced with the tremendous problem of containing these elements in a manner which would not restrain the country's potential growth rate. An evaluation of the precise techniques which they might use to meet this challenge clearly is outside the scope of the present study; however, some of the implications will be raised in later sections.

DEBT-CUT MODEL

The debt-cut model assumes that the initiation of the disarmament program will occur at a time of a predominantly conservative political and economic philosophy. This ideology places primary emphasis upon the elimination of the federal government as a participant in economic affairs. Those who hold it generally also stress the desirability of sharp curtailment of the federal debt. It is reasonable to assume, therefore, that the disarmament program would be viewed as an excellent opportunity for achieving this goal. Taxes would be kept unchanged, and the full annual decreases in armament expenditures would be applied to reducing the federal debt.

The conservative philosophy views the present distinction between the federal agencies and the federal government proper as a legal device for fostering greater governmental intrusion into private affairs. Consequently, the debt-cut model presumes that the authorities would attempt to diminish the responsibilities and activities of the federal agencies. This would lessen their need for funds. The debt-cut model assumes, therefore, that the participation of United States government agencies in the capital market would be negligible by 1975.

The three major holders of the federal debt are the federal and state retirement funds, commercial banks, and individuals.

The first group, the retirement funds, probably would compensate for the loss of "governments" as a primary investment outlet by placing a larger portion of their funds in state and local securities, corporate bonds, and, to a lesser extent, residential mortgages.

Individuals normally attempt to maintain a certain balance in their portfolios. This entails holding specific proportions of their assets in cash, in savings accounts, in federal government bonds, in tax exempts, in corporate bonds, and in corporate stocks. The actual proportion in which these assets are held depends upon the relative priorities that individuals place upon safety versus speculative opportunities in the balancing of their portfolios.

Government securities are not far removed from savings deposits in the spectrum outlined above. In order to maintain the requisite portfolio balance, individuals undoubtedly would immediately transfer to their savings accounts a great portion of the funds received from the retirement of the federal debt. This would place the savings institutions under greater pressure to find investment outlets. As a result, interest rates would fall to lower levels. The lower level of interest rates would encourage borrowing by private enterprise as well as by states and localities.

Considering the emphasis on individualism implicit in the conservative approach, it is extremely likely that in such a period individuals would be attempting to set up their own businesses in great numbers. The introduction of automation is already bringing the economy closer to the day when working hours will be shorter, permitting more and more people to hold two jobs if they choose. Furthermore, the growth of a wealthy and consumer-oriented economy means that greater reliance must be placed on the service fields, which should continue to grow quite rapidly. This area is typically the domain of individuals or small businesses.

The fulfillment of the drive toward independence via the small business route would require capital. The relatively lower interest rates prevailing under this model would enable individuals to borrow part of the funds. However, the continuous reductions of the public debt would provide them with more and more funds which they could draw upon directly. As they got more deeply involved in their business enterprises, their notions of proper portfolio balance would change. They would become more willing to invest these funds directly. Their lessened dependence upon the capital markets would result in a smaller rise in outstanding primary securities between 1970 and 1975 than would be the case under the conditions of any of the other models.

The unprecedented nature of this shift in the economy is evident if the ratio of the federal debt to GNP is traced through the decade under review. The debt-cut model assumes that the program of de-emphasizing the public sectors of the economy would be carried through successfully and that the economy would remain fully employed despite the drastic declines in the public debt. The scheduled drops in disarmament expenditures would pull the outstanding federal debt down from $290 billion in 1965 to $221 billion in 1970, and then to $89 billion in 1975. Nevertheless, GNP would grow from $610 billion in 1965 to $938 billion in 1975. This would produce a declining ratio of public debt to GNP as follows: 48 per cent in 1965, 29 per cent in 1970, and only 9 per cent in 1975.

To turn to the commercial banks, the retirement of the federal debt would result in a loss of both deposits and assets. Unless the Federal Reserve stepped in to alter the situation, commercial bank participation in the capital markets would be substantially reduced in the decade following 1965. By 1975 the participation of commercial banks in the capital market would have risen to $350 billion under the debt-cut model, or 16.2 per cent of total holdings of primary securities compared to 15.5 per cent in 1959, and 16.8 per cent in 1975 under the tax-cut model.

Since total capital market activity should rise less rapidly under this model, the percentage of commercial bank participation in the total should remain relatively the same. However, all of the other models project increased participation in the capital market on the part of commercial banks by 1975 as compared with 1970.

One further aspect of the debt-cut model must be considered. The expanding private economy would require a rising volume of short-term money market instruments in order to function effectively. This would pose a problem to the Treasury authorities. The conservative approach generally has been to lengthen the federal debt as much as possible, but the Treasury is aware of the needs of the business community for short-term instruments. Considering the somewhat lower level of interest rates that would prevail under the debt-cut model than under the other models, Treasury authorities might decide that greater concentration of the outstanding federal debt in short-term instruments is permissible. However, even if this were done, the total reduction in the federal debt would pose limits on the amount of short-term Treasury securities available to the community. Therefore, the Federal Reserve, in conducting its open-market operations, would be forced to rely more heavily on other short-term instruments, such as bankers acceptances or even, perhaps, some form of commercial paper.

SUBSIDIARY MODELS

As indicated before, we have, for comparative purposes, prepared alternative models: a judgment model, assuming no disarmament occurs; a government-spending model, in which federal nondefense spending fully offsets the defense cuts; and a combination model, in which the three main types of adjustment to defense cuts are combined. While, for lack of space, these are not shown in our table, we may take this opportunity to discuss the main characteristics and projections under these models.

In the government-spending model, we would find a great expansion of federal spending on education, roads, urban renewal, parks, foreign aid, etc.; and nondefense federal purchases would rise to 4.2 per cent of GNP in 1975, compared with 1.5 per cent in 1959, and 1.1 per cent under the debt-cut adjustment model.

However, since the capital market is more concerned with the borrower (the federal government in this case) than with the ultimate purpose of the loan, this will not necessarily have much bearing on the pattern of outstanding securities. Hence, on the financial side, this model is not too different from the 1959 situation or the judgment model. The financial contrast with the debt-cut model is, however, striking.

In light of the many crosscurrents of opinion, attitude, and evaluation, and the large role of compromise in our political structure, the combination model appears to represent the most probable type of adjustment to a disarmament program. This, as its name implies, assumes a combination of tax cuts, debt reductions, and substitution of alternative forms of federal spending for the reduced expenditures on defense. The secular rise in the role of government in economic affairs over many years suggests that special weight should be given to an increase in other federal expenditures in such a combination model. This model allows for about equal emphasis as between tax reductions and debt cuts.

The combination model would avoid the pressures resulting from the extreme use of any one technique, and would present the monetary authorities with far fewer problems than those which they would face in either the tax-cut or debt-cut situations.

LIQUIDITY IMPLICATIONS

It is useful to contrast the various approaches to disarmament in broad relation to their effects on liquidity. Liquidity may be envisaged, in its widest meaning, as the adequacy of one's monetary resources to meet one's financial needs quickly and easily. The highest degree of liquidity clearly involves direct ownership of all of the requisite funds. A lesser degree is attained when the funds, while sufficient in amount, are not held outright but are readily accessible. The economy is in a tight liquidity position when the desired financing is neither possessed nor available.

This more abstract definition of liquidity is broader than, but consistent with, the usual definition in terms of holdings of cash and under-one-year Treasury securities. Short-term monetary instruments are evidences of liquidity in that they can be readily converted into cash and are, therefore, most surely and most easily available for the financial purposes required. To that extent they meet the test of "availability" incorporated into our definition. However, they might not meet the "sufficiency" clause unless they were also adequate in amount to meet the purposes for which they were required.

The economy as a whole is generally considered to be liquid when some level of net free reserves is being maintained, indicating that the available financial resources exceed the economy's effective demand for financing. Conversely, the economy is characterized as illiquid, or in a tight liquidity position, when the over-all demands for funds exceed the supply. This is generally evident when the commercial banks are dependent upon net borrowed reserves. This application of the concept of liquidity corresponds to our definition.

In a perfectly liquid economy, where all or most of the required funds are owned outright, there would be little need to resort to the capital markets for financing. Demand would not press heavily on supply; the pressures on interest rates would be limited; and interest rates would remain relatively low.

As the economy became less liquid and the demand for financing began to build up relative to its supply, recourse to the capital markets would occur more frequently. There would be greater impetus to roll funds over quickly, at higher and higher interest rates. The more intensive use of the capital markets would produce an expanding volume of primary securities. In the economy of tight liquidity the uptrend in interest rates would be accompanied by rapid rises in the volume of primary securities relative to the growth in the economy as measured by GNP.

The different adjustment models would have different liquidity implications. In 1959, the ratio of primary securities to GNP was 2.55, close to the general full-employment ratio of primary securities to GNP of 2.5. The various models outlined in this paper fall within a range around the central value. The spread is from a high of 2.67 for the 1975 tax-cut model to a low of 2.30 for the 1975 debt-cut model.

The high ratio in the tax-cut model would result in part from the bidding up of the prices of securities by speculative elements. Interest rates would be higher than in the debt-cut model, since the economy would be less liquid—there would be less funds available to meet all of the demands of the economy.

The greatest departure from the "norm" is to be found in the debt-cut model. It could come about only if a larger proportion of the financing of business were done directly by individuals, as savers invested a large portion of their funds directly, bypassing the capital markets.

PRICE IMPLICATIONS

The assumption of price stability has been built into each model—even though the selective adjustments which the economy would make are widely different. This assumption certainly does not square with the facts of the past decade, and there are persuasive reasons for assuming a continuing upward price trend. Nevertheless, many factors may operate to hold prices in line. The relative labor shortage, which characterized much of the postwar period, seems to have ended. Additions to the labor force will be rising sharply within a few years. Industrial capacity has lately tended to grow faster than output, putting another dampening force on price increases. International competition has imposed still further discipline on our pricing policies. The list of inflation-retarding forces could readily be extended.

On the other hand, the possibility of continuing inflation cannot be entirely dismissed, and must be taken into consideration. What, then, would be the impact of moderate inflation on the various estimates? Under these circumstances the pattern of the future might very well be comparable to that of the past decade. Hedges would be sought, thus bidding up the market value of stocks. The growth

FINANCIAL STRUCTURE OF THE U.S. - 169

of investment companies, too, would probably be stimulated. Inventory demand probably would rise, pushing up the demand for bank loans (which could be made only if the Reserve authorities provided the means to validate the inflation). Conversely, life insurance companies and mutual savings banks would probably suffer relatively. Adjustments to reflect these possibilities could readily be incorporated into the various models.

CONCLUSIONS

The preceding sections have outlined the methodology and major assumptions behind the financial projections of the various disarmament adjustment models, as summarized in Table 1. The considerable degree of detail in the table may impart a spurious note of precision to the numbers. We urge that each entry should rather be regarded as a central value within a small range of variability, and that attention be focused mainly on the broad characteristics and organization of the financial structure as projected.

It may be asked which of the individual models can be looked upon as more than an empty hypothesis, with a real chance of implementation. Such a question transfers the discussions to the political area. This increases the uncertainties and makes it possible to comment only in rather general terms.

1. The tax-cut model—This probably would be the most popular single-factor adjustment. Nevertheless, one may anticipate skepticism as to the adequacy of the reaction of the taxpayer with added dollars to spend. Fears of a declining marginal propensity to consume would likely result in supplementation with other adjustment policies.

2. The debt-cut model—This would seem to be the least likely to be put into effect—from a political viewpoint. The national debt has always been something to talk about, but when surpluses accrue, the debates usually shift to tax cuts rather than debt cuts.

3. The government-spending model—Some sentiment undoubtedly would be expressed for a sizable increase in the level of federal spending. There would be a better chance of this technique being followed than that of the debt cut, but it probably would not

TABLE 1 – PROJECTED GNP FINANCIAL STRUCTURE UNDER ALTERNATIVE ADJUSTMENTS
TO DISARMAMENT
(Billions of 1959 dollars)

| | 1959 | | 1975 | | | |
| | ACTUAL | | TAX-CUT ADJUSTMENT MODEL | | DEBT-CUT ADJUSTMENT MODEL | |
	VALUE	PER CENT OF TOTAL	VALUE	PER CENT OF TOTAL	VALUE	PER CENT OF TOTAL
GNP	$ 482.1	100.0	$ 938.0	100.0	$ 938.0	100.0
Government purchases	97.1	20.1	136.7	14.5	138.7	14.7
Investment, including net foreign	71.0	14.7	147.0	15.6	156.0	16.6
Personal consumption	313.8	65.0	654.0	69.7	643.3	68.5
SECURITIES OUTSTANDING	1,232.1	100.0	2,500.0	100.0	2,160.0	100.0
Corporate bonds	85.3	6.9	220.0	8.8	225.0	10.4
Corporate stocks	446.4	36.2	850.0	34.0	750.0	34.7
State and local	63.7	5.2	100.0	4.0	125.0	5.8
Federal government securities	290.9	23.6	290.0	11.6	89.0	4.1
Non-guaranteed federal debt	7.9	0.6	30.0	1.2	1.0	a
Family mortgages	131.0	10.6	420.0	16.8	410.0	19.0

Other mortgages	60.0	4.9	150.0	6.0	145.0	6.7
Business credit	53.3	4.3	150.0	6.0	140.0	6.5
Consumer credit	52.0	4.2	190.0	7.6	185.0	8.6
All other credit	41.6	3.4	100.0	4.0	90.0	4.2

DISTRIBUTION OF
PRIMARY SECURITIES

	1,232.1	100.0	2,500.0	100.0	2,160.0	100.0
Life insurance companies	103.9	8.4	245.0	9.8	245.0	11.3
Savings and loan associations	57.6	4.7	220.0	8.8	230.0	10.6
Mutual savings banks	37.5	3.0	85.0	3.4	85.0	3.9
Corporate pension funds	24.1	2.0	90.0	3.6	90.0	4.2
Credit unions	4.8	0.4	25.0	1.0	25.0	1.2
Federal and state retirement funds	68.7	5.6	82.0	3.3	82.0	3.8
U.S. government agencies	22.8	1.9	28.0	1.1	b	a
Fire and casualty insurance companies	32.0	2.6	75.0	3.0	75.0	3.5
Investment companies	15.5	1.3	80.0	3.2	60.0	2.8
Miscellaneous nonbank institutions	31.5	2.6	90.0	3.6	65.0	3.0
Commercial banks	190.5	15.5	420.0	16.8	350.0	16.2
Federal Reserve banks	27.0	2.2	35.0	1.4	30.0	1.4
All other owners	616.2	50.0	1,025.0	41.0	823.0	38.2

a Under 0.05 per cent.
b Under $50 million.

have as much political support as the tax-cut approach. As stated here, all of the outlays are assumed to be on the income and product account basis. In reality, however, there might be considerable sentiment to increase non-GNP (transfer) payments. In all likelihood, an increase in federal outlays would result in a relatively slower growth at the state and local levels because of the transfer of functions to the federal level.

4. A combination approach—The technique most likely to be adopted would be a combination along the lines previously discussed.

In summary, this chapter was not designed to present a financial blueprint for adjusting the economy to the process of scheduled disarmament. Instead, it has set forth a number of possible avenues to explore—along with the pressures and circumstances that would prevail in each case. Consequently, it should be looked upon primarily as a tool for further analysis, rather than as a timetable for action.

10

The Expansionary Effects of Shifts from Defense to Nondefense Expenditures*

Leslie Fishman†

Because the low expansionary effect of defense spending has been generally ignored, there has been a widespread tendency to exaggerate the deflationary impact of cuts in defense spending. Once the low expansionary effect of defense spending is recognized, it becomes clear that the substitution of other types of expenditures, whether public or private, should create more activity and employment than was lost through the cutback in defense spending. This would greatly ease the practical problems of adjustment to disarmament, and would eliminate the adverse effects of the "balanced budget multiplier"—according to which a reduction of public expenditure, even if fully offset by tax reductions, would be deflationary because of leakages into private savings.

The key issue here is the extent to which defense spending gen-

* This is a less technical restatement of the argument first presented, partly in mathematical form, in "A Note on Disarmament and Effective Demand," *Journal of Political Economy*, April 1962. I am indebted to Professor Benoit for aid in the reformulation of some of the arguments.
† LESLIE FISHMAN is currently a visiting lecturer in the Department of Applied Economics, University of Cambridge, on leave from the University of Colorado.

erates collateral activity as compared with consumer expenditure or private investment.

In his *General Theory of Money, Income and Employment* of 1936, Keynes urged that the most meaningful analysis of effective demand can be made by considering consumer spending and investment spending separately. Consumer spending is carried on by households for the satisfaction of needs; moreover, it is stable and varies primarily with income and expected income. In contrast, investment spending is done by business units interested in maximizing profits, and it usually increases productive capacity. Moreover, investment spending is extremely variable and is paid for out of savings or borrowed savings (and, perhaps, newly created money). The crucial relation that indicates whether an economy is on the upswing or downswing is that between output and spending. When spending exceeds output, production is stimulated. When output exceeds spending, production tends to be curtailed. An increase in consumer spending usually results in an equal increase in both amounts—spending and output. On the other hand, an increase in investment spending increases, in the short run, only spending and NOT output. It is not until the new plants and equipment are in place and operating that production and output are increased. Therefore, investment spending gives the economy a special kind of boost, an increase in new spending without a simultaneous matching increase in output.

Defense spending can be divided into similar categories—consumer spending (that results from the spending of wages and salaries of the armed forces and Department of Defense personnel and workers directly or indirectly employed on defense contracts) and investment spending (purchase of facilities to make missiles, aircraft, and the purchase of Defense Department buildings). An *increase* in either type of spending will cause or "induce" further investment—IF there is little or no excess capacity already in existence in those industries where demand is expanding. To meet the increased demand, new facilities must be built, and this is what is meant by "induced investment."

Much of the recent increase in defense spending has come from complex weapons systems and warning systems that require very special plants and equipment for their production. These production facilities are, in most cases, created especially for the manufacture of a new system and for a single contract. The weapons systems and detection systems often become obsolete even before they become operational. Therefore, no arms producer would risk private capital to build manufacturing facilities to produce these rapidly-obsolescent weapons or the special materials and machinery required for their production. Thus, relatively small amounts of private investment are induced from this type of defense investment. In contrast, an expansion of defense purchases of shoes or clothing might readily lead private firms to expand their facilities—an example of investment induced by consumer-type defense spending. Undoubtedly, some of the defense investment involves purchases from regular commercial channels of standard commodities (cement, steel, aluminum, electrical equipment, etc.). But these outside purchases of standard items will not be as high a proportion of defense investment as they would be of private investment or of consumer purchases. Thus, relatively little induced investment results from an increase in weapons system spending. The new facilities required for the Nike-Zeus complex, for example, would hardly lead private suppliers to expand their plants with their own money in order to fulfill future Nike-Zeus contracts that may come about in another five years.

Much of the recent increase in defense spending has gone into investment in arms-producing facilities and weapons systems themselves, but the kind of boost to the economy that we have come to expect from increases in investment has not materialized. The induced investment flowing from such expenditures is far less than from ordinary private investment.

Let us now consider expenditure as an outlet for savings. Keynes stressed the fact that prosperity and full employment depended upon making sure that the savings of our economy were fully returned into spending streams, through the channeling of these savings into investment. Thus, when a person saves part of his income, he withholds that much purchasing power from the spending stream. If that saving is then made available to businesses (or housebuyers) for investment purchases, no leakage in spending results. If, however, there are not enough borrowers (whom lenders can take a chance with) in order to absorb all of the savings funds, then spending and effective demand will be insufficient to absorb all of last period's output, and the economy will tend downward.

Defense investment, from this point of view, is peculiar, because the entire investment is paid for by the government—NOT out of the savings market (unless the government runs a deficit). Defense investment does NOT put back into active channels the savings of businesses and individuals, because arms-manufacturing facilities are almost invariably financed out of current taxes—which is equivalent to a restriction of consumption spending. Moreover, the profits earned on defense contracts intensify the problem of the investment-savings balance since these profits raise the total of savings for which investment outlets have to be found.

To recapitulate, defense investment is less stimulating to the economy than private investment because: (1) It induces relatively little additional private investment; and (2) it does not use private savings, and thus does not return to the spending cycle those funds which are potentially idle. As a partial offset to these negative aspects, there is a positive aspect which, particularly in the long run, is important. Arms investment, because it is so specialized, does not appreciably increase the nation's capacity to produce for the private market; and, hence, arms investment does not tend to create excess capacity in consumer goods industries—although private investment often does.

Let us now turn to an application of the effects that flow from these two characteristics during a transitional period of disarmament. In the event of general and complete disarmament on the READ model, federal spending for security and related programs would be reduced by some $32 billion. Congress and the President could respond to such a situation by adopting one or several of the following alternatives (many other less important policies could also be added, but they all would be variants of those discussed below):

1. A substantial reduction in income taxes (can be utilized up to a maximum of some $45 billion)

2. A substantial reduction in corporate profits taxes (up to the total, which is about $25 billion)
3. A substantial increase in government spending (for health, education, transportation, resource development, etc.)
4. A substantial decrease in the federal debt (up to the maximum held by nonfederal, nongovernmental agencies, which is about $220 billion)

A substantial reduction in income taxes will put a large amount of money into the hands of consumers. Previously, when this has occurred, consumers responded by spending a high proportion of the additional money. Consumers will tend to spend this additional income on cars, refrigerators, furniture, clothes, housing, etc. The fear often expressed during the Great Depression, that consumers will run out of needs, is no longer to be taken seriously—especially if one considers the fact that the average American family income (with a single earner) is below $6,000 per year. If the entire $32 billion reduction in security and associated expenditures were passed on as an income tax cut, this would amount to only $164 per person per year, based on a 1965 population of 195 million. There are very few people in the United States who would have difficulty thinking of additional purchases they would like to make for $164. Consumers will use the additional income to upgrade their standard of living, and this spending is likely, over the disarmament period, to be greater than 90 per cent of any income tax cut.

How much investment spending will be induced by increased-consumer spending? About $1 to $3 of new capital is required to increase consumer goods output by $1. This is referred to as the "capital-output ratio" and is extremely high for industries like petroleum, and low for industries like food processing. However, for an over-all rough average, the ratio of 2 to 1 will do. This means that if consumer spending were to increase by $10 billion, the investment required to make possible the additional output by consumer goods would be about $20 billion—*if* existing capacity is being fully utilized. This is an important qualification for the United States economy today. If there were substantial amounts of excess capacity in industries where demand was expanding, the idle capacity would first be utilized before new investments were undertaken. Only after existing capacity was nearly fully utilized would new investment be induced by the increased demand—and then financing and an optimistic profit outlook would be required to justify the investment before it became a reality.

How does this analysis apply to disarmament? In the event that all of the $32 billion decrease in arms and associated spending per year resulted in an income tax cut, consumer spending would increase by about $29 billions. Such a substantial increase in consumption would undoubtedly tax severely the existing capacity in most industries, and would probably induce a considerable amount of private investment—which arms spending does NOT do. With a savings leakage of about 10 per cent, and with an average capital-output ratio of 2:1, the total induced investment would just equal the total savings leakage (half of 10 per cent, or 5 per cent, equals 1 out of 20) in the absence of idle capacity.

Under present circumstances, with idle capacity estimated at between $30 to $50 billion, it might seem that the increase in consumption would be fully absorbed in higher use of existing capacity with no stimulus to investment. In fact, the overcapacity is not uniformly spread over the whole field of industry, and even $29 billion of increased consumer spending would undoubtedly strain capacity in *some* industries, stimulating investment at least in these industries, and indirectly in others. Moreover, it is a legitimate hope that by 1965—the assumed date of the beginning of disarmament—most of the excess capacity will have disappeared, either via higher levels of demand or via technological obsolescence.

The crucial point to remember, however, is that if our economy is underemployed and general and complete disarmament occurs, income tax reductions can be used to increase purchasing power, income, and total employment. When a stimulus to the economy is needed, arms reductions coupled with income tax reductions will provide just such a stimulus. The greater the arms cut, the greater the stimulus.

On the other hand, cuts in the corporate profits tax would have just the opposite effects: They would dampen spending and considerably increase the supply of savings available for investment.

They would lead to either increased dividend payments or to increased corporate savings, or some combination of these two. Higher dividends would increase personal savings considerably, since dividend payments are heavily skewed toward the higher income–higher savings groups. Higher corporate savings would similarly aggravate the savings-investment disbalance, and would, therefore, be extremely deflationary in nature. There is, however, one possible, if unlikely, alternative policy which corporations could follow, which would have just the opposite effect: that is the policy of reducing prices and passing the benefits of the tax cut on to the consumer. If corporate directors, as a result of tax cuts, foresaw a great surplus in savings and a surfeit in the capital market, or if competitive pressures became very great, a price-cutting policy might conceivably be attempted in enough cases to provide a real economic stimulus. But given the sticky nature of prices, particularly in the administered sectors of the economy, it is difficult to anticipate how serious or pervasive such price cuts are likely to be. The effects of such price cuts on total output would vary with the extent of the cuts and the elasticities of their demand (that is, with the responsiveness of the demand to the price cuts). Considerable increase in output and in utilization of plant capacity would undoubtedly result from serious price cuts in major sectors of the corporate economy. Moreover, the competitive position of many American industries in foreign markets would greatly improve. But realistically speaking, increases in dividend payments and corporate savings rather than price cuts have historically been the response by boards of directors when confronted with similar situations. In a similar case in the future, the corporate profits tax reduction would be deflationary in nature and should be used only when such a policy is appropriate.

The third alternative Congressional policy is a substantial increase in nonmilitary government spending. To make the example concrete, let us assume the increased spending takes place in the transportation industry. An increase of, say, $10 billion a year in all phases of the transportation industry would be a significant stimulus to many industries—cement, road-building equipment, aircraft, shipbuilding, steel, locomotive manufacturers, automobile manufacturers, freight car manufacturers, etc. In all of these fields, considerable induced investment is likely to result—if a long-range program is adopted by the federal government. This induced investment is likely to be greater for federal nonmilitary spending than it was for its arms-spending, and to the extent that it is, the net effect will be stimulating to effective demand, to income, and to employment. The consumer respending (resulting from the wage and salary expenditures) is likely to be the same for both the arms and the transportation expenditures. But the induced investment effects will be quite different and, in the case of transportation, are likely to be quite significant.

The fourth and final policy alternative, reducing the federal debt, would be the most severely deflationary of the four. Retiring the federal debt would mean taking the purchasing power out of the pockets of the taxpayers and placing it in the hands of the present debt holders. Since the debt holders purchased government bonds and debentures because they wanted a secure and almost riskless form of investment for their savings, it is almost certain that if the United States Treasury were to redeem their bonds and debentures, they would immediately look for another similar investment. Since the American tax burden falls heavily on low- and middle-income-group consumers, the tax payment restricts consumption rather heavily. The net effect, then, of reducing the debt would be to transfer this purchasing power from the taxpayers (heavy consumers) to the debt holders (heavy savers). Such a policy is extremely deflationary and—if full employment and high output levels are our goals—should be used only to offset a potential inflation.

We now can summarize the effects of all four policies. An income tax cut is quite buoyant, particularly if it emphasizes the lower- and middle-income groups. A corporate profits tax reduction is quite deflationary, except if it were to result in price reductions—not a very likely possibility. Increases in government spending for nonarmaments is likely to be mildly buoyant and stimulating. Finally, reduction of the federal debt is likely to be extremely deflationary. With such a collection of alternative policies to choose from, Congress and the President should be able to assess the economic situation at the time of disarmament and compose several groups of policies that would maintain prosperity and full employment. Since all four alternatives are politically attractive—with all but increased federal spending being in extremely good favor with both political parties—a composite prescription to maintain full employment should be relatively easy to arrive at to meet any situation. Several examples will illustrate how this might be done.

If, when disarmament takes effect, the United States economy is already at full employment, it would be important to emphasize the deflationary policies of a corporate profits tax reduction and a reduction in the federal debt. However, to make sure these deflationary policies do not send us into a recession, some decreases in income taxes and/or increases in other federal expenditures should also be allowed for. It would obviously be desirable to embark on these policies gradually, with flexibility built into the administrative machinery. The deflationary emphasis would dominate the first phase of the transition. However, if it appeared that a slowdown was setting in under the impact of the increased savings, then some of the buoyant policies would be undertaken to bring the economy back to full employment.

On the other hand, if disarmament takes effect when the economy is already burdened with substantial amounts of unemployment, then income tax cuts and increased government spending in nonarms industries would be the policies to emphasize. After these policies had become effective, if it was apparent that inflation threatened, then the other two policies could be utilized—reduction of the debt and corporate profits tax reduction.

In summary, it would appear that disarmament, far from providing us with a bleak and depressing economic outlook, would actually permit the government to use a whole battery of policies to maintain full employment and prosperity. It would require astute evaluation of the economic situation and a wise application of the tools in the government bag, but it appears that maintenance of full employment will be more easily accomplished under complete and general disarmament than it will be with a $60 billion military budget that is responsive to the military and political situation and not to the economic needs of the nation.

11

Measures to Deal with Labor Displacement in Disarmament*

Adolf Sturmthal†

The displacement of workers caused by a substantial measure of disarmament comes under the general heading of frictional unemployment—rather than seasonal or cyclical unemployment. This means that it results from imperfections in the labor market in connection with substantial shifts in the demand for labor. Some authors use the term "structural" unemployment to designate that portion of frictional unemployment that may represent a long-run addition to standard frictional unemployment. In that sense, disarmament-created unemployment may be called structural. Aggregate demand for goods and services in the economy as a whole may or may not drop, according to whether or not the funds no longer spent for armaments are spent for other purposes. If there is a drop in aggregate demand, some unemployment comparable to

* This is a considerably abbreviated version of the original research report, with some of the main arguments foreshortened and much of the supporting and clarifying detail omitted. Those interested in a more extended treatment should consult Richard C. Wilcock and Walter Franke, *Unwanted Workers—Permanent Lay-offs and Long-term Unemployment*, New York: Free Press of Glencoe.
† ADOLF STURMTHAL is Professor of Labor and Industrial Relations at the University of Illinois, currently on leave and teaching at Yale University.

cyclical unemployment will also occur, resulting from the insufficiency of aggregate demand.

The magnitude and character of the unemployment that might be created by disarmament have been discussed earlier in this volume. Accordingly, we shall simply assume that a large number of job shifts will be necessary, however successful public and private policies may be in creating an adequate number of new job opportunities. Solutions for the unemployment problem will be further complicated, during the foreseeable future, by the rapid growth of the labor force. During the next few years, more than a million additional members of the labor force will have to be accommodated annually. Between 1965 and 1975 the annual rate of growth of the labor force will average close to 1.5 per cent.[1] If output per manhour continues to increase at its long-term rate of growth, present output could be produced by a working force shrinking at a rate of 3.5 to 4 per cent a year. In other words, unemployment created by disarmament has to be viewed against the background of an economy in which between 3 and 4 million jobs per year must be created if rising unemployment is to be avoided.

The cornerstone of any policy designed to absorb displaced defense workers as rapidly as possible must be a set of measures aimed at reducing over-all unemployment to a "tolerable" minimum. However, the nature of disarmament-created unemployment is such as to require special caution in applying the standard full-employment criteria and policies. An increase in expenditures designed to offset the cut in defense spending almost certainly involves the expansion of sectors of the economy different from those affected by disarmament. If the displaced labor is to be absorbed it is necessary that the rate of offset spending be harmonized with the possibilities of expansion in the least elastic sectors of the economy affected by increased spending. This rate is determined by the volume of idle capacity and by the mobility of capital and labor—to be employed in the expanding sectors of the economy.

[1] *Population and Labor Force Projections for the United States, 1960 to 1975*, Dept. of Labor, Bulletin No. 1242.

APPROACHES TO EMPLOYMENT POLICY

The traditional view on labor adjustments, held by a decreasing but still significant number of people, relies on the mechanism of the labor market itself to provide a solution for unemployment problems. Given certain assumptions about the elasticity of the supply curves of labor and about fiscal and monetary policy, this result will indeed occur—*after* a period of transition. However, the probability that the assumptions will be matched by reality is not very high; nor will modern industrial societies as a rule sit quietly for an indeterminate "period of transition," which may extend over many years, while unemployment persists in concentrated form in certain areas.

This applies particularly to the unemployment which may be created by successive stages of disarmament: first, because the event is predictable (in its main outlines, though not in its details) once a disarmament treaty is signed; and second, because lack of preparation for tackling the problem may become a serious roadblock for any administration endeavoring to pursue a policy of disarmament. Our attention thus shifts to possible short-run policies.

United States policies regarding displaced workers can be usefully subdivided into two main groups: assistance policies and policies designed to improve the economic situation of a given area or occupation. Under the heading of assistance come unemployment insurance and public assistance. Labor market organization belongs to the second category. There are obvious connections between the two groups of policies; for instance, assistance tends to increase effective demand and thus affects the economic situation as a whole. Yet the classification is useful for practical purposes.

Unemployment insurance is deficient in several respects. In the first place, some of the states have quite inadequate programs, particularly as regards the duration and the level of benefits. Second, substantial numbers of employees are not covered by the insurance. This applies to some 13 million wage earners, including state and local government employees and employees of nonprofit firms. Disarmament-generated unemployment is likely to affect a number of noncovered employees. Third, the level of benefits, particularly the maximum, is clearly insufficient. As a consequence of inflation on the one hand and the rise of real wages on the other, benefits have dropped in relation to average weekly earnings. Thus in 1939, all but two states, and all but 15 per cent of covered workers received minimum weekly unemployment benefits covering 50 per cent or more of their average weekly wage. By 1959 this was true of only fourteen states and 23 per cent of covered workers.[2]

With concentrated unemployment of the kind which disarmament might call forth, the drop in unemployment benefits in relation to average earnings could become an important deflationary factor. This danger is aggravated by the insufficient duration of benefits, which under federal legislation can amount to twenty-six weeks at the most.[3] Indeed, this may well be even more serious a problem than the *level* of benefits.

The relatively short duration of unemployment benefits appears even more serious in connection with public assistance. In several states no regular assistance is provided for needy families with employable members. In others, assistance is available only to a limited extent. The inadequacies of unemployment insurance are thus rendered more acute by corresponding inadequacies of the public assistance system. The prolonged unemployment which disarmament might cause would bring these shortcomings into sharp focus.

In the organization of the labor market, counseling services should play a key role in order to provide for a maximum matching of demand and supply of labor of different categories and to enable young people to develop according to their ability. An important tool for this purpose is the United States Employment Service, which maintains a counseling staff. Equipped with the long-range forecasts of employment needs made by the Labor Department, these services could be of tremendous value in "steering" young people at the beginning of their job-training and thus

---

[2] Data from Bureau of Employment Statistics, Department of Labor, cited in the report of the Special Senate Committee on Unemployment Problems, S. Res. 196, 86th Cong., 1st sess., 1960, p. 95.

[3] Some states have provisions for extension when unemployment exceeds a specified level.

facilitating the adjustment of the labor supply to the changing demand. Hardly less important would be counseling on the occasion of job changes.

The fact is, however, that the counseling services are used by only a fraction of those who could benefit from them. Equally serious, from the point of view of an orderly labor market, is the fact that the *placement* facilities of the Employment Service are relatively little used. Moreover, the current use is overwhelmingly to fill unskilled jobs, in spite of the fact that a number of Employment Service offices have added special placement facilities for professional, technical, and scientific workers to meet the increasing need for workers of this kind.

PROBLEMS OF LABOR MOBILITY

While information on job openings is the first requirement, it is by no means the only one. Willingness and ability to move to the job is equally necessary—since moving the worker to the job is the object. The term "mobility" may refer to movement to a similar job in a different locality, or to a different occupation, or to a different plant or firm within the same occupation and locality.

Geographic mobility increases with the pull of job opportunities, with the increase in knowledge of the labor market, and with the degree of assistance in moving. This may involve moving to a different country—but for American workers international migration is likely to remain numerically insignificant, unless foreign aid, in the wake of disarmament, expands far beyond anything that can at present be foreseen. There may be considerable movement across state lines. Generally speaking, the American worker has been exceedingly mobile, though the bulk of the population remains relatively stable. It is true, however, that "job changes from one local labor market area to another are much less frequent than those from one occupation or industry to another."[4] The trend toward home ownership is thought by some to have reduced geographic mobility, since the forced sale of a house leads often to substantial losses. Such blocks to geographic mobility may be

---

[4] Herbert S. Parnes, "Extent and Character of Labor Mobility," *Readings in Unemployment*, Special Senate Committee on Unemployment Problems, S. Res. 196, 86th Cong., 1st sess., 1960, p. 1209.

partly offset by growth of the habit of commuting for considerable distances and by the development of modern transportation, which makes this possible.

To what extent should individual geographic mobility be encouraged? Should jobs be brought to the workers, as the saying goes, rather than the workers to the jobs? At the level of principles it is fairly easy to state that while it is desirable for a free society to maintain a state of full mobility, conditions should be such that relatively few workers should feel the need to make use of this right. Under permanent full employment, with a perfectly organized labor market, this ideal state might be approximated. But we are dealing here precisely with a problem that arises because these conditions are imperfectly achieved.

Given the personal and social costs involved in the uprooting of families and the shifting of populations, one is tempted to say that the jobs should go where the workers are. It is not, however, possible to apply such a rule in all situations. Shifts in industrial location may be advisable, or even indispensable, from the economic point of view. The costs of maintaining or creating jobs in inappropriate locations may be higher than the community is willing to bear, and clearly no democratic society would wish to give the government permanent authority to dictate industrial location policies.

It is unlikely that rapid and substantial shifts in the volume and direction of aggregate demand will always be faithfully reflected in changes in the location of economic activities. Space does not permit a full exploration of the complicated issues arising out of this fact. Some of the principles to be taken into account in considering these problems may, however, be stated. When an area shows promise that in the long run it will be self-sustaining, then making the investments that may be necessary to bring the jobs to the workers will pay off. Investment already existing in the form of social overhead must, of course, be taken into account. Areas with surplus labor which, even in the long run, show little likelihood of attaining economic self-sufficiency, will call for moving workers rather than capital. In case of doubt, the suffering associated with uprooting families and associations justifies a bias in favor of moving capital rather than labor.

Occupational mobility is usually regarded as inversely proportionate to socioeconomic status; the number of occupational changes is greater for common laborers than for managerial or professional workers, while the latter have the highest geographic mobility. Service workers, with a particularly low occupational mobility, are an exception to this rule. However, in the situation we are considering—substantial unemployment created by disarmament—a special type of occupational mobility is likely to be necessary, i.e., the crossing of occupational frontiers.

A rough guess at the nature of occupational changes that a substantial measure of disarmament would involve indicates the difficulties of the problem. Four main groups of employees would be concerned: (1) a relatively small group of unskilled and semiskilled workers; (2) a number of young men, at the beginning of their occupational careers, being released from the armed forces; (3) experienced officers and career men from these forces; (4) a number of persons of high skill or professional competence—mechanics, electricians, technicians, engineers, scientific and administrative personnel. Of these, a certain number, as set forth elsewhere in these studies, may be gradually absorbed by international agencies engaged in the inspection and supervision of disarmament measures. Some of the remaining displaced people may be able to find jobs in the same or former occupations. For the rest, getting a new job may involve working not simply for different employers but also in different occupations.

Little systematic empirical evidence exists as to the behavior of workers in changing occupations. There is some indication that the professional group is relatively more "closed" than others, though there is some interchange at all levels. The most common type of intergroup shift appears to be from one manual category to another.[5] Perhaps the most instructive experience is that of World War II, when substantial movements of workers from one occupation to another occurred without much time loss or difficulty —under the pressure of relentless demand. Jobs were "broken down," so that the component operations could be carried out by workers who did not possess the training necessary to carry out

---

[5] See Margaret S. Gordon, *"The Mobility of San Francisco Workers, 1940– 1949,"* unpublished report, University of California Industrial Relations Section, quoted in Parnes, *op. cit.*

the whole operation. A good deal of learning occurred on the job, sometimes in formal, more often in informal, ways. Re-engineering of work processes can many times help solve the problem.

The core of the problem of occupational mobility is clearly in the group of scientific personnel, and even there some degree of elasticity seems to exist, e.g., physical chemists turn into physicists, physics teachers, and science writers. In the case of disarmament-created unemployment of scientific personnel, the long-run upward trend in the demand for such personnel will be of some assistance.

Mobility within an occupation, or within the same industry, offers problems of the loss of fringe benefits, including pension rights. A cutback of defense spending may affect different parts of a plant or firm differently if the operation combines defense and nondefense work; and here problems of seniority arise. Private and social costs differ. Job protection for older workers and those more difficult to employ in different occupations may be costly for industry but preferable from the social point of view. If the burden is disproportionate, either for employees or employers, the social interest may require public intervention, through subsidies or in other ways.

POSSIBILITIES OF OCCUPATIONAL RETRAINING

Mobility, however refined and improved, of labor or of capital, needs to be supplemented by a program of training and retraining of the labor force—first, because a series of cutbacks in defense spending would require a permanent restructuring of the labor force to adjust it to the new set of demand schedules for labor; second, because this process would be superimposed upon a radical and rapid change in the composition of the labor force, which has been under way in this country for many years and seems destined to continue for considerably longer. The Area Redevelopment Act of 1961, which represents an effort to alleviate the unemployment problem of depressed areas by reviving economic activities there, provides, among other things, for weekly retraining payments and the establishment of vocational training facilities where needed.

Training and retraining have been the object of extreme but contradictory attitudes. Frequently, retraining has been presented as the cure-all of unemployment. It is well-known that the demand for unskilled labor has been falling over a long period, and that the demand for semiskilled labor—not so long ago the fastest-growing group in the labor force—has leveled off to a constant proportion, while the share of white-collar, professional, scientific, and technical workers has greatly increased. From these facts it is inferred that any individual's chances of employment are low if he has little or no skill, and high if and when he acquires higher skills. This reasoning is reinforced by analysis of the unemployment figures, which show that unskilled and, to a slightly lesser extent, semiskilled workers form a larger proportion of the unemployed than of the total labor force. Thus, to raise the standards of skills of as many as possible of the displaced workers appears as the logical conclusion for a program to deal with unemployment.

The trouble with these recommendations, of course, is that they do not affect the aggregate volume of employment—except, perhaps, insofar as the training process itself involves expenditures. Unless there is an excess demand for labor of the newer types, the principal result will be to change the personnel that is unemployed, or as the French put it, *mêler les fortunes!*—to redistribute fate. This may be of help to the individual who is unemployed, but retraining per se cannot be regarded as a contribution to solving the unemployment problem, except to the extent that real and adequate job openings exist.

At the other extreme are the voices of those who when retraining is suggested respond with the query, "retraining—for which jobs?" This may sound negative, but retraining, in order to be a remedy for unemployment, cannot stand by itself; it must be part of a total program, in which increasing the aggregate volume of effective demand for goods and services is the foundation stone. The particular measures taken to create full employment will usually provide some indications as to the nature and perhaps even the location of the future jobs.

Since retraining represents a sizable capital investment for the acquisition of skills, it may be questioned under what circumstances it "pays off." Can every worker profit from retraining? One limit is set by the aggregate demand for labor, another by the educational background of the worker, another, perhaps, by age. An experiment at the Armour Company's Oklahoma plant brought a report that of 170 persons laid off who were given tests to determine whether they could profit from vocational training only 60 showed promise for jobs locally available.[6] A Belgian experiment with coal miners led to the conclusion that retraining helps only an elite group.[7] However, the United States Office of Vocational Rehabilitation has been carrying on retraining on a limited scale since 1920 and has retrained more than a million workers. It proceeds on a careful individual basis and, according to an article in *Fortune,* July 1961, "officials were 'shocked at the casual approach' of the Armour experiment in declaring 65 per cent of its applicants ineligible merely on the basis of a battery of impersonal aptitude tests. . . . The agency spends about $2,000 to counsel, train and place one man and it boasts success in 75 per cent of its cases. By contrast, the Armour Fund appropriated no more than $150 per worker."

CONTRIBUTIONS OF EUROPEAN EXPERIENCE

A number of studies during the last few years have dealt with the methods employed in Western Europe to deal with localized "lapses from full employment" or, in our current terminology, with distressed or labor surplus areas.[8] The following summaries of policies pursued may help to place in perspective the problems and policies we are examining.

Britain. British policies of assistance for resettlement date from 1909 but have undergone many changes. The policies apply to areas designated by the Board of Trade in which, in the Board's opinion, "a high rate of unemployment . . . is imminent and is likely to persist (whether seasonally or generally)." Recently areas

[6] Information from *Progress Report, Automation Committee,* on a study set up under agreements of September 1, 1959, between Armour and Company and the two meat-packing unions affiliated with the AFL-CIO (United Packinghouse Food and Allied Workers, AFL-CIO, and Amalgamated Meat Cutters and Butcher Workmen of North America, AFL-CIO).

[7] "Retraining Works—for the Fortunate Few," *Business Week,* June 17, 1961.

[8] See, for instance, Ellen M. Bussey, "Assistance to Labor Surplus Areas in Europe," *Monthly Labor Review,* June 1960; "Aid to Labor Surplus Areas in Great Britain, Belgium, the Federal Republic of Germany and Sweden," *Foreign Labor Information,* Bureau of Labor Statistics, 1960; *Economic Programs for Labor Surplus Areas in Selected Countries of Western Europe,* 86th Cong., 2d sess., 1960.

with an unemployment rate of at least 4 per cent—double the national average—have been so designated. Moving expenses, free transportation, a "lodging allowance" for a maximum of two years in the case of a separation between the worker and his family, and a small amount of financial assistance in the purchase or sale of a house are provided for the worker who is willing to move out of the designated area.

There has been a rising emphasis in the British program on bringing industry to the worker rather than the worker to a new job. This new principle was first embodied in legislation enacted in 1945 and has been retained, with modifications, in the current Local Employment Act of 1960. Assistance is available in the form of loans to business enterprise, grants for up to 20 per cent of investment costs, reduced taxes, and accelerated amortization to enterprises which locate in an area designated as requiring assistance, provided they show a reasonable chance of success and will ultimately not depend on government assistance.

Sweden. The Swedish attack on unemployment is not confined to specially designated areas. Essentially, the program provides for three kinds of policies—assistance for workers' transfer, promotion of new businesses in an area of unemployment, and public works. Unlike the British program, the Swedish one puts chief stress on the relocation of workers and less on the relocation of industry.

Relocation is encouraged by travel and moving allowances, a family allowance in case the worker is separated from his family, and a lump-sum starting allowance. To cope with the housing shortage, the government buys prefabricated houses, furnishes them to relocated workers, and provides mortgage funds. These activities are administered by the Royal Labor Market Board, a joint labor-management committee, whose program, however, requires the approval of the parliament each year. The board also encourages, and advises upon, the formation of new industries in depressed areas, with the help of a loan program for smaller firms.

Belgium. A program of regional employment assistance dates from 1959, operating in designated areas which must fulfill requirements defined in terms of unemployment, out-migration and large-scale commuting. To business firms willing to locate in depressed areas the government provides assistance in the form of loans, grants, guarantees, and tax incentives, plus the purchase or construction of industrial centers and the retraining of labor. In the relocation of workers, special problems are presented by the cultural and linguistic division of the country between the Flemish and Walloon areas. Because of the small size of the country, commuting suffices in many cases. Little emphasis has, therefore, been placed on relocation, though traveling and moving allowances are available.

West Germany. The unemployment problem has been complicated in Germany by the steady influx of refugees, who now represent about a quarter of the total population of West Germany. Yet the exceptional prosperity of the past decade has made for a short supply of labor rather than an excess. Local labor surpluses have existed for short periods, particularly after the Korean War. These have been handled primarily by loans at low interest rates for industrial, tourist, and handicraft enterprises and for local communities, as well as by vocational training, tax incentives, preference in government contracts, transportation subsidies, and other similar measures. Workers are encouraged to move to areas of labor shortage, being given travel expenses where necessary, transportation of household effects, a family separation allowance, and an allowance to tide the worker over until he receives pay from his new job.

Denmark. Here assistance programs exist for industrially less-developed areas, which in practice means all of Denmark except Copenhagen. The inventory of available measures comprises loans, grants, and local—but not national—tax incentives. Like most other European programs, Denmark's emphasizes the movement of industry to the worker rather than the reverse.

Social Fund. The European Economic Community, which came into official existence January 1, 1958 provides in its founding treaty for the creation of a European Social Fund to provide assistance to the member nations in certain of their efforts to help unemployed workers. The activities must be carried on by public agencies, and must involve expenses for reemployment, retraining, and moving allowances intended to maintain at an unchanged level the compensation of workers whose employment is reduced or temporarily suspended as a consequence of the reconversion of the enterprise where they are employed.[9] The fund pays 50 per cent of such expenses, and since its income is derived from contributions of the member nations, it accomplishes the distribution among the community of half of the costs of helping displaced workers to find new jobs.

Coal and Steel Community. When, in 1956, the High Authority of the Coal and Steel Community ordered the gradual shutdown of some unproductive coal mines in Belgium, it provided full wages for four to twelve months as severance pay, rehousing allowances, and full pay during retraining for the workers accepted for retraining. The retraining program so far seems to have enrolled only a tiny percentage of the displaced workers—some 100 out of 7,000!

Relevance of European Experience. In appraising this experience a number of distinctions have to be kept in mind. The policies summarized above have mostly functioned in a general climate of high prosperity and full employment, and were designed to minimize the "pockets of unemployment" that existed within a full-employment economy. Without a similar foundation such policies have slight chances of success.

An objective of several of the European policies—including French regional programs not discussed here—is to direct economic development away from areas of full employment in order to reduce inflationary pressures. The problem in disarmament would be not so much that of directing economic development away from certain areas as directing it into depressed areas—to stave off deflation rather than to prevent inflation.

Several European programs are essentially sets of policies for the economic development of backward regions. This is the case of Sweden or Italy. The job-shift to be solved during disarmament

---

[9] See "Europäische Wirtschaftsgemeinschaft," *Dritter Gesamtbericht* (March 21, 1959 to May 15, 1960), May 1960, pp. 213–216; M. van Dierendonck, "Deux ans et demi de Fonds Social Européen," *Droit Social,* November 1960, especially p. 532.

in the United States would be primarily that of adjusting to a shift in demand rather than a regional lack of development or a lagging rate of economic growth—though these may enter the picture as well and affect it fundamentally. Moreover, administratively, European plans, with the exception of the Social Fund, operate within the framework of relatively centralized governments compared with the federal structure of the American government. Altogether, European experience cannot be transferred bodily to the United States, even though a number of devices employed abroad could be adapted to the American scene.

ADJUSTMENT POLICIES FOR THE UNITED STATES

On the basis of the model prepared in other parts of the READ program, net displacement might amount to between 500,000 and 600,000 employees a year during the first stage of disarmament, and then gradually decrease as the international programs get under way. Such displacement should not be equated with *unemployment*. The amount of actual unemployment would depend in part on how rapidly new jobs were made available.

To deal with this rate of displacement by itself would not be an unmanageable assignment. It is, however, rendered far more difficult by the fact that if disarmament comes during the sixties, it will add to the pressures on a labor market with a built-in tendency toward an excess supply of labor, due to large classes entering the labor market and to a high rate of technological displacement.

Experience indicates, moreover, that unemployment has tended to have a highly differentiated effect upon various groups in the labor force. Unskilled workers, older workers, colored persons, new entrants into the labor market, and women are a higher proportion of the unemployed than of the labor force. To some extent this means that discrimination is a luxury that employers can afford when there is an excess supply of labor on the market.

Unemployment created by progressive and supervised disarmament will have many features in common with frictional, and some with cyclical, unemployment. It will be heavily concentrated in certain industries, occupations, and regions. But it will also be somewhat diffuse and general—similar to the unemployment created by the downswing of the business cycle. Moreover, unless certain stringent assumptions are made regarding the volume of aggregate spending, any substantial volume of defense layoffs is likely to reflect upon the general business situation.

Combining some of the features of frictional and of cyclical unemployment, the displacement of workers by a program of progressive disarmament will make imperative the combination of two sets of policies: general full-employment policies to establish the volume of effective demand at a satisfactory level; and specific policies tending to absorb the local, industrial, and occupational "pockets" of unemployment which will continue to exist even when aggregate demand for goods and services has been raised to the level required for full employment. It is understood that the repercussions of one set of policies on the other must be taken into account if inflationary pressures are to be kept at a minimum.

A consistent full-employment policy is the foundation for the specific measures that may be aimed more directly at the pockets of unemployment. Almost equally fundamental is the correct timing of these measures. It may not be possible to foresee the date, the volume, and the details of the first stage in the disarmament program, but foresight and, consequently, preparation are possible for the succeeding stages. It should therefore be the obligation of the authority in charge of the anti-unemployment program to map out the strategy in dealing with the second stage of disarmament, while taking the appropriate measures for dealing with the problems created by the first stage.

The immediate and emergency measures of the first stage would thus be accompanied by attempts to forecast the probable size of the displacement likely to occur during the second and later stages, not only in large aggregates, but also according to the various skill groups involved and the industries and regions concerned. On the basis of these forecasts, specific programs can be established to deal with the pockets of unemployment which are likely to develop in spite of general full-employment policies.

Initial Steps. The first-stage measures themselves can be classified in two groups: (1) immediate but permanent measures and (2) temporary emergency measures.

Under the first heading come improvements in unemployment

benefits, dealing with coverage, duration, and size. With a view toward the second disarmament stage, benefits should be tied up with a retraining program in such a way that participation in such a program will be encouraged rather than regarded as a reason for a cutoff of benefits. This new approach is already foreshadowed in recent legislation.

The public assistance system should be modified, so that, when necessary, families with employable but unemployed members can become eligible for assistance.

A complete overhaul of the United States Employment Service is needed, in order to increase its acceptability among employers and job-seekers, and to widen its effective coverage to include skilled workers, white-collar people, technicians, and professional persons. Vocational counseling combined with forecasts of changing needs in American industry should be expanded and closely related to the placement functions of the service. Steps of this sort are already being taken.

An early retirement program might be established, particularly for older workers who without extensive retraining would appear unlikely to find another job. Such a program should be voluntary. Beginnings in this direction have been made in recent social security amendments and in some collective agreements.

A set of measures should be adopted to increase labor mobility primarily during the first stage of disarmament. Fundamentally, the policy we recommend relies on the enhanced mobility of capital rather than that of labor, but in the first stage, when detailed and specific plans for handling unemployment cannot be adequately prepared, individual mobility should be encouraged—up to a point. There is a danger that the workers most likely to take advantage of opportunities elsewhere represent manpower of high quality in competency, initiative, and other respects. The loss of these men may make it difficult in the long-run aspects of our program to bring jobs to the remaining workers. Yet since, at this stage, in the absence of well-prepared plans for the future, society may rightly hesitate to commit capital irrevocably, labor mobility must be encouraged.

The catalog of methods to encourage geographic mobility is

well-known. It comprises various kinds of allowances—travel, separation, moving, first expenditure, and the like. In this respect the example of various European countries can be of help. Government assistance in selling houses would be a desirable contribution to the solution of a problem that is characteristically American, at least in its size. Neil Chamberlain has proposed that a public authority, under certain conditions, offer to buy up workers' houses at or near cost in order to remove this hindrance to geographic mobility.

A distinctly temporary emergency measure would be the stockpiling of industrial output. Within the framework of a disarmament policy, the selection of material to be stockpiled would of necessity be limited in range. Moreover, this measure should be clearly limited in time and not develop into an industrial counterpart of the agricultural support program. For the period of transition, the stockpiling of peaceful industrial goods for foreign aid or future domestic consumption—seems justified and advisable until a long-range program can take effect.

Shorter Work-hours a Solution? Shortening the hours of work as a device to reduce the number of fully unemployed persons has been proposed so many times in the past that it is almost certain to arise again as a slogan during the disarmament process. Shortening the working hours may take the form of a reduction of the work week or of a longer vacation period, more holidays, or some combination of these.

The objection to all these proposals is that shorter hours are merely a device to distribute unemployment more widely and in a sense turn everyone into a short-hour worker. This represents no real solution. Shortening work hours—a process that has been going on during the last century or longer—should come about as a voluntary decision in favor of more leisure rather than more income, and not be imposed by inability to earn additional income because of lack of jobs. The task is not to distribute unemployment more widely but rather to reduce it to the minimum consistent with flexibility.

Yet if society is unable for longer periods to reduce unemployment to tolerable levels, then the pressure for shorter working hours is likely to become irresistible. If this solution is to be avoided, society must provide a better method of tackling the unemployment problem. An orderly transition to shorter hours, particularly in the industries and areas with long-run labor surplus, may prove unavoidable. The reduction of hours should then lag slightly behind the rate of productivity increase.

Long-range Plans. A long-range program requires most elaborate preparations. What is involved may be described most properly as a restructuring of the American labor force. The main problem to be faced is that of coordinating the process by which unemployment is absorbed with the retraining process and with policies aimed at influencing the location of enterprises. Close coordination among these three programs is necessary. Retraining for unknown jobs is meaningless. Job creation without a labor force that is properly adjusted to the new jobs is inflationary. Jobs separated in space from the unemployed manpower are likely to go unfilled for long periods.

During the first phase of disarmament, therefore, it will be imperative to determine precisely the policies by which the pockets of unemployment will be absorbed—assuming, of course, that general full-employment policies have mopped up most of the excess labor supply. On the basis of full-employment measures to be taken during the second stage there should appear the general outlines of the structure of the labor force that will be required. It is only then that a successful retraining program can be organized. In reverse, the nature of the labor supply available after retraining or, put differently, the limits within which retraining can effectively restructure the labor force, will have some bearing upon the characteristics of the job-creation process. Displaced coal miners can probably never be turned into tool and die makers or watch mechanics. What is needed is thus a close correspondence between the job-creation process and the potential labor supply. A vastly expanded vocational training program will have to be developed, hopefully in cooperation with the United States Employment Service.

The third element in this coordinated program relates to the location of industry. While the general political and psychological climate of this country will undoubtedly reject a system of licensing new industrial plants or plant expansion after the British model, various other measures could be taken to influence plant location. Tax reduction, making available buildings and other industrial facilities, outright subsidies—all could be employed to bring the plants to the workers, within the limits of the principles outlined above. By the concerted efforts of these three policies—job creation, retraining, job location—a major contribution could be made to restructuring the American labor force according to the pattern made necessary by a system of progressive disarmament.

A large part of this process will most probably occur without more than minor public help. The experience of World War II and of the Korean War shows that the American economy and its labor force have a remarkable ability to adjust to rapid and substantial changes. What is required is, in the first place, a sufficiently high level of over-all demand for goods and services. Without this, little can be achieved. The second requirement is that as far as government help enters the adjustment process, a broad geographic viewpoint be maintained. It is not merely the parochial needs of local or area-wide labor markets that must be considered in retraining programs and other assistance measures. The opportunities to be brought to the attention of potential job-seekers and made financially accessible to them should not be those of the area alone but also those of more distant regions of the United States.

Legislative Foundations. The present legal instruments at the disposal of the authorities consist of the Area Redevelopment Act of 1961 and the Manpower Development and Training Act of 1962. They operate in combination with the Employment Act of 1946, which imposed upon the federal government the obligation to maintain a high level of employment.

The Area Development Act provides for the establishment of an Area Development Administration to stimulate economic development, in a variety of ways, in regions with high chronic unemployment or underemployment. At the heart of the program is the ability of the Development Administration to grant loans for the purchase or development of land and facilities, including machinery and equipment, under unusual circumstances, for industrial or commercial usage. This may include the construction of new buildings, the rehabilitation of abandoned or unoccupied buildings, and the alteration, conversion, or enlargement of existing buildings.

Such financial assistance is available only when there is no other source of funds and when there is reasonable assurance that it can be repaid. It is limited to 65 per cent of the aggregate cost to the applicant. Individual enterprises and redevelopment groups can obtain loans for a twenty-five-year period.

While the Area Redevelopment Act contains some provisions for training, this feature is more central in the Manpower Development and Training Act, which established a three-year retraining program (July 1962 through June 1965), with $419 million allocated for the selection and training of workers and $16 million for such purposes as program planning and manpower surveys. Estimates were that 110,000 would be trained during the first year, 160,000 in the second, and 300,000 in the third.

The United States Department of Labor, through the federal-state employment service system, is responsible for testing, counseling, and selecting workers for occupational training. Priority is given to the unemployed and underemployed, including workers in low-income farm families "who cannot reasonably be expected to secure appropriate full-time employment without training." Employed workers who need job improvement are also eligible, however. Priority in referral for training goes first to those who can be trained for jobs in the local labor market area and, second, for jobs within the state of residence. Training periods vary from two weeks to fifty-two weeks. Training allowances go to unemployed heads of households with at least three years of employment experience.

Two general types of training are permitted. Training in public and private schools is arranged by state vocational education agencies under agreements with the United States Department of Health, Education, and Welfare. Priority goes to public schools. Secondly, the Department of Labor develops or arranges for on-the-job training programs, in cooperation with the states, private and public agencies, employers, trade associations, labor organizations, and other qualified industrial and community groups.

FUTURE PERSPECTIVE

Adaptation to disarmament would not be the only adjustment taking place during the disarmament period. Adjustments to the exceptionally large age classes that will be entering the labor market during the 1960's or to the changes imposed by the technological reorientation of the American economy and by automation seem likely to be more far-reaching over the long run than adjustments required by a disarmament-imposed restructuring of the labor force. This realization may help us keep our sense of proportion, but it will not make the task any easier. Indeed, it means that the restructuring of the labor force imposed by disarmament will reinforce rather than counteract the long-run changes in the composition of the labor force which we have been witnessing over the last few decades. Whether disarmament will involve a shift to greater private spending or to enlarged public activities will most probably make little difference in this respect: The expansion of service activities that will occur in either case has been a long-term significant trend of our economy for a considerable length of time.

It is, therefore, perhaps wise to speak in general of the problem of the restructuring of the American labor force and to regard disarmament as just one of several significant factors in the process. Put simply, the question to be raised is how this process can be advanced in such a way that those most directly concerned undergo the least suffering without undue loss of potential output.

Seen in this light, training and retraining, without losing their importance, become simply facets of the far broader issue of American *education for the new forms of our industrial society*. It is in this light that long-run plans to fit the labor force to the future requirements of the American economy ought to be made. This vast topic extends beyond the confines of our assignment.

Implementing the program that has been outlined above requires an administration on the federal level, with special authority to obtain cooperation from the states. In addition, the federal administrator—who should have cabinet rank and be appointed by the President with the consent of the Senate—should be assisted by an advisory committee on which management, labor unions, and independent labor experts are represented.

12

Alternatives to Defense Production

Emile Benoit

The story is told of Rosie the Riveter, working in a West Coast shipyard in World War II, who, during a luncheon break, expressed decided reservations about the then Pope. When challenged, she explained that she and all her family had been unemployed for years, until the defense boom had suddenly provided them with well-paying jobs. She said she found it hard to understand how the Pope, who was supposed to be a good Christian, could be praying right out in public for peace.

To the noneconomist, the process by which new jobs are created to take the place of old ones appears both mysterious and unreliable. The economists, on the other hand, have sometimes attributed too much to the reallocative virtues of the free market. While the market is a superb instrument for reallocating displaced resources in relatively small doses, provided the level of aggregate demand is sustained, it is less effective if the amount of displaced resources becomes indigestibly large, or when there is a slump in the level of aggregate demand.

In fact, our economy has a second mechanism for directing and redirecting resources, which, while not as important as the free market, plays an essential role in a modern private enterprise economy. This is the mechanism of the government budget, which enables the government to redirect resources from one government use to another or from one group of citizens to another, or by net cuts in government purchases to free resources for nongovernment uses. If the cuts are made without corresponding cuts in taxes, then the resources freed from government use and not positively directed to other uses may not readily find re-employment. On the other hand, if there are parallel tax cuts as expenditures are reduced, resources are not only freed by the government, but positively directed toward the groups of taxpayers who are left with larger disposable incomes. (These effects, and the effects of budget cuts offset by debt reduction, are further considered in Chapter 15.)

The widely-expressed fear that tax cuts would *not* raise the expenditures of the individuals and businesses that receive them has little apparent justification. The percentage of personal disposable income which is spent by consumers is one of the more stable of economic phenomena. Since 1950, the annual rate has varied only between 92 and 94 per cent; and in no quarter has the ratio dropped below 91 per cent. We know less about the percentage of *additions* to disposable income that will be used for consumption, but budget studies suggest that at least two dollars out of three will be spent; and there is some evidence that spending out of windfall gains may not diverge much from the average propensity to consume out of normal income.[1]

---

[1] Thus, Ronald Bodkin found, in one sample of veterans' families, that the marginal propensity to consume windfall income from unanticipated National Service Life Insurance dividend payments was 0.97, and concludes that the tendency to spend windfall income is as high as, if not above, the marginal propensity to spend out of normal income ("Windfall Income and Consumption," *American Economic Review,* September 1959, p. 608). A later study by M. E. Kreinen, suggesting a contrary conclusion, can be readily explained. This case concerned restitution payments to Israelis by the German government in compensation for the damage inflicted on the recipients, their families, and their property by the Nazis. Since the amounts involved were large in relation to income (88 per cent), and since the payments must symbolically have stood for partial restitution of lost family security, it is not surprising that they were treated as additions to capital, rather than to income. Thus, I believe this evidence is entirely irrelevant in determining the propensity to consume out of income ("Windfall Income and Consumption—Additional Evidence," *American Economic Review,* June 1961, pp. 338–390).

The propensity of business to invest may be roughly measured by corporate investment in new plant and equipment as a percentage of "cash flow," i.e., net after-tax profits plus depreciation and amortization. Business propensity to invest is more variable than personal propensity to consume: it was 55 per cent in 1950, 81 per cent in 1952, and under 62 per cent in 1961. Even so, except in depressions, one can count on it to be over 50 per cent, and if we could raise aggregate demand and eliminate excess capacity, we should be able to attain again the 75 per cent average achieved in the 1951–1957 period. Moreover, nearly a third (31 per cent) of cash flow was distributed in dividends during the fifties—and dividends, in turn, affect both personal consumption and personal investment. Thus, cuts in corporate taxes will raise aggregate demand even though the precise effects are not easy to measure.

Apparently, then, adequate and dependable mechanisms exist by which redundant defense resources may be shifted either to other government programs by changes in the pattern of budget expenditures or to private use by tax reductions. Many persons, however, hesitate to draw any favorable implications from this fact because they have the general impression that there is nothing of any urgency left to do which could justify or motivate additional expenditure. It may be helpful, therefore, to consider a variety of high-priority needs to which unutilized resources could be shifted.

The term "need" is, to be sure, necessarily somewhat subjective.[2] No claim is here made as to the objective validity of the following list of "needs" and expenditure programs. It is presented simply as a summary of what well-informed students of current social and economic conditions consider desirable and appropriate uses of additional resources. Most of these programs have been set forth as national objectives in an official United States document sent to the United Nations.[3] The chief purpose of this presentation is to

[2] The point is illustrated in extreme form by the story of the impecunious gentleman who was trying to borrow a small sum from a casual acquaintance on the plea that "After all, a man must live!" but was turned away with the supercilious retort: "I fail to see the necessity!"

[3] *The Economic and Social Consequences of Disarmament; U.S. Reply to the Inquiry of the Secretary-General of the United Nations, Part II*, U.S. Arms Control and Disarmament Agency, March 1962.

emphasize the immense backlog of valuable uses for the resources that may be released from the defense sector by disarmament.

CONSUMPTION AND INVESTMENT

While the American standard of living is by far the highest in the world, it hardly justifies the appellation of "affluent," and a great many Americans do not enjoy that standard. Per capita personal income after taxes had not yet reached $40 a week in 1962, and many families live on far smaller amounts. In 1960, 3.33 million families, predominantly city families, had an average income *per family* of only $23.50 a week, and there were nearly 4 million individuals, living alone, with an average income of less than $20 a week.[4] To raise this poverty-stricken one-eighth of American households even to a hardly tolerable level of $40 a week per household would require an increase in annual consumer expenditures of $6.4 billion. There will be need of another extra $6.6 billion a year merely to keep up with population growth, even if average income levels do not rise. Incidentally, some people tend to be critical of consumption increases, identifying consumption primarily with automobiles, television sets, etc.; in fact, durable goods plus gas and oil account for only around 17 per cent of consumption, which also includes such items as private education and health expenditure, travel, and various cultural activities.

Growth in consumption will undoubtedly have to derive mainly from increases in the number of persons employed and from wage increases. These will be obtained primarily as a by-product of a more dynamic growth policy. But an effective attack on severe poverty in the lowest income group would also require special programs, emphasizing health services, education, rehabilitation and retraining programs, psychiatric and social counseling, and special youth assistance and employment programs, as well as more generous social security benefits and relief payments. Resources released from defense uses could be channeled to these uses by expanded federal welfare programs, including federal welfare grants to states and localities.

[4] *Survey of Current Business,* Department of Commerce, July 1962, p. 16.

For general stimulation of consumption, the simple expedient of a general reduction of personal income taxes is available. Because of the comparatively broad base of this tax today, across-the-board reductions would benefit a large majority of the population, and would stimulate consumption in the broad middle-income group of households with incomes between $5,000 and $15,000, which now includes half of all families, and about 60 per cent of all taxable income.

Consumption increases in the long run can be sustained only out of current production; therefore, a high priority must attach to the strengthening of our capital equipment and to the further improvement of our education, vocational training, and R&D programs, upon which our future productivity and welfare will most vitally depend.

Our rate of productivity growth was far too low in the 1950's to enable us to advance as rapidly as most other leading industrial countries and to maintain the strength of our balance of payments.[5] Our need to modernize and expand our industrial plant in order to remain internationally competitive is becoming a matter of serious concern to well-informed people. We will need to speed up our annual plant and equipment outlays during this decade by about $16.3 billion over the 1961 level if we want to maintain full use of capacity and the high average ratio of new investment to corporate cash flow achieved from 1951 to 1957.

RESIDENTIAL CONSTRUCTION

Housing in this country barely meets our present needs. Current vacancy rates are 1.2 per cent of home-owner units and 7.7 per cent of rental units. Over 3 million of these total units are in a dilapidated condition. To keep pace with the growing population and to insure that every American household can be adequately accommodated by the end of this decade, we should be building 2

---

[5] On the relationship between the slowdown of United States productivity rates and our balance-of-payments difficulties, see my *Europe at Sixes and Sevens: The Free Trade Association, the Common Market, and the United States,* New York: Columbia University Press, 1961, Chapter 4.

million units a year by 1970, at a cost of $25 billion (1961 dollars)—an $8.8 billion increase over 1961 levels. These figures assume the elimination of dilapidated units, no change in the current vacancy rates, and a slight increase in home ownership. They also assume a continuation of the population shift from rural to urban areas and the replacement of housing demolished as a result of public improvement programs, etc. Present projections indicate that effective demand will probably fall short of the level required to purchase this much housing, and low-income groups will clearly require housing subsidies. The Housing Act of 1961 authorized $2 billion for new housing projects, and this program will undoubtedly absorb much larger sums as it continues.

URBAN NEEDS

The explosive growth of our metropolitan areas will be one of the major domestic problems of this decade, during which the urban population is expected to increase by about thirty-six million. While suburban areas will also require rapid capital improvements and increased transportation, housing, school, and recreational facilities, it is the central cities of the rapidly expanding new metropolitan areas which will show the greatest growth. Over two-thirds of our population now live in big urban areas. The revitalization of the older cities in these areas, and the expansion of the newer ones, will call for vast expenditures for improvement, modernization, and rebuilding. Approximately $2 billion of federal grant authorization has been reserved for urban renewal projects, exclusive of the $2 billion earmarked for new projects by the Housing Act of 1961. Obviously, such sums only scratch the surface of the problems, and must be viewed as preliminaries to much larger programs.

The problems of urban transportation and traffic congestion are becoming almost terrifying in magnitude and complexity. With only a 75 per cent population increase in urban areas between 1935 and 1959, transit rides declined by 20 per cent but automobile travel increased by 180 per cent. One transportation specialist estimated that an additional $1 billion a year will be needed to obtain satisfactory urban transit and suburban railroad facilities during the decade.[6] The Housing Act of 1961 authorized $25 million of grants just to make studies of the problem.

With a rapidly expanding population, the need for more water and sewer facilities is becoming acute. In the last few years, total contract awards for construction of municipal water facilities and for sewer and sewage-treatment facilities have ranged between $1 billion and $1.5 billion annually. On the basis of estimated present and potential needs, we shall soon have to be spending about $5 billion a year for these purposes. Our cities also confront a growing problem of solid-waste disposal. Current total national expenditures for urban collection and disposal are approximately $2 billion annually. This figure will have to be raised by about 50 per cent to meet increasing needs.

There are many other community needs in these urban areas—recreational facilities, police and fire stations, the solution of air pollution problems, etc.—that are growing rapidly along with the increasing population, increasing automobile traffic, and increasing congestion. It is difficult to obtain any precise notion of the cost of obtaining and maintaining adequate programs in these fields, but we do know that such programs usually cost more than can be foreseen and that the costs of delay may be even higher.

NATURAL RESOURCES

The United States is richly endowed with natural resources, but positive programs are needed to conserve and develop them to keep pace with our growing requirements. Our margin of safety in some fields, especially with regard to water, is uncomfortably narrow. Periodic serious water shortages have already appeared in many communities. The 1961 report of the Senate Select Committee on National Water Resources points out that whereas in 1954 our daily water requirements utilized only about 27 per cent of our total streamflow, by the year 2000, it will absorb more than 80 per cent of the total streamflow. To achieve this, along with some associated programs for navigation, flood control, power generation, irrigation, water supply and waste disposal, recreation,

[6] Unpublished report referred to in *Economic and Social Consequences of Disarmament,* p. 19.

wildlife and fisheries protection, as well as some for urban water and sewage disposal will require average expenditures of around $5.5 billion a year.

A tentative estimate of the Department of the Interior, for the cost of a program of reforestation, reseeding, forest recreational area development, watershed and erosion control on forest land, and public land acquisition sets the total at $3.6 billion during a period of ten years. The Department of Agriculture has outlined a ten-year forestry development program, costing more than $2.5 billion; and the Bureau of Public Roads calls for the construction of public highways through national forests at a cost of $2.7 billion by 1971.

A ten-year program for soil and watershed conservation would involve expenditures of $4.6 billion, though this figure would probably include some overlapping of the program of the Select Committee on National Water Resources. A program for the conservation of federal range lands would require the expenditure of $1.2 billion over a ten-year period.

To manage, protect, improve, and rehabilitate our national park system within the next decade will require about $1.1 billion. For additions to the park system, the President recently recommended an eight-year program of land acquisition, totaling $500 million. He also recommended a $50 million increase in annual federal grants for open-space lands in urban areas.

An adequate program for maintaining and improving fish and wildlife habitats would cost $380 million during a 10-year period, including $150 million for land acquisition.

Altogether, the total federal costs of these proposed programs for the conservation and development of national resources would be about $40 billion over a ten-year period—$16 billion more than the current rate. State, local, and industrial programs for water development, estimated to cost about $8 billion annually, are not included in this figure.

EDUCATIONAL NEEDS

By 1970, school enrollments in kindergarten through the twelfth grade, will require annual expenditures of $10 billion more than the 1960–1961 expenditures. This estimate makes provision for additional capital facilities and for more teachers with higher salaries.

Institutions of higher learning, giving degrees, will require expenditures by 1970 of $10 billion above present levels to accommodate the prospective growth in the student body. This estimate allows, too, for increases in outlays for capital facilities and for salary increases necessary to attract increasing numbers of competent teachers. But $10 billion would do little more than maintain the present standards of education, and American life in the 1970's will make considerably greater demands on education than it is currently doing. The labor force will require more skill and technical know-how, and the accelerating rate of additions to knowledge in the fields of technology, science, etc., will call for more extended study by larger numbers of educated people. Our needs for elaborate and expensive laboratories, visual aids, computers, and research equipment grows rapidly; and there is increasing need for adult education courses of varied types, including refresher courses for businessmen and technical people as the pace of our acquisition of knowledge quickens. The National Science Foundation estimates that to maintain our present world position in science, we will have to double the number of persons receiving Ph.D's in science and engineering by 1970. The added annual cost of the necessary facilities would average $1.6 billion during this decade.

HEALTH SERVICES

There is already a high degree of effective demand for medical care in the United States. In 1959–1960, 5.4 per cent of our gross national product was devoted to public health, personal health services, construction of medical facilities, and medical research. However, there are still many Americans who cannot afford, and do not obtain, a satisfactory amount and quality of medical services; and this is even becoming an important political issue.

An improved and better-distributed level of medical care in the United States will involve an increase in health personnel, greater investment in health facilities, more coordination among health services and improved systems of financing personal health services.

In 1960 there were 140 physicians for every 100,000 of the

population, but this ratio, while insufficient, is declining. In the case of dentists, the decline is even more rapid and has continued steadily since 1940. To maintain even the existing ratios of physicians and dentists to the population would require an additional expenditure of $1 billion (at present prices) by 1970 to expand existing medical and dental schools and to set up new ones.

During the next decade, 23,000 additional hospital beds each year will be required to maintain the current ratio of 7.7 beds per 1,000 population. To provide even a slight improvement in this ratio—to replace, renovate, and modernize hospital plants, to maintain outpatient care facilities, and to increase rehabilitation facilities—would require the expenditure over the next decade of at least $6 billion above present levels.

About 6 per cent of our population live in counties with no organized local tax-supported health services, often because of limitations in staff and financial resources. To provide adequate public health services by official state and local health agencies, it has been estimated that a minimum expenditure of at least $4 per capita is required. To achieve this would require that present levels of annual expenditures be increased by $383 million.

The dangers of air pollution are becoming widely recognized as a serious health hazard in many urban communities. At present we are spending about $300–$400 million per year in an effort to control it. To provide proper protection we will need at least to double this amount by 1970.

The reports of two expert groups[7] have suggested that by 1970, personnel and other resources will be available to justify an expenditure of $3.0 billion a year on health research, with incalculable potential benefits to the nation's health. This research could be rapidly stepped up if the research facilities and personnel now devoted to defense activities could be released.

[7] Secretary's Consultants on Medical Research and Education, *The Advancement of Medical Research and Education Through the Department of Health, Education, and Welfare,* Department of Health, Education, and Welfare, 1958; Committee of Consultants on Medical Research to the Subcommittee on Departments of Labor, Health, Education, and Welfare of the Senate Appropriations Committee; *Federal Support of Medical Research,* 1960.

OTHER SOCIAL SERVICES

Although our population benefits from a valuable program of social insurance protection, coverage remains incomplete and the level of benefits in relation to income continues to shrink. Since 1940, benefits under the national Old Age, Survivors, and Disability Insurance program have risen less than a third as much as increases in general wage levels. To relate such benefits to increases in productivity, it would be necessary to increase the annual outlays by more than $11 billion before 1970. Private pension benefits (now running at close to $2 billion annually) also require improvement: Very few of them are adjusted to changing price or wage levels. If disarmament comes to pass, an increased number of persons may find retirement unavoidable; it would be helpful if the benefit levels were such as to make it unnecessary, as is so often the case today, for the pensioner to supplement his benefits by applying for public relief to meet minimum needs.

In 1960, only $0.8 billion was paid out under public and private sickness insurance programs despite the very wide coverage already existing for these programs. If there had been a nationwide system of sickness insurance, covering all wage and salary workers in private industry and providing benefits equal to two-thirds of weekly wage loss after a one-week waiting period, the benefits paid would have amounted to $2.2 billion in 1960. A program such as this would require benefit payments in 1970 of $3.3 billion (in 1960 prices).

Payments for wage loss and medical benefits under the state and federal workmen's compensation laws amounted to $1.3 billion in 1960. These payments replaced less than two-fifths of the wage loss in the average temporary disability case, and an even smaller proportion in fatalities or permanent injuries. They also reflect incomplete coverage and limited medical care. A system which provided medical care for the duration of the disability, replacement of two-thirds of wage loss (after a one-week waiting period), and survivors' benefits to widows for life, and to children to the age of eighteen, would have cost, it is estimated, an additional $700 million in 1960. Such a system would provide an important attack on the problem of poverty in the United States, which is frequently tied up with injury or death of a breadwinner.

The 7 million persons in the United States who are currently receiving public assistance under one program or another, and the 7 million persons who might also receive assistance in 1970, require an additional $1 billion a year to assure reasonable levels of living, according to a 1958 study.[8] Medical care expenditures through public assistance also need substantial expansion.

In the field of community and social services there is a need that is real, though difficult to estimate and to document, for expansion in the services of public and private agencies to meet the needs of a complex and growing urban economy. For example, vocational rehabilitation services are currently helping 100,000 disabled people back to work, but there are 275,000 persons disabled annually who without rehabilitation services will not be able to work. Public expenditures for existing child welfare services amounted to $211 million in 1960, but could usefully be doubled by 1970, with an additional $60 million for expansion of day care services for children.

Most of the benefits of increased social expenditure will be obtained only if they are guided by improved research and administered by effective administrators and social workers. This research, and the training of the necessary personnel, could usefully absorb some of the resources released by defense cuts.

FOREIGN ASSISTANCE

We have, so far, concentrated on identifying the needs for additional resources within the United States. It should never be forgotten, however, that the severity of our material needs is small in comparison with those of the larger part of mankind. We are led by feelings of compassion and moral obligation, as well as by alleged considerations of long-term self-interest,[9] to devote a small

---

[8] "Unmet Needs in Public Assistance," *Social Security Bulletin,* Department of Health, Education, and Welfare, April 1960.
[9] Our actual material self-interest in this is, I believe, far less than professed, but according to the current vogue in rationalizations, we feel the need to convince ourselves and others that even minor acts of benevolence must have "good," i.e., selfish, reasons.

part of our annual savings to foreign development assistance. Between 1957 and 1961, it amounted to about 5 per cent of gross national savings.[10]

I suspect we do not yet know enough about the marginal productivity of such aid to justify the elaborate calculations frequently made in estimating how much more aid is required to enable developing nations to achieve self-sustaining growth. More searching analysis of the economic development process suggests that factors other than external capital availabilities may be decisive. In any case, the effective limits on United States economic aid to underdeveloped countries would appear to be set by quite different considerations: (1) With respect to the private part, it would be the net profitability of investment in underdeveloped countries relative to that in industrial countries, discounted by the heavier political risks; and (2) with respect to the public part, the willingness of legislatures to make such appropriations, taking into account the balance of public sentiment on the question and the visible evidence as to whether or not past programs have been effectively administered and have served a useful purpose politically as well as economically.

If disarmament is achieved, we would eliminate $1 billion a year of foreign military expenditure—or more if, by that time, the United States government had not succeeded in the very difficult task of cutting it down to that level. We would also eliminate defense-related economic aid, which now costs in the neighborhood of $300 million. It would be relatively easy and natural to devote these savings to increased regular foreign aid—which could, of course, be tied if we were still under balance-of-payments pressure.

An increase of this size ($1.3 billion) added to the 1961 level of United States development assistance of $4.6 billion, would bring the total only $400 million short of what was required to com-

---

[10] The figure includes private investment in, and public grants and loans (exclusive of defense assistance) to, underdeveloped countries and multilateral agencies. Source on aid estimate is OEEC: *Development Assistance Efforts and Policies in 1961, The Flow of Financial Resources to Countries in Course of Economic Development in 1960, and The Flow of Financial Resources to Countries in Course of Economic Development, 1956–1959;* and on gross savings: *Economic Report of the President, 1962.*

prise 1 per cent of the probable GNP in the mid-sixties and, thus, to conform to the minimum standard which has sometimes been urged in international discussions and has been recommended by, e.g., Jean Monnet's Action Committee for a United States of Europe. This is a standard it would be desirable to meet, if only because it would provide appropriate pressure on our allies to follow suit. If it is achieved, we would be spending around $6.3 billion a year by the mid-sixties, about $2.4 billion more than in 1960. An assistance figure tied to such a formula would, moreover, rise by about $300 million a year and reach $7.5 billion by the end of the decade. Over the decade as a whole, such a program implies an annual figure some $2 billion over the 1960 level.

I believe, however, that much larger amounts could probably be arranged with the right type of cooperation between the industrial and the underdeveloped countries. I have elsewhere proposed "economic development treaties," which would commit the United States to supply specified quantities of assistance (private and public) over a decade, in exchange for all-out cooperation by a developing country in achieving ambitious (and clearly defined) growth objectives agreed upon in advance.[11] A mechanism of this sort might mobilize a great deal more assistance by providing concrete goals against which the success of the effort being made could be measured and the deficiencies identified and eliminated. Hopefully, also, we may in the mid-sixties tackle in earnest some of the technological barriers to economic growth discussed in the next section.

RESEARCH AND DEVELOPMENT

The National Science Foundation has urged an expanded program of basic research in the 1960's that would involve additional expenditures averaging $900 million a year.

The expansion in the civilian space program has been so embroiled in controversy that the rate of build-up during the decade is hard to predict. In the READ model, the expansion in the

---

[11] In testimony before the Subcommittee on Foreign Trade Policy of the House Ways and Means Committee, *Hearings on Private Foreign Investment,* 85th Cong., 2nd Sess., December 5, 1958, pp. 495–499.

expenditures of NASA and of the civilian side of the AEC (which does some work for NASA under contract) was estimated at something short of $7 billion, i.e., from an annual rate of $0.9 billion in 1960 to an annual rate of $7.9 billion by 1971. The build-up has been going faster than projected in the READ model, but the relevant question of how much expansion will occur between 1965 and 1977 is not necessarily affected by this. *Total* expenditures in the NASA program during the 12 years are estimated at $80 billion, which would appear to be a fairly ambitious figure. Nevertheless, some opportunities for further expansion may seem worth taking.

In the event of disarmament, enough military R&D might be demobilized in the latter part of the 1960's, not only to meet the expansion requirements of NASA and the AEC, but to create something of a glut in the R&D market. As Nelson cogently demonstrates in Chapter 7 the surplus could sooner or later all be reabsorbed by industrial R&D in private enterprise. Whether it is wise to wait until this happens may be questioned. Even a temporary slack in the demand for R&D could have unfortunate, even dangerous, consequences. It could weaken the individual and institutional incentives and pressures upon which we rely to develop the rapidly increasing corps of first-rate scientists and engineers, upon whom our future achievements and security will primarily depend. The lead time in this area is so long that even a temporary letdown can be most difficult to make up. We are already falling behind, and there is some evidence of a slackening in the rate of adoptions of science and engineering courses, which require a high level of ability and more effort than many other courses of study leading to better-remunerated employment.

I also believe that there are important positive advantages in preserving some of the working scientist-technician-management teams and organizations now functioning in the defense effort, and utilizing their outstanding skills and expert knowledge in seeking solutions to fundamental problems of national importance. Some of the specific projects on which they might work are mentioned in the concluding chapter.

The above makes no allowances for the continued expansion in

TABLE 1 – ADDITIONAL NATIONAL EXPENDITURES REQUIRED DURING THE 1960'S
(Billions of dollars)

PROGRAM	ADDITIONAL AVERAGE ANNUAL COST	CONTENT OF PROGRAM
Ending serious poverty in the United States	$6.4–8.8[a]	OASDI benefits to match increased productivity; cash sickness insurance programs extended to all workers, with improved benefits; complete medical care and improvements for beneficiaries under Workmen's Compensation laws; reasonable standard of living for public assistance recipients and increased counseling services; extension of child welfare services[b]
Industrial plant and equipment	16.3	To maintain average ratio of new investment to corporate cash flow achieved during 1951–1957[c]
Health	7.8	Replacement, renovation, and modernization of hospital and clinics; increased rehabilitation facilities; provision of minimum level of community health services, adequate medical care for public assistance recipients; intensified program of air pollution control; medical research as deemed feasible with available personnel and facilities[d]
Education	1.6	Additional investment needed in universities to double number of science and engineering Ph.D's[e]
	10.0	Increased capital facilities to match population growth; training additional teachers, increasing salaries[f]
Housing	4.5	Replacement of demolitions, improvements in home ownership, elimination of dilapidated units[g]
Urban water, sewage, and solid-waste disposal	4.5	To correct present unsatisfactory practices and to meet increasing needs[h]
Urban transportation	1.0	Investment for urban transit and suburban railway plant and equipment[i]

Water resource development	7.9	Programs to meet deficiencies, obsolescence, and growth[j]
Natural resources	1.6	Land acquisition and physical improvement to forests, range lands, parks and recreation facilities, fish and wildlife habitats[k]
Research and development	0.9	Expanded basic research facilities in colleges and universities[l]
	0.5	R&D expenditures implied by the $1.6 billion of additional plant and equipment outlays[m]
	?	NASA, civilian AEC, and special R&D programs of national importance
Foreign assistance	2.0	To maintain a 1 per cent ratio of foreign assistance to GNP.
Total	65.0–67.4+	

[a] This range represents the difference between the amount necessary to raise the weekly income of the lowest-income one-eighth of all households up to $40, and the cost of certain specific programs indicated in the following column.

[b] *The Economic and Social Consequences of Disarmament, Part II,* U.S. Arms Control and Disarmament Agency, 1962, pp. 24–26; *Survey of Current Business,* Department of Commerce, July 1962, p. 16.

[c] *Economic Report of the President,* 1962 pp. 192, 196.

[d] *Economic and Social Consequences of Disarmament,* pp. 22–25.

[e] *Investing in Scientific Progress,* 1961–70, National Science Foundation, 1961, p. 28.

[f] *Economic and Social Consequences of Disarmament,* p. 21.

[g] *Ibid.,* p. 17; *Survey of Current Business,* July 1962, p. S-9.

[h] *Economic and Social Consequences of Disarmament,* pp. 19, 23.

[i] Still unpublished report referred to in *ibid.,* p. 19.

[j] *Loc. cit.*

[k] *Ibid.,* p. 20; *Survey of Current Business,* July 1962, p. 20.

[l] *Investing in Scientific Progress,* p. 28.

[m] See p. 220, above.

industrial R&D, upon which our future productivity gains and product improvements in most of our industry will heavily rely. The step-up in new investment discussed earlier in this chapter would presumably require, by itself, a rise of about $0.5 billion in the annual rate of R&D expenditures in the coming decade.[12]

The various programs presented in this chapter are summarized in Table 1. The total is, of course, huge: around $66 billion a year during the 1960's—exclusive of the very large amounts that may be called for in the space program and other special R&D programs of national importance. Because of the rather broad terms in which most of these estimates have been defined, the total is not too meaningful, but it does signify that probably more than twice the estimated resources released by disarmament would have high-priority alternative uses, in the judgment of persons who have given the matter careful attention.

The problem then will not be to find important alternative uses for resources released from the defense effort: It will be to achieve a consensus on priorities, and to endow the chosen programs with enough purchasing power to make them effectively able to bid for and absorb the released resources. The problems in doing so lie primarily in the fields of monetary-fiscal policy. Some of the principles that might appropriately guide policy in these fields in order to facilitate economic adjustments to disarmament will be discussed in the last chapter.

[12] On the assumption, explained by Richard Nelson in Chapter 7, that $1.00 of investment final demand generates 3.5 cents of R&D spending.

PART IV

International Aspects of Disarmament

13

Balance-of-Payments Adjustments

*Robert W. Stevens**

INTRODUCTION

While this study was in preparation the United States government
and some of its allies took a number of steps which are intended to
reduce significantly the net impact of military activity on our balance of payments—and, therefore, to reduce the net impact that
disarmament sometime in the future might be expected to have.
The specific measures that have been taken stem from a widely-
held opinion that United States foreign military expenditures had
grown too large to be financed indefinitely by the underlying commercial surplus in our balance of payments. In fact, the reduction
of net foreign military expenditures has become one of the focal
points in the Administration's current efforts to strengthen the
United States balance of payments. Consequently, while total military expenditures are now rising, their net effect on the balance
of payments is being reduced. These efforts, if successful, will mean
that our over-all foreign accounts will reap some of the financial
benefits that might have been expected to accompany disarmament
—despite the fact that total military spending will be rising.

The year 1958 was originally chosen as a benchmark year

* ROBERT W. STEVENS, an economist with Standard Oil (New Jersey), is a
specialist in international trade and finance who previously served in the
U.S. Economic Cooperation Administration and successor agencies.

against which to assess the probable foreign-payments effects of disarmament, in part because it was the year for which the READ input-output studies were available. Official concentration on reducing the impact of military activity on the balance of payments, which began late in 1960, has of course altered the significance of the 1958 data. For some purposes, however, 1958 data are still relevant, and for these purposes they have been retained, with qualifications added where necessary. Even if there had been no post-1960 campaign to reduce the net impact of military activity on the balance of payments, foreign-payments data for a past year such as 1958 could, in any event, have been applied only in a rough, schematic way to some future year of possible disarmament. This is because, in addition to the notorious fluctuations which occur in the flows of foreign payments, there are continuous changes in *defense-related* foreign transactions due to changes in the intensity of the cold war, shifts in military strategy, troop deployment, weapons systems, productive technology, and so forth. In short, the effects of possible disarmament on defense-related foreign payments and receipts would depend upon the particular pattern of military activity prevailing at the time it is introduced.[1]

At the outset of this chapter it should be noted that I have concentrated on the direct balance-of-payments effects of possible disarmament, leaving mainly to others an assessment of the economic effects it might have *within* countries. Possible income and employment effects in countries which export defense-related goods or which receive defense-related foreign aid are largely by-passed. Similarly, I have not gone into the effects of possible disarmament on world prices or the international flow of investment capital.

MILITARY EXPENDITURES AND OVER-ALL BALANCE-OF-PAYMENTS EQUILIBRIUM

In the years 1958–1961 net defense-related payments to foreign countries by the United States were roughly equal to the large

[1] The term "defense-related" is used in this chapter in its common-sense meaning to denote foreign expenditures and receipts which have a military purpose. These include transactions in both military goods and non-military or "soft" goods such as imports used in the manufacture of military equipment.

deficits in our over-all balance of payments.[2] The rough equality be-tween these two sums was only a coincidence in the context of bal-ance-of-payments accounts but it does highlight the fact that large defense-related foreign expenditures were a leading cause of the unsatisfactory condition of our balance of payments and of the weakness of the dollar during those years. The relationship also establishes a strong presumption that the direct effects of dis-armament would greatly strengthen the U.S. balance of payments.

Ever since the beginning of the Korean conflict in 1950–1951 U.S. military expenditures abroad have been high and since 1956 they have been running at the very high annual rate of some $3 billion.[3] Final estimates of the over-all payments deficit for 1962 will probably lie in the neighborhood of $2.0 billion, a sum smaller than the probable net cost of foreign defense-related transactions in 1962. For the future, meanwhile, Secretary of Defense Robert S. McNamara announced in mid-1962 that the government ex-pects, through a combination of measures, to reduce net foreign military expenditures from $2.6 billion—their level in the fiscal year 1961—to $1.0 billion a year by the fiscal year 1966. Between fiscal 1961 and fiscal 1963, the goal is to reduce the net adverse balance by about $1 billion, to $1.6 billion.[4] Thus, despite the fact that total military expenditures are rising, the government has set the target of reducing their net adverse effect on the balance of pay-

[2] As shown in the official United States balance-of-payments accounts published by the Department of Commerce, the average over-all deficit in 1958–1961 was $3.4 billion per year, while net payments for military transactions averaged $2.8 billion per year. Data compiled for the purpose of this READ study indicate that other net defense-related payments may have averaged some $0.7 billion per year. Details of this and other estimates contained in this chapter are available from the author in mimeographed form upon request.

[3] As reported by the Department of Commerce, gross military expenditures averaged $3.1 billion per year in 1956–1961; military receipts averaged $0.3 billion, leaving average net military expenditures of $2.8 billion per year.

[4] See the testimony of Assistant Secretary of Defense Charles J. Hitch before the Subcommittee on International Exchange and Payments of the Joint Economic Committee, December 12, 1962. Published in "Outlook for U.S. Balance of Payments," Hearings before the Subcommittee on December 12, 13, and 14, 1962, Washington, 1963, p. 50.

ments by a very significant amount. In principle, at least, a major step toward equilibrium in the United States over-all balance of payments will be taken if the government only achieves its present target rate of reduction in net military expenditures. Table 1 summarizes U.S. over-all payments and receipts, ar-

*TABLE 1 – DEFENSE-RELATED AND OTHER TRANSACTIONS IN THE UNITED STATES BALANCE OF PAYMENTS, 1958*ᵃ
(*Billions of dollars*)

GOODS AND SERVICES		NONDEFENSE-RELATED	DEFENSE-RELATEDᵇ	TOTAL
Exports		22.3	1.0	23.3
Imports		17.2	3.9	21.1
	Balance	+ 5.1	−2.9	+ 2.2
Capital, aid, etc.		− 4.7	−1.0	− 5.7
Over-all balance		+ 0.3	−3.8	− 3.5

SOURCE: Derived from Table 4. Minor discrepancies are due to rounding.
ᵃ Net goods and services transferred as grants, valued at $2.3 billion, are excluded.
ᵇ Defense-related transactions as here defined comprise: (1) United States military expenditures abroad and foreign military expenditures in the United States; (2) United States net defense-related foreign aid; (3) United States exports and imports directly and indirectly serving defense uses.

ranged to show the net impact of defense-related transactions in 1958. The United States was clearly "a net importer" of defense-related goods and services in that year, with defense-related imports accounting for about 18 per cent of total imports and earnings from defense-related exports for about 4 per cent of total export earnings. In addition, there was a large defense-related outflow in the capital and aid accounts, leading to a deficit on defense-related items slightly larger than the over-all deficit on all transactions.

Britain, which is second only to the United States in the scale of its foreign military expenditures, and which provides the world's other main international reserve currency—the pound sterling—has also experienced foreign payments difficulties in recent years. Britain's foreign military expenditures in 1958–1960 averaged the sterling equivalent of about $400 million a year net and $525 million a year gross, with gross military expenditures amounting to some 3.0–3.5 per cent of all overseas payments on current account.

Thus, in the late 1950's, the western world had drifted into an anomalous position in which the two countries that provide its major reserve currencies had allowed their foreign military expenditures to become overextended, threatening not only the financial standing of the dollar and the pound but, through these key currencies, the financial stability of the whole western world. The final link in this curious chain was provided by the fact that military payments by both countries tended to be concentrated in West Germany.[5]

The United States, British, and West German governments have now essayed to reduce the unsettling effects of interallied military spending on relationships between the dollar and pound on the one hand, and the deutschmark on the other. The principal step has been an agreement by West Germany substantially to increase its arms purchases in both English-speaking countries. In addition, both the United States and Britain are cutting back their own foreign defense-related expenditures, with the British replacing troops formerly stationed in large foreign military bases by mobile "floating garrisons," supplemented by increased air transport facilities for United Kingdom–based troops.

From the viewpoint of balance-of-payments equilibrium, the rapid rise of foreign defense-related expenditures by the United States and Britain in the 1950's may be likened to a sudden and drastic shift of national tastes toward imports. Such a change would naturally weaken a country's established foreign-payments position unless there were compensating developments. In the present case, the approach taken of increasing total spending while

[5] In a recent analysis of this problem the Secretariat of the United Nations Economic Commission for Europe reached the following conclusion: "Over the decade of the fifties [United States military expenditures] have almost exactly equalled, in the aggregate, the total loss in international liquidity experienced by the United States . . . [and military expenditures—chiefly by the United States] are almost wholly responsible for the present imbalance in West Germany's balance of payments" (*Economic Survey of Europe—1960*, 1961, Chap. I, pp. 39 and 41).

redistributing the financial burden on the dollar and the pound was adopted for several reasons. The NATO allies wished to increase their military effort in connection with crises over Berlin and other areas, the Germans proved unwilling to absorb more of the *existing* costs of supporting United States or British troops in Germany because that would be reminiscent of the early postwar occupation costs, and—finally—the contemplated increase in United States arms sales probably reflects a genuine United States comparative advantage in the production of military equipment.[6]

EFFECT OF DISARMAMENT ON UNITED STATES IMPORTS
AND EXPORTS

In the event of disarmament, defense-related foreign expenditures would be partially replaced by expenditures for arms control, inspection, and enforcement. The United States, Russia, and the major countries of western Europe would presumably spend large sums, either directly or through international institutions, in one another's countries, and observation posts would be stationed throughout the world at points determined on strategic and scientific grounds (see Chapters 2 and 3). For a time, expenditures for inspection and control might increase faster than foreign military expenditures would taper off. The disarmament model described in Chapter 2 foresees a United States share in the cost of international control agencies beginning at $3.7 billion in 1971, and rising to $7.1 billion in 1977. Only a part of such costs, however, would consist of *foreign* expenditures. The larger part would undoubtedly be spent on pay for internationally sponsored deterrent forces stationed in the United States, for American-made detection equipment, for research and development work, etc. Even the part spent abroad should not, in any case, subject the dollar, pound, or deutschmark to the international financial pressures recently associated with foreign military spending, since payments of this sort for arms control would flow in both directions—into and out of the major countries.

[6] This would be expected in view of the large scale of expenditures in this country on research, development, and production for military purposes.

THE EFFECT ON UNITED STATES IMPORTS

In recent years the import content of military activity in the United States has been much higher than that of nonmilitary activity, and it seems likely to remain higher as long as the United States maintains a sizable number of troops overseas.[7] In the event of disarmament, therefore, United States imports of goods and services would probably decline even though the level of total economic activity remained high.

Defense-related foreign expenditures for goods and services are shown by major categories and major geographical areas in Table 2. In the official balance-of-payments accounts most of the items

TABLE 2 – UNITED STATES MILITARY AND OTHER DEFENSE-RELATED EXPENDITURES ABROAD FOR GOODS AND SERVICES, 1958

(Millions of dollars)

BY MAJOR CATEGORY	
1. Troops, personnel, post exchanges, etc.	890
2. Construction	321
3. NATO infrastructure	81
4. Other services	772
5. Offshore procurement for military aid	212
6. Equipment	49
7. Indirect components, materials, etc.	615
8. Other goods	949
9. Total	3,890
BY MAJOR REGION	
10. Western Europe	1,995
11. Canada	588
12. Latin American republics	148
13. Rest of world	1,159
14. Total	3,890

SOURCE: *Survey of Current Business*, Department of Commerce, January 1962 for lines 1–9, except line 7 and adjustment to line 8, which are derived from Table 3; lines 10–13 are from both sources. Minor discrepancies are due to rounding.

[7] In 1958, military and other defense-related imports (including United States troop expenditures abroad) amounted to 7.6 per cent of all defense purchases ($44.8 billion) while other imports came to 4.4 per cent of all nondefense purchases ($399.7 billion).

in this table are grouped into a single item, "military expenditures," and are shown as a United States foreign payment for services. These military expenditures include purchases by or for United States troops stationed abroad, Defense Department and some other imports (including uranium), which are shown here rather than with other merchandise imports, construction expenditures abroad, and (rapidly declining) purchases abroad for transfer to allies abroad under United States aid programs. Table 2 includes, in addition, an estimate of "components, materials, etc.," (indirect imports) whose derivation is explained below. By countries, total defense-related expenditures as shown in Table 2 were largest in 1958 in (in order) West Germany, Canada, Japan, France, the United Kingdom, Italy, Spain, Korea, and the oil-exporting countries of the Caribbean Sea and the Persian Gulf.

In October 1960, the Defense Department reversed a long-standing policy and began to favor procurement in the United States rather than abroad, applicable both to imported goods and to those purchased for use overseas. In addition to this decrease ordered in United States foreign military procurement, a planned regrouping of United States armed forces stationed in Europe is expected to have, as one implication, reduced United States expenditures in Europe for support units and military dependents.[8] These measures, and others, are reducing the cost per man of maintaining United States troops abroad, but they are now being partially offset by the increased number of troops abroad in connection with the crises in Berlin and Laos.

Most imports by private firms which are combined with labor and materials of United States origin and then sold to the armed forces are not included in the military expenditures item in the balance of payments. The order-of-magnitude values of these imports in 1958 have been estimated with the aid of data generated in the course of the input-output, or interindustry, analysis described in Chapter 2. They are shown in Table 3 by broad categories and by major geographical regions.

[8] See *New York Times* report, on March 24, 1962, of General Lauris Norstad's testimony before the House Foreign Affairs Committee, March 23, 1962.

TABLE 3 – INDIRECT DEFENSE-RELATED MERCHANDISE
IMPORTS, 1958[a]

(Millions of dollars)

MAJOR COMMODITY GROUPS		
Aluminum, copper, and nickel		150
Iron ore, steel mill products, ferroalloys, and other nonferrous metals		135
Petroleum and products		170
Rubber, lumber, wood, and paper products		45
All other		115
	Total[b]	615
APPROXIMATE REGIONAL DISTRIBUTION		
Canada		155
Latin American republics		165
Western Europe		130
All other		165
	Total[b]	615

[a] Detailed notes on these estimates are available in mimeographed form from the author upon request.

[b] Same as line 7 of Table 2.

Allowing for the great hazards attending estimates of this sort, it appears that in 1958 total defense-related imports were about one-fifth larger than the value of military expenditures carried in the official balance-of-payments accounts. The size of these additional "indirect imports" is limited for several reasons. Military equipment is ordinarily procured from domestic sources as a matter of course, besides being subject to buy-American restrictions.[9] Beyond these basic restrictions the Defense Department is required by the "Berry Amendment" of 1954 to purchase in the United States those foods and textile fibers which are available here.[10] Moreover, all food imports into the United States are excluded from these estimates on the ground that people do not eat more food because they are in military service.

[9] Except that military imports from Canada are exempt from the Buy-American Act.

[10] For a penetrating commentary on these restrictions see Lawrence A. Knapp, "The Buy-American Act: A Review and Assessment," Columbia Law Review, March 1961.

Metals and petroleum are prominent among defense-related imports, reflecting the substantial military requirements for telecommunications and transportation equipment. The leading minerals imported for military use in 1958 were steel, copper, aluminum, nickel, lead, zinc, tungsten, manganese, chromium, uranium, petroleum, and some "exotic" materials with special heat-resistant qualities.[11] These commodities have highly varied market structures and very different records of price and output behavior. Each would require individual, detailed analysis for a satisfactory estimate of how it might respond to disarmament.[12]

The world markets for minerals, which have long been very responsive to changes in military activity, would be severely affected by disarmament. After World War II many minerals remained in tight supply; then came the Korean conflict, accompanied by rearmament and the building up of strategic stockpiles, and bringing an intense scramble for many minerals. In the years since the Korean conflict, however, available capacity has come to exceed the demand for most minerals, and prices have remained chronically weak for several years. The new weaponry caused a shift away from conventional types of armament so "the metal content of a unit of defense expenditure was sharply reduced"[13] and now, even in the absence of any progress toward disarmament, questions have arisen about how to go about *reducing stockpiles*. The conclusion is unmistakable that the markets for most minerals, which are already under some pressure to adjust to relative overcapacity, would come under sharply intensified pressure with disarmament.

[11] For an informative survey of the defense-related demand for minerals in 1958, see Samuel G. Lasky, "Minerals, Defense and Growth," *Challenge,* August–September 1958.

[12] There have been many changes since 1958, of course. For example, in October of that year lead and zinc import quotas came into effect under the escape clause of the Trade Agreements Act, and in March 1959, mandatory quotas replaced voluntary quotas for oil imports on national security grounds. No new contracts for uranium imports are being signed, and deliveries under existing contracts are running down, etc.

[13] *Commodity Survey 1960,* United Nations, 1961, p. 72.

EFFECT ON UNITED STATES EXPORTS

The United States, with the world's largest armaments industry, is expecting a substantial increase in its foreign sales of military goods in 1962. In case of disarmament in some future year, United States defense-related exports would certainly decline, but probably by less than the decline to be expected in defense-related imports. Our defense-related exports are of two general types: those granted under the Military Assistance Program (MAP) to foreign countries whose improved military posture the President believes important to the United States and those which are paid for, either as commercial exports or under government programs.

Exports under MAP reached a peak of $4.2 billion in 1953, when NATO countries were the principal recipients, and have since fallen off to $1.6 billion in 1961, when they were distributed among some fifty countries in all parts of the world. Korea was easily the largest recipient in that year, followed by Italy, Turkey, and Taiwan.

The tapering off of MAP grants in case of disarmament would have no direct effect on the United States balance of payments and probably relatively slight economic effects in the United States and in the former recipient countries. These exports are usually excluded from balance-of-payments analyses because, being granted directly to foreign governments, they do not affect the financial balance between the United States and the rest of the world. They are carried twice in the full balance-of-payments accounts, once as an export and once as a unilateral transfer, so their effect on the net balance is zero. The value of these aid transfers as carried in the balance-of-payments accounts is partly nominal.[14] Much of the military hardware of which they mainly consist is surplus to United States needs and is transferred from stocks held by the armed forces. The countries now receiving these grants would pre-

[14] Detailed discussions may be found in Robert E. Asher, *Grants, Loans and Local Currencies: Their Role in Foreign Aid*, Washington: The Brookings Institution, 1961, pp. 56–58; and *Semi-Annual Report, January–June 1960*, U.S. Advisory Council for International Monetary and Financial Problems, p. A-23.

sumably be disarming or stabilizing their defense forces and thus would no longer "need" military grants.

The MAP grants, like other United States aid, now go mainly to underdeveloped countries, and in some of these the pace of steps toward disarmament would need to be carefully planned. Strains are certain to arise if large numbers of men are released from military service to find their own way in traditional societies already plagued by severe poverty and underemployment. Much ingenuity would be needed to convert people's interests and energies from military activity into the attack on poverty that would be the appropriate sequel to disarmament.

One currently important element of MAP is the Mutual Weapons Development Program, designed to mobilize the allied powers' scientific skills for keeping ahead in the arms race. This activity could be converted to an international authority's continuing weapons research program, or to civilian R&D programs as foreseen in Chapters 2 and 7.

Defense-related exports for which payment is received are estimated to have earned about $1 billion in 1958. These exports, which, of course, do affect the balance of payments, are now rising, in contrast to the decline which has occurred in MAP shipments. They fall into three main categories, of which only the first is shown separately in the official balance-of-payments accounts; the latter two were estimated indirectly, making use of relevant published data.[15] The three categories are (1) government military sales ($296 million in 1958), (2) commercial exports of defense-related goods, and (3) defense-related exports financed by non-military aid (estimated at $400 million and $340 million, respectively, in 1958). These exports are now higher than in 1958 and, barring disarmament, will probably continue to increase.

Government military sales approximately doubled, from some $200 million in 1953–1956 to $406 million in 1961, and official estimates early in 1962 were that they might reach $1 billion in that year. In early years Canada was the principal buyer under

[15] The sources and methods used are available in mimeographed form from the author.

TABLE 4 – UNITED STATES BALANCE OF PAYMENTS, SHOWING SIGNIFICANCE OF MILITARY AND OTHER DEFENSE-RELATED ITEMS, 1958

(Millions of dollars)

1. Total exports of goods and services	25,606
2. Less: Transfers under military grants	2,281
3. Equals: Goods and services, adjusted	23,325
4. Less: Exports of other military goods and services[a]	696
5. Exports financed by defense-related foreign aid	340
6. Equals: Nondefense-related exports of goods and services	22,289
7. Total imports of goods and services	21,053
8. Less: Indirect defense-related imports	615
9. Military expenditures[b]	3,247
10. Equals: Nondefense-related imports of goods and services	17,191
BALANCE ON GOODS AND SERVICES	
11. Total (lines 1 minus 7)	+4,553
12. Excluding military transfers (lines 3 minus 7)	+2,272
13. Of which: Nondefense-related (lines 6 minus 10)	+5,098
14. Defense-related (lines 12 minus 13)	−2,826
15. U.S. government grants and capital outflow	−5,379
16. Military grant aid	−2,281
17. Nonmilitary grants and capital outflow	−3,098
18. Of which: Nondefense-related	−2,128
19. Defense-related	− 970
20. Repayments of government loans	+ 544
21. Private U.S. long-term capital	−2,538
22. Foreign long-term investments	− 27
23. Remittances and pensions	− 722
BALANCE ON BASIC ACCOUNTS	
24. Total (lines 12 plus 17, 20–23)	−3,569
25. Of which: Nondefense-related (lines 13 plus 18, 20–23)	+ 227
26. Defense-related (lines 24 minus 25)	−3,796
27. U.S. private short-term capital and unrecorded transactions	+ 74
OVER-ALL UNITED STATES BALANCE	
28. Total (lines 24 plus 27)	−3,495
29. Of which: Nondefense-related (lines 28 minus 26)	+ 301
30. Defense-related (line 26)	−3,796

SOURCE: Council of Economic Advisors, Economic Report of the President, Jan. 1962, p. 295, and READ analysis.

[a] Military transactions as reported by the Department of Commerce plus an estimate of defense-related goods exported outside of Defense Department channels.

[b] Adjusted to avoid duplication with line 8.

United States government sales programs, but since 1957 sales to West Germany have been rising in importance. Late in 1961 the Bonn government agreed to buy about $700 million of United States arms and military supplies annually, in an agreement that was later extended to cover the period through the calendar year 1964. This amount is said to be about double the value of such purchases in recent years and would approximately cover the cost of maintaining United States troops in the Federal Republic. Also late in 1961, it was announced in Washington that France had agreed to buy $50 million of military equipment in the United States "that it might ordinarily not buy here,"[16] and late in 1962 Italy ordered over $100 million of military equipment in the United States. Exports of defense-related goods through commercial channels and those financed by defense-related foreign aid may also be rising—particularly the latter, since procurement in the United States rather than abroad by foreign aid agencies has now been stressed for some time.[17]

EFFECTS OF DISARMAMENT ON FOREIGN AID

The American public has a "mind-set," according to which foreign aid is thought to be civilian in character and aimed primarily at raising living standards abroad. But for more than a decade much of our foreign aid has been designed to enable the recipient countries to maintain larger military forces than they could maintain without it, and such aid is definitely defense related.[18] It is of such a magnitude that there would need to be a fundamental review and reshaping of all of our foreign assistance programs in the event of disarmament.

16 *New York Times*, December 1, 1961.
17 A Commerce Department study of U.S. exports from 1959 to 1962 points out that, "The sharp and uninterrupted rise since 1959 in non-aid exports of military-type equipment has been among the largest of any category." *Survey of Current Business*, December 1962, p. 23.
18 United States foreign aid is customarily divided into two main categories: military grant-transfers, supplied to some fifty countries, and nonmilitary, or "all other," aid, going to some sixty countries. Military aid has been declining for several years, as pointed out on page 233 above. The discussion in this section centers mainly on subcategories of nonmilitary aid as they were in the late 1950's.

Among the various categories of nonmilitary foreign aid, different people might draw the line in different ways between those which are defense related and those which are not. The distinction I have drawn, using the foreign aid nomenclature of the period 1957–1961, is based upon the dominant intent of the United States Administration and Congress in extending the aid rather than upon whether its *effect* was subsequently judged to be mainly "economic" or "military."[19] Using this criterion, defense support aid is clearly defense related,[20] while technical assistance, Export-Import Bank loans, Development Loan Fund loans, and the sale of surplus agricultural commodities for local currencies are regarded as not being defense related.[21] The major recipients of defense support aid in 1957–1961 were (in order) Korea, Vietnam, Pakistan, Turkey, Taiwan (Formosa), and Spain.

While the dominant intent of most foreign aid categories can be plausibly described as mainly politico-military (defense related) or politico-economic (not defense related), there is no easy way to classify the category known as special assistance. Its intent was recently summarized in the following way:

[19] At present (fall of 1962) a shift is occurring away from grant aid to loan aid repayable at low interest rates over a long period. At the same time defense support (or "supporting assistance" as it is now called) is declining as a fraction of the total, since it is much the largest category of grant aid.

[20] One of the United States foreign aid officials who invented the phrase "defense-support" recalled, some years later, "a winter afternoon when . . . two of us, searching for ways to explain the foreign aid budget in the new [Korean crisis] atmosphere, invented that confusing but politically effective phrase 'defense-support' to justify economic aid as a handmaiden of the military build-up in areas like South Korea, Formosa, and Vietnam" (Harlan Cleveland, "The Convalescence of Foreign Aid," *American Economic Review*, May 1959, p. 217).

[21] I have treated *all* defense support aid as defense related and *all* aid in the other categories mentioned in the text as being not defense related. This solution has the advantage of simplicity, and it is compatible with an interest in the *intent* of aid rather than its *effects* or its *composition*. Studies of the *effects* of defense support aid have suggested that as much as one-third to one-half of it contributes to economic development by providing such facilities as docks, warehouses, roads, irrigation, etc. (see, for example, the discussion in Thomas C. Schelling, "American Aid and Economic Development: Some Critical Issues," in *International Stability and Progress*, New York: Columbia University, June 1957, pp. 127 ff.)

To develop or maintain economic stability in countries in which some U.S. support is essential to continued independence or identification with the free world. . . . To secure or maintain U.S. military facilities or other rights in a country or to deal with economic and other problems arising out of the existence of such facilities; to initiate or accelerate programs in health and education which further U.S. policy objectives by their humanitarian nature and by contributing to economic improvement.[22]

Against this background of a clearly mixed intention, the decision was taken to regard special assistance as one-half defense related and one-half not defense related. In 1961 this category of aid was extended to some fifty-five countries plus Berlin, the Indus Basin, an international malaria eradication program, and the Central Treaty Organization (CENTO). The largest individual recipients in 1957–1961 were (in order) Jordan, Morocco, Tunesia, Bolivia, Yugoslavia, and Libya.

Thus, a concept of defense-related nonmilitary aid has emerged: it is the sum of defense-support aid plus one-half of the special assistance category. When it is applied to United States foreign aid for the period 1957–1961, as in Table 5, it appears that about one-third of all nonmilitary grants and credits were defense related in those years. When military grants are added to the picture, the two categories together accounted for perhaps two-thirds of total United States foreign aid.

The distinction on the basis of intent that has been drawn in this manner through the total United States foreign aid picture cannot be sustained at all on the level of aid to individual countries. Among individual countries nearly all defense-support aid goes to countries on the periphery of the Sino-Soviet bloc, and many of these would be receiving United States aid for politico-economic reasons even if politico-military considerations were not dominant. During some of the years when India was neutral, for example, it received more United States aid than any other single country. Also, in the aid programs of many individual countries there are strong interrelationships between economic and military

---

[22] *Mutual Security Act of 1959*, H. Rep. 440, 86th Cong., 1st Sess., June 5, 1959, p. 34.

TABLE 5 - UNITED STATES FOREIGN AID, SHOWING
RELATIONSHIP OF MILITARY AND OTHER DEFENSE-
RELATED AID TO TOTAL AID
(*Millions of dollars*)

	1957	1958	1959	1960	1961[a]
1. Total U.S. government foreign aid, net	5,087	4,886	5,295	4,640	4,229
2. Less: Investments in international financial institutions			1,375	153	172
3. Equals: Total aid programs, net	5,087	4,886	3,920	4,487	4,057
4. Less: Military grants, net	2,483	2,368	2,031	1,881	1,518
5. Equals: Nonmilitary aid, net	2,604	2,518	1,888	2,606	2,539
6. Plus: Returns, repayments, etc.	719	580	1,067	631	1,295
7. Less: Net accumulation of foreign currency claims	619	270	256	521	189
8. Equals: Nonmilitary grants and credits, gross	2,704	2,828	2,699	2,716	3,645
9. Less: Defense-related, nonmilitary grants and credits[b]	1,115	970	960	925	1,115
10. Equals: Nondefense-related, nonmilitary grants and credits[c]	1,589	1,858	1,739	1,791	2,530
11. Defense-related aid as per cent of nonmilitary grants and credits[d]	41	34	36	34	31
12. Military and other defense-related aid as per cent of total aid programs[e]	71	68	76	63	65

SOURCE: *Statistical Abstract of the United States,* Department of Commerce, except lines 9–12. Discrepancies due to rounding.

[a] 1961 is not quite comparable to earlier years due to new Agency for International Development categories.

[b] Estimated expenditures of defense support and one-half of special assistance.

[c] Export-Import Bank, Development Loan Fund, Technical Co-operation, "Other" ICA Aid, and one-half of special assistance.

[d] Lines 9 ÷ 8.

[e] Lines (4 + 9) ÷ 3.

objectives which cannot be sensibly disentangled (see footnote 21). Finally, much of the aid that has been classified as defense related goes to countries with which we have the closest political and defense relationships. At a time of possible disarmament, defense-related aid to these countries would certainly not be cut off while our aid to other, previously neutral, countries continued, unaffected by disarmament.

Today's defense-related aid has a resemblance to lend-lease aid extended during World War II. In part it consists of military hardware (the MAP part) and in part of soft goods in a military context (the defense-related nonmilitary part). Lend-lease aid, it will be recalled, was cut off abruptly when World War II fighting ceased. At a time of disarmament defense-related foreign aid would probably not be terminated so abruptly; but, at the very least, it would require a new justification under the altered circumstances. Certainly, at such a time, a thorough review and reconsideration would be required of the aims, the amounts, and the distribution by country of foreign aid as a whole. And who can say in advance how Congress would respond to requests for foreign aid if, at a time of disarmament, the atmosphere were shorn of the continuing danger of imminent military conflict?

EFFECTS ON OTHER COUNTRIES: THREE MAIN TYPES

At a time of disarmament or of a significant cutback in military expenditures, countries having defense-related transactions with the United States would be affected in one of three main ways.[23] First, in some countries—mainly in western Europe—the loss of receipts from the United States would be at least partly offset by reductions in their own foreign defense-related expenditures, in the United States or elsewhere. Second, in the minerals-exporting countries—such as Canada and certain countries in Latin America, Africa, and Asia—a loss of receipts from the United States would be intensified by similar losses of defense-related income from other disarming countries. Third, for certain countries now receiving substantial defense-related aid from the United States—such as Korea, Vietnam, and Taiwan—a lessening of world military tensions would presumably bring some loss of strategic importance, accompanied by a decline in their current relatively large shares of the world's available foreign aid.

[23] It is assumed in this chapter that adequate total demand would be maintained in the United States and, therefore, that impulses transmitted via our balance of payments would be only those direct ones originating in defense-related sectors. A trade-off matrix was developed, using the 1958 interindustry data, to indicate how United States use of some leading minerals might be affected by a shift from military to nonmilitary demand. The matrix suggests that the patterns of production that might ensue after disarmament would not fully restore the United States demand for minerals imports.

In western Europe most of our defense-related payments are included in the military expenditures category and reflect the large number of United States troops stationed in Europe. In 1958, at $1.6 billion these expenditures were equal to the United States deficit on all bilateral transactions with western Europe, but in most of the European countries they amounted to less than 5 per cent of all export receipts. Within the region, 90 per cent of our defense-related payments went to West Germany, France, Britain, Spain, Italy, and Benelux. As indicated earlier, defense-related payments are increasingly flowing in both directions across the North Atlantic, reducing *net* United States defense-related payments to Europe.

Reserves of gold and dollars are now very high in most of the western European countries, and in case of disarmament a loss of net dollar income would not be the main economic problem. Instead, most of the countries would face adjustment problems within their own economies and would be concerned about establishing burden-sharing arrangements with some of the underdeveloped countries whose export incomes would decline with disarmament and who would look to western Europe for adjustment assistance.

In the second group of countries—mainly the minerals exporters —disarmament, or even the prospect of it, would be seriously depressing. The demand for defense-related materials would fall in all countries simultaneously, and this shrinkage in world markets would be additional to the shrinkage that has already been caused by the virtual cessation of purchases of roughly the same materials for national stockpiles. The countries most seriously affected would be those which export uranium, petroleum, rubber, nickel, bauxite, copper, and other defense-related metals. Canada is one of these countries, and the others are widely scattered through Africa, Asia, and Latin America. In some cases, the defense-related minerals exports account for a large fraction of total exports, as in the case of Jamaica's bauxite, Chile's copper, and Venezuela's petroleum. In most cases, countries which depend heavily upon minerals exports are already suffering weakness in their foreign payments, and disarmament would bring substantial new strains. Besides the loss of export volume which they would suffer, prices would probably fall, in the typical case, and there might well be a simultaneous decline in the flow of investment capital to minerals-producing areas from the industrially developed countries. In these circumstances there would be an urgent need to work out some arrangements whereby the unintended economic burden of disarmament falling upon these countries could be partially borne by the major disarming powers themselves. Among possible approaches to this problem are accelerated research to find new uses for the affected materials, temporary increases in foreign aid, increased diversification of exports from the affected countries, and—as a last resort—temporary commodity price stabilization agreements. The most appropriate combination of measures would depend upon individual market circumstances prevailing at the time of disarmament.

Canada is a country which might experience severe economic difficulties in the event of disarmament. Some of its major exports are defense related, and it has suffered serious foreign-payments difficulties even in the absence of any early prospect of disarmament. Its net defense-related receipts from the United States were about $500 million in 1958, an amount roughly equivalent to one-eighth of total United States purchases of goods and services from Canada in that year.

Several Latin American republics are also heavily dependent on defense-related exports to the United States. The leading commodities in 1958 were petroleum, copper, iron ore, lead, nickel, zinc, and ferroalloys—mainly from Venezuela, Chile, Peru, and Mexico. While these particular countries were highly dependent on United States defense-related expenditures, the relative dependence of the Latin American republics as a whole was not great in 1958, amounting to only about 3 per cent of their exports to the United States in that year. This dependence is low partly because about half of Latin America's exports to the United States are foodstuffs, which are not included in the definition of defense-related imports. Furthermore, in 1958, our imports of primary commodities were low because there was a recession in that year and inventories were declining. Whatever Latin America's exact dependence upon defense-related exports may be today, it is certain that the region's total export earnings are quite inadequate to meet the demands of its rapidly growing population for higher standards of living. Therefore, any loss at all in export income might have serious consequences.

The third group of countries consists of those receiving large amounts of foreign aid because of their strategic importance in the cold war. As indicated above, about one-third of our nonmilitary foreign aid is defense related in intent. Many countries receiving this aid are devoting a high proportion of their meager resources to military programs financed jointly with the United States, and their shares of the available foreign aid might be severely reduced if their strategic importance should diminish. It would be pointless now to try to forecast what might happen to aid programs in particular countries at a time of disarmament, but it is possible to single out individual countries where large receipts of defense-related nonmilitary aid would undoubtedly come under very close scrutiny at such a time. Receipts of such aid were much larger in 1958 than receipts from total exports of goods and services in Korea, Laos, Vietnam, and Jordan,[24] and were also very significant in Cambodia, Taiwan, Pakistan, and Bolivia. If United States military purchases are added to the flow of United States defense-related aid, then Turkey, Spain, Iceland, the Philippines, Greece, Libya, and Morocco must be added to the countries whose dependence on United States defense-related spending was between about 10 and 25 per cent of the value of their total exports in 1958.

A summary of United States defense-related foreign transactions in 1958 classified by four main geographical regions is shown in Table 6. The largest sums involved were military expenditures in western Europe, but more difficult economic adjustments at a time of possible disarmament would probably arise for some of the countries producing defense-related materials—mainly minerals—for which demand would shrink in all countries simulta-

[24] In considering the individual countries mentioned in this paragraph, the definition of defense-related aid must be borne in mind, along with the hazards of seeking to apply the concept to individual countries (see pages 237 and 238).

TABLE 6 – UNITED STATES BALANCE OF PAYMENTS AND DEFENSE-RELATED FOREIGN TRANSACTIONS, BY AREA, 1958

(Millions of dollars)

	CANADA	LATIN AMERICAN REPUBLICS	WESTERN EUROPE	REST OF WORLD	TOTAL
OVER-ALL BALANCE OF PAYMENTS					
1. Exports of goods and services[a]	4,779	5,806	6,785	5,829	23,199
2. Imports of goods and services	3,770	4,837	7,269	5,075	20,951
3. Goods and services balance[a]	+1,009	+ 969	– 484	+ 754	+ 2,248
4. All other transactions	–1,004	–1,132	–1,116	–2,871	– 6,123
5. U.S. Over-all bilateral balances	+ 5	– 163	–1,600	–2,117	– 3,875
6. Errors and omissions, etc.					+ 436
7. U.S. over-all balance, all areas					– 3,439
DEFENSE-RELATED TRANSACTIONS					
Payments by the U.S.					
8. Defense-related indirect imports	155	165	130	165	615
9. Military expenditures[b]	428	23	1,840	984	3,275
10. Defense-related aid	0	20	60	890	970
11. Total defense-related payments	583	208	2,030	2,039	4,860
Receipts by the U.S.					
12. Military transactions[c]	36	21	171	68	296
13. Other military goods exports[d]	48	28	232	92	400
14. Defense-aid financed exports[e]	0	7	20	313	340
15. Total defense-related receipts	84	56	423	473	1,036
16. U.S. defense-related payments, net	499	152	1,607	1,566	3,824
17. Net defense-related payments as per cent of total payments for goods and services[f]	13%	3%	21%	31%	18%

source: United States Department of Commerce, Office of Business Economics, *Survey of Current Business*, March 1960, and READ analysis.

a Excluding military grants.   b Adjusted to avoid duplication with line 8.   c Service receipts in official balance-of-payment statements.   d Same regional distribution assumed as line 12.   e Same regional distribution as line 10.   f Lines 16 ÷ 2.

neously, and for countries which might experience a loss of strategic importance and of foreign aid receipts. Income and employment would decline in these countries along with export earnings. Since most of them are relatively underdeveloped and already have balance-of-payments problems, it would be more difficult for them than for the more industrialized countries to make the necessary adjustments.

It is this group of countries which seems likely to experience the most serious balance-of-payments difficulties from disarmament. First of all, the decline in their United States dollar earnings from defense sales might be matched by declines in defense imports from other countries.[25] Second, their earnings from international disarmament inspection and enforcement activities would not be substantial, since comparatively little recurrent new procurement, especially of metal-using products, would be involved. Third, these countries, which generally lack adequate diversification, are also particularly sensitive to world industrial recessions, and would be doubly affected if—relaxing our assumption of constant over-all demand—we allow that disarmament might result in recessions or extended periods of slower industrial growth in the developed countries. Fourth, large stockpiles overhanging the markets for many of their exports will continue to depress prices. This effect would be intensified with disarmament, particularly if the industrialized countries begin to liquidate their stockpiles rather than meeting their current requirements through imports.

It is to be hoped that the industrially developed countries, mindful of their international responsibilities and commitments, would provide adequate adjustment assistance—which they would be well able to afford at a time of disarmament—to these generally underdeveloped countries for which disarmament would mean the loss of established flows of foreign exchange income.

---

[25] United States defense-dependent imports were estimated at about one-half of the world's total in *Economic and Social Consequences of Disarmament,* United Nations, Department of Economic and Social Affairs, 1962, pp. 65–66.

14

Development Aid and Disarmament

Wilson E. Schmidt*

In the event of a secure disarmament, could and should more resources from the advanced countries be devoted to stimulating
the development of the poor countries of this globe?

The new directions to our foreign policy at the time of disarmament, the depth of our concern for the fate of other peoples, the
then current levels of aid, the feasibility of administering larger
volumes of assistance, the reaction of public opinion to the relief
provided by disarmament, and, of course, the ability of the underdeveloped countries to employ added assistance usefully—all of
these and more will determine what can and will be done. We
cannot hope to predict the strength of these factors for some un-
specified date in the future, but we can at least sort out some of
the matters which will have a bearing on the decision and spell
out some possible problems in undertaking vigorous action.

* WILSON E. SCHMIDT, Professor of Economics at George Washington University, has done much work in the fields of economic development and
international economics. He has served the United States government and
private business as a consultant in Africa and Latin America.

RECENT AID LEVELS

A recent estimate put the level of gross capital formation in the underdeveloped countries at about $29 billion.[1] Though one must, for a variety of reasons, have a high tolerance for error to use such figures, it would seem that the advanced countries currently play a considerable role in financing the capital expenditures of the underdeveloped world.

According to Paul Hoffman, the annual flow of capital for development from the advanced countries stood in 1957–1958 at a level of about $4 billion, exclusive of the Soviet bloc's contribution; if this is added, the total rises to $4.7 billion.[2] Rosenstein-Rodan sets the levels of aid for 1959–1960 at about the same levels, namely $4 billion annually, exclusive of the Soviet bloc's estimated contribution of $0.5 billion.[3] Each of these estimates is the product of considerable adjustment to the basic data. The most comprehensive data are provided by a recent study of the Organization for European Economic Cooperation.[4] It puts the annual net flow of capital from the advanced countries, either directly or through multilateral organizations, at $3.5 billion during 1950–1955 and $6.8 billion during 1956–1959.

Of the total net aid estimated by OEEC, the United States provided during 1956–1959 approximately 55 per cent. Rosenstein-Rodan, in an effort to determine fair shares, calculated that the United States ought to give 65 per cent of the total assistance to developing countries, exclusive of the Soviet share. He employed for this estimate the rate of progression in the United States federal income tax. An alternative criterion might be the basis on which we share income internally; this would imply a smaller relative burden for the United States than the figure derived from the

[1] Paul Rosenstein-Rodan, "International Aid for Underdeveloped Countries," *Review of Economics and Statistics,* May 1961.

[2] *One Hundred Countries, One and One Quarter Billion People,* Albert and Mary Lasker Foundation, Washington, D.C., 1960.

[3] Rosenstein-Rodan, *op. cit.*

[4] *The Flow of Financial Resources to Countries in the Course of Economic Development,* 1961.

federal income tax because the total tax system, including local and state taxes, is significantly less progressive.

If the burden of aid should be borne on the basis of some progressive income tax principle, the distribution of this aid has not followed a similar standard. Hoffman provides estimates for the amount of aid per head in relation to national income, exclusive of private foreign investment. For selected nations with per capita incomes below $100, external governmental assistance in 1957–1958 was $1.70 per person. For certain nations in the range of per capita income of $100–$200, government aid was $2 per person. And for those above $200, it was $3.20. This suggests that motives other than those of strict egalitarianism dominate aid programs—which brings us to the next topic.

DOES DISARMAMENT JUSTIFY LARGER FOREIGN AID EXPENDITURES?

The answer to this question depends, at least in part, on what one believes are the motives for, and purposes served by, aid programs to the underdeveloped nations.

Employment Arguments. There are many Americans who support foreign aid partly, at least, because they believe that it helps maintain employment in the United States. More narrowly, there are persons who view foreign aid as a means of ridding ourselves of embarrassing surpluses of agricultural products. For these proponents of aid, the possibility that disarmament may bring a recession at home urges a substantial expansion of aid.

Presumably the unemployment argument would justify aid for only a very limited period of time. The tax cuts which would accompany disarmament and/or the shifts in government expenditures to other employments would stimulate the economy in due course, and when the nation had made its adjustment to the decline in military expenditures, foreign aid would no longer be required as a prop to the economy.

The practical fact is that the lead-time, including the programming cycle in aid agencies, for large-scale projects is so long that a prospective period of temporary unemployment would hardly justify expanded aid. The obvious solution would be to get ready with projects on the shelf, but this runs into the practical difficulty that it is impossible to develop projects without the complete cooperation and knowledge of the countries in which they would be carried out. Unwelcome pressure would be placed on the United States to finance the project before disarmament, given the pressures for development, and the shelf would normally be bare.

Even if one assumes that it might take as much as five years for the American economy to adjust to disarmament, the amount of real benefit to the less-developed countries of foreign aid for this period is not likely to be great. Current discussions of development assistance tend to emphasize the need for a continuing aid program, perhaps for fifteen to twenty or more years, before the less-developed lands can be placed in a condition of self-sustained growth. Furthermore, even those who would never justify foreign aid on humanitarian grounds would probably feel a twinge of guilt for the serious economic effects on the poor countries of a sharp cessation of aid once the unemployment rationale had disappeared, with the return to high employment in the United States.

Political Arguments. Those persons who see aid largely as a political instrument, the monied arm of foreign policy, may find in disarmament a justification for either a reduction or an increase in foreign aid, depending upon the particular circumstances surrounding disarmament. As one State Department-International Cooperation Administration memorandum put it several years ago, the main thrust of foreign assistance is to maintain peace, or at least to avoid a major nuclear war, and to preserve and expand the number of countries which are friendly, or at least not hostile, to the United States. The mechanisms by which foreign aid is thought to serve this political objective are varied. One line of argument contends that by stimulating economic growth and by providing economic opportunities to the discontented in poor countries, we reduce the chances that the underdeveloped nations will adopt Communist "solutions" to their poverty and can avoid the political instability which would open the doors to internal subversion by alien powers. Another line of argument holds that foreign aid provides the occasion for the "presence" of the United States within a foreign country, giving us more of the proximity necessary to affect the policies of foreign governments which bear on matters concerning our national interest—ranging from trade relations to United Nations voting positions. In effect, the points of contact between representatives of our government and foreign governments are increased by foreign aid, providing a subtle reminder of our importance and a greater opportunity to present and to support the United States policy position throughout foreign governments.

Still another strand in the political instrument theory emphasizes the competition between the United States and the Soviet bloc in gaining the favor of the less-developed countries; inasmuch as one of the instruments of the bloc is foreign aid, we must compete with the bloc at some adequate aid level. If chief emphasis is given to the political arguments for aid, the need to increase aid in the event of disarmament depends upon the circumstances surrounding that disarmament. If the Soviet bloc should merely shift the form of the cold war from military expenditures to economic and political efforts to gain the favor of other countries in the world, then disarmament would strengthen the case for aid on political grounds. If the bloc chose to compete on nonmilitary grounds, and if our security were to depend upon preventing the establishment of hostile governments abroad, we too should have to compete on nonmilitary grounds.

But if the cold war should recede on all fronts rather than merely shift its form, the case for foreign aid which rests its logic on the foreign policy benefits to be gained from aid would be sorely weakened, if not destroyed. Even if the cold war should continue but take only one form, namely a competition to determine which type of system and society can grow the more rapidly, the foreign policy benefits from aid would be sharply reduced, though if the size of aid were taken as a measure of affluence, foreign aid still would receive support in the political context.

Humanitarian Arguments. Finally, there are those who see foreign aid as a reflection of a humanitarian spirit, as an obligation of the rich nations to the poor. The grinding poverty of the southern half of the globe becomes a call for humane action. Would disarmament strengthen or weaken the case for foreign aid on humanitarian grounds?

So far as the advanced countries are concerned, the reduction in armament expenditures would make them richer in real terms, leaving aside a possible recession which would ultimately pass from the scene. If one employs the gap in standards of living between the rich and the poor nations as the criterion for aid levels, the lifting of the burden of armament would support greater aid expenditures on humanitarian grounds.

On the other hand, with respect to the underdeveloped countries, the effect of disarmament on their "deservedness" is not as clear. The possibility of a recession in the event of disarmament suggests that the import demands of the advanced countries for the products of the poorer nations would fall off, depressing their standards of living. But, after the internal adjustments to disarmament in the advanced countries were completed, the tax reductions which might accompany disarmament would place in the hands of the people immense amounts of purchasing power, some of which would leak into foreign markets. Inasmuch as the available evidence suggests that the propensity to import goods is smaller for the federal government than for the economy as a whole, a shift of purchasing power from the public to the private sector is apt to increase the total level of imports.[5] In recent years, Americans have shown a much greater awareness of foreign goods, and there is increasing evidence that the less-developed nations are shifting toward light consumer-goods manufactures in their exports. This suggests the possibility that over the long pull the export earnings of the poorer nations might be enhanced by disarmament in the advanced countries. Also, relief from the threat of war would mean that less credence could be given to claims by American industry for protection from foreign imports; so it would be easier to avoid rais-

[5] See Lawrence A. Knapp, "The Buy-American Act," *Columbia Law Review*, March 1961. The federal government's propensity to import services appears to be quite high, but these services are not so important to the less-developed countries.

ing trade barriers, and it might be possible to bring some down. Unfortunately, all of this is rather speculative, simply because our comparative advantages have been shifting rapidly in recent years, making predictions of our import patterns quite difficult.

For some underdeveloped areas, disarmament may weaken the case for foreign aid on humanitarian grounds. If disarmament should be general and thereby put an end to the need for large armies in some of the poorer nations—such as Korea, Taiwan, Vietnam—the gain in resources available for development in those countries would be substantial, and the need for external assistance would be reduced. While there are only a few countries to which this argument might apply, our economic assistance to them is so large that whatever increased contributions might be justified for other poor nations on humanitarian grounds could conceivably come out of reductions in economic assistance to these few heavily militarized nations; hence, even a net reduction in over-all economic development aid might be possible.

On the other hand, if one contends that the military expenditures of the advanced countries not only protect their freedom but also insure the freedom of the poorer nations, disarmament strengthens the case for foreign assistance. Merely to maintain a constant level of help, including that presently provided through our domestic military expenditures as well as through military aid, it would be necessary to increase economic aid expenditures when the military threat passes.

CAPITAL NEEDS AND GROWTH RATES

Suppose we decide that some of the resources freed by disarmament ought to be devoted to accelerating economic growth in the poorer countries. How much should be provided? One approach to answering the question is to establish a rate of growth in income or output for the less-developed countries which is regarded as desirable, and to calculate the amount of aid necessary to achieve this objective.

Paul Hoffman suggests that we should strive to increase the rate of growth in the less-developed countries from the 1 per cent per capita rate that he estimates prevailed in the 1950's to 2 per cent per capita. This objective recommends itself to Hoffman because it is approximately the rate of growth in output per head enjoyed by the United States in 1870–1929. According to Hoffman, the combined income of the less-developed nations today is roughly $100 billion. To make that income grow at 2 per cent rather than at 1 per cent, we would have to inject enough added capital to raise income by $1 billion per annum. Believing that it takes, on the average, $3 of extra capital to produce $1 of extra income (a capital-output ratio of 3), he concludes that we ought to increase the flow of capital into the less-developed nations by a minimum of $3 billion annually.

Somewhat earlier, Max F. Millikan and Walt W. Rostow estimated that it would take an additional $3.5 to $4 billion annually to raise the rate of growth to 2 per cent per annum per head.[6] The method of making this estimate may be illustrated as follows: For India, Pakistan, and Ceylon, the national income was set at $27.9 billion in 1953. Net capital formation in the area ran about $1.7 billion. If we injected $1 billion of aid, the level of capital formation would rise to $2.7 billion, or to about 10 per cent of the area's national income. Assuming a capital-output ratio of 3, the 10 per cent of the national income which would be invested would raise income by 3.3 per cent. Inasmuch as the population was estimated to be growing at 1.3 per cent, the 3.3 per cent growth rate would leave an increase in per capita income of approximately 2 per cent. Repetition of this procedure for all of the various underdeveloped regions indicated that an additional $3.5 to $4 billion annually would be required.

More recently, Millikan and Rostow have raised the requirement by 20 to 25 per cent, due chiefly to the deterioration of the terms on which the less-developed countries sell their products in world markets. At maximum, this would suggest an annual requirement of $5 billion.[7]

[6] *A Proposal: Key to an Effective Foreign Policy,* New York: Harper & Row, 1957.
[7] Millikan and Rostow, *United States Foreign Policy: Economic, Social, and Political Change in the Underdeveloped Countries and Its Implications for United States Policy,* Cambridge, Mass.: Massachusetts Institute of Technology, March 30, 1960.

A very early estimate made by United Nations experts placed the annual requirement for external assistance well in excess of $10 billion.[8] This proposal sought a 2 per cent rate of growth in per capita income, and involved assumptions about shifts in population between agricultural and industrial production and estimates of the required amount of capital per worker outside of agriculture. These assumptions indicated a need for about $19 billion of capital formation, of which about $5 billion would be covered out of savings within the less-developed countries. This left an annual gap of $14 billion, but the authors, recognizing that savings might rise, set their final figure for the deficit nearer to $10 billion.

The large difference between this estimate and the one previously mentioned lies chiefly in two factors. The United Nations estimate included the needs of China, which, if dropped, would cut the deficit by $4.7 billion. Furthermore, the estimate implies a relatively high capital-output ratio, on the order of 7½ ; if a less conservative figure is employed, perhaps 4 or 5, the annual external assistance requirement falls, on the basis of the data employed, to between $4.7 and $7.1 billion.

GATT STUDY

The staff of the General Agreement on Tariffs and Trade gives an estimate of annual external capital requirements which reaches $13 billion.[9] The figures they employ suggest that per capita income in the less-developed countries rose, between 1950 and 1958, at the rate of 1.8 per cent per annum—much higher than the estimates employed by Hoffman. Their objective is to raise income per head at the rate of 3.2 per cent rather than the 2 per cent sought in the previous studies. They explicitly assume that the rate of saving is 7 per cent of income in 1960, and that the underdeveloped countries will save 25 per cent of the increments in their income in subsequent years. With these assumptions, two estimates of external capital requirements are offered, one involving a capital-output

[8] *Measures for the Economic Development of Under-developed Countries,* 1951.
[9] *International Trade,* Geneva, 1959, p. 50.

ratio of 3 and the other a capital-output ratio of 2.3, which is the figure employed in India's Second Five-Year Plan. At the higher capital-output ratio, external capital requirements are put at slightly less than $13 billion annually during the 1960's. At the lower capital-output ratio, the requirements start at an annual rate of $7.4 billion and taper off to $4.1 billion toward the end of the 1960's. Inasmuch as the authors of these estimates judge the levels of capital flows during 1956–1958 to have been between $5 and $6 billion annually, the first estimate would clearly require a substantial increase in assistance. In fact, these estimates may be on the conservative side, because the assumption that the underdeveloped countries could save 25 per cent of the increase in their incomes is probably on the high side if we assume the absence of repression.

The GATT study also provides a rather startling estimate of import requirements, which displays the heavy tasks which lie before both the less- and more-developed countries if faster growth rates are to be achieved. On the basis of the 5 per cent annual increase in imports sustained by the underdeveloped countries in the 1950's, if they merely maintain their 1950 growth rates in the future, their import requirements by the end of the 1960's will be on the order of $43 billion, compared to an estimated normal level of imports for 1960 of $27 billion. If the growth rate is accelerated to 3.2 per cent, the calculated level of imports at the end of this decade is as high as $55 billion. The job of providing foreign exchange to cover the possible $28 billion increase in imports will fall upon export earnings and external capital.

DOES CAPITAL INSURE GROWTH?

None of the estimates given so far really faces the question of whether or not the provision of the required amount of capital will in fact produce the desired rate of growth. By assuming a capital-output ratio of a given magnitude, these estimates assume that a certain amount of capital will in fact produce a certain amount of output. Yet for numerous reasons this is in doubt. Various factors limit the effectiveness of capital when injected into the less-developed areas.

Raymond Mikesell includes on his list of the factors in underdeveloped countries which restrict their capacity to absorb capital (1) the shortage of entrepreneurs who are willing and able to organize new ventures; (2) a lack of well-conceived projects—from an economic and engineering point of view—in the public sector; (3) a shortage of trained labor, supervisors, plant managers, and other complementary skills and experience; (4) the time required for the formulation of projects, for conducting engineering and economic surveys, and for the actual implementation of projects with the help of loan funds; (5) the difficulty of maintaining a proper balance in the pattern of investment and output in various sectors of the economy, so as to utilize effectively the capital provided to any one sector; (6) the existence of governmental policies that reduce business incentives and discourage foreign capital from entering the country; and (7) social conditions which inhibit labor mobility and productivity, domestic savings and investment, and changes in the structure of the economy.[10] Millikan and Rostow convey the same thought when they see a limit in the capacity to absorb capital because of the lack of "modern men and institutions."[11] This has caused them to cut down the additional amount of aid which might be absorbed from $5 billion, which at maximum was required to achieve a 2 per cent growth rate, to $2.5–$3 billion annually.[12]

In one of the most detailed estimates of possible aid levels, Rosenstein-Rodan explicitly allows for limits on absorptive capacity by estimating what he believes to be feasible rates of growth instead of assuming a particular growth rate which is believed to be desirable.[13] Under this procedure, it was necessary to establish a probable rate of growth for each country rather than for the less-developed world as a whole or particular regions. Using a capital-output ratio and estimated savings rate, it was possible for him to deduce the required level of external assistance if the feasible rate

[10] *Problems of Latin American Economic Development,* A study prepared at the request of the Committee on Foreign Relations, U.S. Senate, 1960, p. 60.
[11] *United States Foreign Policy,* p. 51.
[12] *Ibid.,* p. 83.
[13] Rosenstein-Rodan, *op. cit.*

of growth were to be achieved. With a few exceptions, the estimates were based on a capital-output ratio of 3, and it was assumed that the proportion of increased income that would be saved would generally be twice the average proportion of total income which was saved in 1960.

When Rosenstein-Rodan aggregated the external requirements of the individual countries, he found that the less-developed countries could absorb annual capital, including private foreign investment, of $5.7 billion during 1961–1971 and $4.7 billion for 1971–1976. He acknowledges the tentativeness of these estimates: "In view of the nature of the statistical information available the margin of error in our computations may be estimated at plus or minus 25%." His estimates are particularly sensitive to errors in measuring the current national output, the average savings ratio, and the capital-output ratio. For example, if the capital-output ratio were only 10 per cent lower than assumed, namely 2.7 instead of 3, and if the rate of growth consistent with absorptive capacity were 4 per cent, the external capital requirements would be lower by over 20 per cent.

RIDDLE OF PRODUCTIVITY

Even with Rosenstein-Rodan's method of feasible growth rates, several difficulties remain. The capital-output ratio is not clearly a stable parameter of economic development. For one thing, the ratio between an increase in capital and the subsequent rise in output depends significantly on the kinds of investments undertaken. In agriculture, the amount of capital required to produce additional output is usually quite small in contrast with overhead facilities such as power.

Furthermore, the relationship between capital and output is probably not the central determinant of the rate of economic growth, if there is a key determinant at all. Moses Abramovitz has noted that capital played a relatively unimportant role in raising output per head in the United States between the 1870's and 1953.[14] Over that period, the amount of capital and labor avail-

[14] *Resource and Output Trends in the United States Since 1870,* New York: National Bureau of Economic Research, 1956.

able to each person in the United States increased about 14 per cent; had the productivity of men and capital together remained constant, output per person would have grown only 14 per cent. He suggests that increased productivity, which would comprise skills, entrepreneurship, technology, and improved methods of social and economic organization, accounts for virtually all of the actual rise in output per head of 300 per cent. Odd Aukrust's analysis of the Norwegian data for the period 1900–1950 confirms this view. He found that a 1 per cent increase in the labor force raised national output by 0.75 per cent, a 1 per cent rise in capital raised output by 0.20 per cent, but a 1 per cent increase in the other factors which affect output—Abramovitz's productivity—raised output by 1.8 per cent. Clearly, there is much more to the process of accelerating economic development than the accumulation of what we normally call capital.

THE QUESTION OF LIMITS

It would seem from the discussions of Mikesell, Millikan and Rostow, Rosenstein-Rodan, and many other writers on economic development that there are limits to the amount of additional capital which can be effectively employed for development in the poorer nations. But for several reasons, any estimate suffers from exaggerated preciseness, not only because of the uncertain reliability of the data employed but from the very fuzziness of the concept of absorptive capacity.

Aid for Consumption. First, there is no way of knowing whether or not aid will be employed for economic development, i.e., for capital formation rather than consumption, and there is great danger in assuming that what is labeled as development assistance in fact serves economic growth. To take the other side of the coin, suppose that in order to reduce starvation the United States offers foodstuffs to a country suffering a drought. The motive is clearly to support consumption. In the absence of the foodstuffs provided under the aid programs, the foreign government, because of political sensitivity and compassion, might well cut back licenses on capital goods imports in order to free foreign exchange to buy imported food. But the provision of foodstuffs under the aid program would permit the foreign government to continue imports of capital goods; consequently, aid in the form of consumer goods would sustain economic development. Aid for consumption thus becomes development assistance because, in the absence of the aid, development would be slowed. By a reverse process development aid may become aid for consumption if the donor finances projects which would otherwise be undertaken by the foreign government and if the foreign government uses the released resources for non-development purposes.

It is not at all clear that external assistance *should* avoid the financing of increased consumption. If a country had no chance of making effective use of external aid for development, the humanitarian argument for aid still might support aid for consumption. But even where there is an opportunity for effective development assistance, we should remember that the process of capital formation generally increases consumer incomes in the short run by injecting added streams of spending into an economy; part of the increased incomes will seep into world markets in demand for imports of consumer goods. These imports require financing, and the funds might properly come out of the aid program instead of out of the resources of the recipient country, inasmuch as they derive from the capital formation induced by aid.

Aid donors may be forced to accept the risk that some of their aid may be employed for consumption. By limiting assistance to specific, visible investment projects, we run the risk that the most viable and quick-yielding investment opportunities will be starved for resources. In those countries with massive public-sector capital programs, the private domestic investor is often hard put to obtain foreign exchange for his purposes because the government has reserved so much for its own use. There are means by which foreign exchange, provided through aid, can be channeled to private domestic investors, e.g., through development banks; but these are rarely sufficient to meet the whole private-sector requirement. Consequently, the provision of foreign exchange by the purchase of local currency in the foreign exchange market with aid funds may be an essential method of providing aid to the private sector, although it will not be possible to trace the end use of the funds.

Aid to Remove Bottlenecks. There is something to be said for providing aid which is not "used" at all. Most of the poor countries impose controls on international payments and receipts. These provide protection to inefficient domestic industries, wasting the scarce resources of the poor countries; and, because these controls require administration and compliance, they divert large amounts of executive talent, both within governments and in private enterprises subject to the controls, from more productive tasks. To get rid of these controls, it is necessary that the underdeveloped countries have sufficient foreign exchange reserves to tide them over adverse shifts in their international payments and receipts. It is widely felt that reserves equal to six months' imports are essential for this, though any estimate is of course conjectural. If the GATT estimates of prospective imports by the underdeveloped countries, previously noted, are anywhere near the mark, and if the underdeveloped countries only maintain the present ratios of reserves to imports and thus continue their growth-denying exchange controls, the required accumulation of reserves is substantial, perhaps $6–$8 billion over the next ten years. The reserve accumulations necessary to permit removal of the controls are, of course, even larger. If the poor countries are obliged to accumulate those reserves out of their own export earnings, they will have to sacrifice imports of an equivalent amount, thereby retarding domestic consumption and investment. If the advanced countries were to provide funds for reserves on the condition that the less-developed nations remove their controls and take the steps necessary to sustain their removal, these sacrifices could be avoided; and their economies would receive a new stimulus for progress by being opened to the rigors of international competition. The funds would not be used for development projects; but, nonetheless, they would make an inordinate contribution to the recipient's growth.

One reason for the alleged limit to absorptive capacity lies in the absence of sufficient complementary facilities and faculties with which to employ added capital. Why not provide those complementary inputs along with the aid? For example, if the lack of entrepreneurial capacities is specified as a bottleneck, could we not employ more American personnel in developing investment opportunities and undertaking the necessary feasibility studies? Currently, a number of private American firms do precisely this for foreign governments or for aid agencies, and the advent of disarmament would clearly increase the number of people available for this kind of work. As one of the most experienced project analysts has written: ". . . it is not basically a shortage of capital which retards the rate of industrial development . . . the shortage of good, well-developed projects is in many cases the limiting factor on economic growth."[15] The author of this statement has drawn up over 100 projects, and he illustrates what can be done to provide entrepreneurial capacity through the cooperation of citizens of the advanced countries.

If the bottleneck is a shortage of technical or managerial skills, could we not employ personnel from the advanced countries to run and supervise operations in enterprises in the less-developed countries? The answer is obviously "yes" if we are willing to pay the high price for the services required; and since the question of price has to do with the supply function of aid, it does not bear on the possibility of absorbing aid. This procedure is employed in projects where lenders, such as the International Bank for Reconstruction and Development, require the borrower to arrange a management contract with some experienced firm because it doubts the capability of the local management. It has been employed in private foreign investment for years. In the nineteenth century, Englishmen ran some of the locomotives in Europe on railroads constructed by Englishmen with British capital. Many American firms abroad today employ nonlocal personnel in top administrative and technical positions; gradually, as the local people gain competence, they are moved into positions of higher authority and responsibility.

FLEXIBILITY OF LIMITS

Yet there remains a limit to what may be done along these lines. How many Americans will a proud, newly independent under-

[15] Murray Bryce, *Industrial Development,* New York: McGraw-Hill, 1960, p. x.

developed nation allow in its political and economic processes? How many Americans can take over key functions in poor nations without inducing foreign governments and citizens to assume that the advanced countries will do everything for them, so that they do not need to increase their own efforts? If development is essentially a do-it-yourself project, how can the backward nations achieve self-sustained growth? Obviously, there are some limits, but it is difficult to predict what they are. The degree of tolerance for outsiders depends upon a host of variables, from the state of general political relations with advanced countries to the qualities of the people sent abroad. And, of course, it depends upon the maturity of the people of the recipient nations. If many of the bottlenecks which appear to limit absorptive capacity could technically be met by foreign personnel, the limit to absorptive capacity is not economic but political, and the precision of the concept is lost.

Even the political limit is subject to manipulation. There is no reason to assume that we cannot train Americans to make better adjustments in non-Western cultures, improving their acceptability in underdeveloped countries. There is a growing awareness of the cultural differences, of the causes of that cultural shock which too often afflicts Americans working abroad for the first time. Further improvements in these areas will do much to increase the absorptive capacity of underdeveloped countries for personnel from the industrially advanced countries, and this would simultaneously increase their absorptive capacity for foreign capital. Furthermore, the absorptive capacity for outside government advisors will rise as governments expand because the number of foreign personnel will become less significant in the total.

The notion of a limit to absorptive capacity generally involves either explicitly or implicitly the idea that there is some minimum yield on projects below which investments will not be undertaken. For example, the Center for International Studies suggests as a standard of effective employment that of Turkey or Mexico rather than the United States.[16] But why Turkey or Mexico? Why not Bolivia? If one sets the standard at the United States level, the rationale is clear: The movement of funds from the United States

[16] Bryce, *op. cit.,* p. 52.

to any place which can use them less effectively would reduce world output because the resources would be shifted from higher-valued to lower-valued employments. But once the United States standard is cast aside, the rationale for shifting resources becomes political or humanitarian, not economic. The question of absorptive capacity becomes a question of how low a standard for effective employment—that is, yield—one is willing to accept.

LOANS OR GRANTS?

There is, of course, an economic limit to aid provided in the form of loans, which stems from the interest rate charged on those loans. Only projects (or, more broadly, development plans) which promise a yield in excess of the interest rate charged will obtain financing. But this is not a limit to absorptive capacity if the benefactors are willing to reduce interest rates or shift to grants. In fact, if we set the standard yield low enough, there is a strong technical argument for grants over loans. Suppose that the yield on capital in an underdeveloped country, after allowance for risk, is 7 per cent. In such circumstances, the following alternative aid offers provide the same present value of benefits to the underdeveloped country: (1) an annual grant of $1 for fifty years; (2) a lump sum grant of $13.80; (3) a loan, repayable at the end of fifty years, of $14.29 at no interest; and (4) a loan, repayable at the end of fifty years, of $100 at 6 per cent interest. If we assume that the yield on capital is higher in the donor nation, the present cost to the donor of the loan alternatives is higher than that of the grant alternatives. For example, if the yield on capital in the donor nation is 8 per cent, the grant alternatives give present costs of $12.23 and $13.80 respectively; the loan alternatives have present costs of $13.94 and $24.47 respectively. Under these circumstances it is cheaper to give money away than to lend it, and the recipient is equally well off as if it had received a loan because each of the alternatives has the same present value of benefits to the recipient.

PRESSURES TO "BUY AMERICAN"

If disarmament should come, it is likely that the reduction in our military expenditures overseas plus a possible recession at home will ease any balance-of-payments problem we may be suffering at the time. As a result, there will no longer be a balance-of-payments excuse for requiring United States aid monies to be expended chiefly for American goods.

But the balance-of-payments excuse may be replaced by severe pressure to limit procurement to United States goods in order to ease the transition to full employment without arms. There are important dangers in such policies, both for us and for the underdeveloped countries. If the aid program, which is already studded with special procurement regulations to help particular domestic groups, becomes even more an instrument for domestic relief, we will find ourselves forcing upon the rest of the world specific goods it would not prefer from free choice. Because the domestic producer needs the support of aid expenditures, he is not competitive. Consequently, our aid dollars do not go as far in purchasing real goods and services as they might. In 1955, for example, a requirement that locomotives and rail cars for India be procured in the United States resulted in India getting 100 locomotives and 5,430 rail cars instead of 100 locomotives and 11,220 cars, and cost the United States government an additional $8.5 million.[17]

If domestic interests succeed in forcing procurement in the United States on an expanded scale during the transition period, and if they can induce the government to sustain these procurement policies—and none of those put into effect to date has been relaxed—a permanent burden is placed either on us, because we must provide more dollars to cover the higher costs of buying aid commodities in the United States, or on the underdeveloped countries, because they get less real benefit from each dollar provided.

DIMENSIONS OF DEVELOPMENT

The term "economic" in "economic development" is grossly misleading. There is growing recognition that the growth and development of a nation is a process of change which cuts across all aspects of its society and culture. The modernization of a country

[17] *The United States Economy and the Mutual Security Program,* Department of State, April 1959, pp. 27 f.

involves shifts in population between rural and urban areas, changes in family and clan relationships, revisions in religious beliefs and practices, and new concepts of political morality and government functions. To be sure, "purely" economic factors, such as the level of capital and savings, have much to do with the process of economic growth, but they are apt to be impotent without cultural change.

If the process of growth involves cultural change, it implies shifts in societies which may create uncertainties and stresses, and these may either favor or hinder further progress. This in turn implies that the personnel involved in foreign aid programs should combine their technical competence with knowledge of the social science disciplines, for only if they are aware of the interaction between the technical changes which they propose to introduce and the total cultural complex can they hope to discern the ultimate effects of their efforts on development. This will require a revolutionary approach in the training of foreign aid officials and will call for further innovations in university curriculums along lines already taking place at some institutions.

Action to meet this requirement presupposes a knowledge of the interaction of culture and economic development which can be transmitted to foreign aid officials in a training program. We are, in fact, far short of knowing enough.

Awareness of cultural differences is not enough. It alone acts as a warning against action along Western lines, but it may stultify action altogether if the foreign aid personnel freeze in fear that their projects will do more harm than good. Hence, we must know how to stimulate useful change—how to use cultural differences to stimulate growth. Some of the things we have to learn are fairly simple —how close should one stand to a foreign person in talking with him? Other things are more complex. We have to know enough to avoid constructing villages which the people tear down to move to another location. We have to learn enough to predict when the construction of two-room houses will lead to the failure of large projects because the polygamous society for which the houses are to be built requires separate housing for each wife.

It is a lamentable fact that, until very recently, the United States government spent almost no funds for research on the process of change in the underdeveloped world. A private enterprise faced with problems as novel and broad as those faced by economic development agencies would be considered negligent if it did not set aside 5 to 10 per cent of its revenues for research.

A corollary of the foregoing is that wherever possible the United States government should shift from the project approach to general balance-of-payments support in providing economic development assistance. The project approach provides an excuse for placing United States personnel "in the bush," where they may stimulate change and protect aid investments, but where neither is absolutely necessary, as in countries where the process of development has a head-start, the scarce personnel capable of instituting modernization should be diverted to slacker "climes" to do their job of initiating basic changes.

NEED FOR HISTORICAL RESEARCH

Many industrial projects are presently not feasible in the underdeveloped countries because of the smallness of their markets. For example, a shoe factory in Puerto Rico at one time made no sense economically because, while there was a large demand for shoes, the demand was so diversified in size, shape, and style that the production runs were uneconomically small.

This problem can be met in part by transferring from the advanced countries obsolete technologies which were economic when their own markets were smaller. To some extent these techniques can be found in the old technical sources; and, conceivably, some of the more advanced of the underdeveloped countries may fruitfully employ technologies which are just going out of use in certain areas here. Yet, for the most part, obsolete techniques are also forgotten techniques. The engineers have brushed them aside long ago, and there are few courses in the history of engineering analogous to the courses in the history of each social science to remind us of former procedures. Hence, we must set about renewing old knowledge for transfer abroad.

This suggestion suffers one major defect: The developing countries often want the most moden techniques as a matter of prestige.

Hence, we must also go in the opposite direction to develop new technologies specifically for the cultural, physical, and economic circumstances of the less-developed countries. In view of the wide cultural differences, we cannot really expect that the technologies of the advanced countries are the most satisfactory and efficient for employment in the poorer nations. Furthermore, in the advanced countries, technologies are a set of interrelated procedures, processes, and ideas, each of which would have little value in isolation. Unless the whole complex of interdependent technologies can be transferred, which is out of the question, the isolated units we provide will require adaptation.

MILITARY CONTRIBUTIONS TO DEVELOPMENT

Finally we must not overlook the possibilities for economic development afforded by the existence of military establishments in the underdeveloped countries. Where governments are weak, corrupt, or inefficient, the military may constitute the only truly organized and disciplined unit of the government which can respond, if it will, to the need for economic development. Even in the event of general disarmament, we may anticipate that the less-developed countries would maintain some military forces, under one name or another, for reasons of internal security. Where United States military assistance has produced extensive and close contact between American military personnel and the military personnel of underdeveloped countries, a ready-made channel exists for foreign assistance to economic growth. In the last decade, the United States armed services have trained, in formal programs, some 160,000 people in underdeveloped areas.

Military units of foreign governments can and do carry on important efforts in the social and economic overhead sphere. In the Philippines, over a decade ago, the military played a decisive role in defeating the Communist Huks through purely civilian activities, including the representation of farmers in courts and the provision of a wide range of public services and facilities. In Ecuador, Guatemala, Colombia, Honduras, Peru, and elsewhere, local military units have carried on significant public works of only civilian application.

Military service provides an opportunity for training in skills useful both to military and civilian purposes, e.g., literacy, communications, finance, maintenance of electric and automotive equipment, etc. Land-clearing and road-building in areas where civilians will not penetrate because of health and other hazards can be undertaken by military units. Those units with land- or aerial-spraying devices can participate in insect, rodent, and disease control programs, some of which are fundamental to economic progress in agricultural areas. Engineering units can support construction activities, including irrigation, safe water supplies, roads, bridges, railroads, waterways, wharves, harbors, and various public buildings; all military units can provide troop labor for these efforts. Signal units can assist in the installation, operation, and maintenance of telephone, telegraph, and radio systems. Medical units can help in public health measures. Air force units can perform aerial mapping and assist in geological surveys.

There are approximately 8,000 officers and men assigned to United States military advisory groups or missions in some forty-six countries; while the country distribution is secret, not an insignificant proportion of them are in the less-developed lands. A check of the Marine Corps personnel data shows that over 5 per cent of the officers have professed or tested knowledge of at least one language spoken in some underdeveloped area. Thus, American military personnel provide a reservoir of persons with experience abroad. Those who have been close enough to non-Western cultures to have had their cultural shock and gotten over it could become valuable assets to international economic development abroad. But these people remain only a reservoir. How they may be effectively employed should be part of the larger effort in research, mentioned earlier, on the process of change in the underdeveloped world.

PART V

Conclusion

15

Economic Adjustments to Disarmament

Emile Benoit*

The present chapter will deal with the measures of public policy required to achieve prompt and efficient redeployment and reutilization of resources released by a future disarmament agreement. The discussion will deal primarily with the United States. The implications for other nations and for their economic interrelations are to be considered in another book.[1] The chapter will present a broad strategy of economic adjustment to disarmament, organized as follows: (1) a discussion of the relative magnitude of the adjustment problem implied by the READ model, in relation to the defense cutbacks after 1945 and after 1953; (2) an econometric analysis of the effects of alternative fiscal adjustment policies, and the selection of an optimum solution; (3) an examination of how the "propensity to reduce the national debt" may complicate the problem; (4) a consideration of the uses and limitations of monetary policies in defense readjustment; (5) a review

* The author is indebted to W. Locke Anderson for helpful criticisms of an earlier draft.

[1] Pursuant to research now being conducted under a grant from the Ford Foundation. However, a summary of certain data on defense burdens of most of the countries of the world is presented in the Appendix, at the end of this chapter.

of structural problems and policies; and (6) a proposal for a new forward strategy to deal simultaneously with the obstacles to the adoption of an optimum fiscal policy, and with certain key structural problems.

DEFENSE CUTS AFTER 1945 AND 1953

As indicated in Chapter 2, certain types of arms control programs, such as arms stabilization or arms limitation agreements, might result in no decrease, or even an increase, in defense budgets. However, general and complete disarmament would certainly reduce security expenditures, even after liberal allowances are made for a United States contribution to the costs of inspection and peace enforcement by an international disarmament organization.

In the READ model, shown in Chapter 2, net reductions in United States security expenditures, after all offsets, are $32 billion (in 1960 dollars) or about 5 per cent of the probable gross national product at the start of disarmament. This is about the same relative size as the $21 billion reduction (again 1960 prices) in defense expenditures between the second quarter of 1953 and the third quarter of 1960. This was also 5 per cent of the GNP at the beginning of the cutback. The post-Korean cutback occurred (with some ups and downs) over a seven-year period, and was heavily concentrated in the first year, while the disarmament process envisaged in our model would extend over twelve years, and would be less precipitous. Both these cases involve cutbacks only about one-eighth as severe as the defense cuts between 1944 and 1947, which came to 41 per cent of initial GNP. While these comparisons are reassuring, it must be recognized that the economic environment has changed considerably since 1945, and even since 1953; our economy might not adjust as easily or as automatically to deflationary stimuli as it did before.

In contrast to the present, inflationary pressure was extreme in 1945–1947. However, the usual explanation, in terms of "wartime shortages" and "backlogs of demand" as the source of the excess demand, may be misleading. In fact, real consumer expenditure during 1941–1945 averaged 10 per cent higher than in 1940, without allowance for the vast supplies of consumer-type goods produced for the armed forces. Even in the matter of consumer durables, the shortages were only relative: real purchases of consumer durables during the war years averaged only a quarter below the prewar level; and taking the whole period, 1941 to 1948 averaged out at the 1940 level. Since a fifth of the prewar labor force went into the armed services, it seems that even during the war, the purchase of consumer durables per civilian adult consumer, or even per household, could not have declined significantly, and the stock of consumer goods must have considerably increased.

The primary source of excess demand, I believe, was the vast increase in purchasing power arising from the $182 billion of federal deficit financing (on income and product account) during the war years, and the resulting accumulation of $157 billion of financial savings of individuals—about $136 billion more than would have occurred if the 1939–1940 volume of savings had continued. In the first three years after the war, purchasing power was further stimulated by tax refunds, transfer payments, and especially by easy credit: Bank loans and mortgage debt rose by about 60 per cent, and consumer debt rose two and a half times. As a result there was a rapid increase in primary liquidity in the economy, which was later dissipated. The money supply, in the sense of cash and demand deposits, which was 41 per cent of GNP in 1940, rose to 47 per cent of GNP in 1945, but fell to 43 per cent of GNP in 1948, 35 per cent of GNP in 1953, and 28 per cent of GNP in 1960.

The marked rise in consumer debt as a percentage of disposable personal income may also have lowered the resiliency of the economy. This ratio has risen from 3.9 per cent in 1945, to 12.4 per cent in 1953, and to 15.6 per cent in 1961. We have no evidence of any absolute and permanent ceiling on consumer willingness to borrow, but there does appear to be less likelihood of as rapid a rate of expansion of credit-financed purchases as formerly. And, of course, the higher levels of unemployment and unused industrial capacity render the economy more vulnerable to deflationary influences than it used to be.

It is possible, of course, that by the time disarmament occurs, the economic situation may be more like that of 1945. This could happen if accentuation of international tensions forced a rapid further build-up of United States defenses, combining large antimissile defenses, big publicly financed civil defense programs, and the enlargement of conventional capacity for limited warfare. A disarmament, at the end of an all-out arms race, in which the United States had demonstrated a decisive willingness and capacity to outbuild its opponents in defense forces and weapons, is not an impossibility. In such a case, the cutbacks might occur in a situation with much of the inflationary pressures that existed in 1945. On the other hand, in such a case the cutbacks would have to be larger than those shown in the READ model, which allows for only a moderate defense build-up in the years prior to disarmament.

Unless the substantial slack in the economy is eliminated, either by an intensification of the arms race, or by the adoption of more dynamic fiscal policies, we face a difficult unemployment situation in the sixties, with a rapid growth of the labor force, and accelerated labor displacement from automation. We would then arrive at disarmament in the mid-sixties under economic conditions more nearly resembling those of 1962, than those of 1945, or even 1953.

Moreover, would even as successful an adjustment to defense cuts as was achieved after the Korean War be satisfactory in connection with a future disarmament? The disturbing aspect of the economic adjustment to the post-Korean defense cuts was the industrial slowdown. Industrial output, which had risen 6.0 per cent per year from 1951 to 1953, rose only 2.6 per cent a year from 1953 to 1961. The unemployment rate rose from 3.0 per cent to a post-Korean War average of 5.4 per cent.

I am not attributing the post-1953 industrial slowdown to the arms cut itself, but to a defective adjustment to the arms cut: to the failure to provide adequate offsets. Between the second quarter of 1953 and the last quarter of 1954, defense expenditures dropped $12.1 billion (annual rates at current prices). Instead of increasing nondefense expenditure programs as an offset, these were also cut back by *one-third* in three years. Federal expenditures (on income and product account) from 1954 to 1957 inclusive, averaged $5.2 billion annually below the 1953 level. The tax cut of 1954 helped, but was far too small to provide a sufficient offset. Federal revenues from 1954 to 1957 (on income and product account) averaged $3.6 billion *above* the 1953 level. With a decline in expenditures and a rise in revenues, there was a total federal budget surplus (on income and product account) of *$11.5 billion* in 1955, 1956, and 1957. This amount of purchasing power was taken by the federal government from private spenders (persons and businesses) and not returned to them via government purchases or other payments. The net effect was, of course, sharply deflationary.

In consequence, there was, despite the record rate of real private investment in new plant and equipment in 1956 and 1957, a quick leveling off in industrial production. The index, in 1956 averaged slightly below the December 1955 level; and for the period 1956–1958, averaged still lower. In effect, three years of industrial growth were wasted—a loss that can never be made good. And the level of final demand, which would have justified the high levels of private investment from 1955 to 1957, was not allowed to materialize. Investor confidence was damaged, and real investment in producers' durable equipment from 1958–1961 dropped 16 per cent below the 1956 level.

The $11.5 billion budget surplus was large enough to explain a good part of the slowdown, on almost any reasonable assumption as to its multiplier effects. The average GNP in the 1956–1958 period fell nearly $29 billion short of what it would have been had a 4.5 per cent growth rate been sustained.[2]

A new industrial slowdown in conjunction with disarmament in the sixties and seventies could be dangerous both to internal morale and to external prestige, in an era of "competitive coexistence," emphasizing economic rather than military rivalry.[3]

The adjustment problem in its essentials, as we view it, falls into

---

[2] The 4.5 per cent is the average rate of growth in real GNP from 1947 to 1953, and is the growth rate picked as feasible in our economy, without exceptional exertions or emergency controls, by Otto Eckstein and others of the staff of the Joint Economic Committee in the well-known report on *Employment, Growth and Price Levels,* Joint Economic Committee December 24, 1959, p. xxvi. I would be inclined to put the figure slightly higher, since I would define full employment at 3 per cent rather than 4 per cent unemployment (see my, "On the Meaning of Full Employment," *Review of Economic and Statistics,* May 1948). The JEC use of the 4 per cent figure is explained by J. Knowles in the report *loc. cit.,* p. 98. Maintaining a lower unemployment figure would, I believe, stimulate upgrading, automation, and more efficient labor utilization generally.

[3] See my "Competitive Coexistence: Can We Win?" *Antioch Review,* Summer 1956.

two major segments. First is the problem of maintaining adequate overall demand for the new goods and services into the production of which the defense resources will be re-channelled. This is essentially, in our type of economy, the domain of fiscal and monetary policies. Second, we have the structural problem of overcoming various obstacles to a prompt and smooth shift of the displaced resources into the new uses.

FISCAL POLICIES FOR DISARMAMENT ADJUSTMENT

The econometric model used for analysis of fiscal impacts is that developed by Daniel Suits and presented in Chapter 6. Applying his multipliers (as shown in Table 1 of his chapter) to our projected $32 billion of defense cutback, we have traced out the effects of seven different fiscal adjustment policies that might be adopted. I believe these alternatives offer reasonably good examples of the chief types of responses that might be considered. There are certain qualifications that should be borne in mind when using these multipliers. First, they neglect the adverse "announcement effects" of publication of the disarmament program on anticipations. Second, they greatly understate the adverse effects on investment of declines in income when actually experienced. The Suits multipliers are much lower than those used by other econometric models. Considerably larger multipliers can be derived from models whose parameters are well within the errors of measurement of the Suits model. The estimated declines in income and employment should therefore be viewed as conservative and minimal: It is possible that the adverse effects could be up to twice as bad as those estimated on the basis of the Suits multipliers. On the other hand, the Suits model makes no allowance for the expansionary effects of using a budget surplus to reduce national debt—implicitly handling the surplus as if it were an increase in Treasury cash or deposits. We have therefore, included alternative and lower estimates of declines in income and employment in cases where there are budget surpluses, in order to allow for this expansionary effect. Some further offset might also be provided by additional expansionist monetary measures, though, as indicated in the next section, these seem

TABLE 1 – IMPACT OF ALTERNATIVE FISCAL PROGRAMS IN AN ADJUSTMENT TO A $32 BILLION DEFENSE CUT

(*Billions of dollars*)

CHARACTER OF ADJUSTMENT		IMPACT		
TYPE OF ADJUSTMENT POLICY	SPECIFIC MEASURES INVOLVED	Changes in GNP	EMPLOYMENT (*millions*)	BUDGET SURPLUS OR DEFICIT (−)[a]
1. Laissez-faire	No offsets	$−48.0[b] −37.0[c]	−5.3[b] −4.1[c]	$+19.8
2. Balanced budget with tax cut	Tax cut $32.0[d]	−12.3[b]	−2.9[b]	0
3. Balanced budget with partial tax cut and new government programs	Tax cut $22.0[d] New government programs $10.0	− 8.4[b]	−2.0[b]	0
4. Three-way split	Tax cut $11.0[d] New government programs $11.0 Debt retirement $10.0[d]	−19.2[b] −14.8[c]	−2.6[b] −2.0[c]	+ 6.2
5. Production stabilization tax cut	Tax cut $43.0[d]	0	−2.0	− 6.8
6. Employment stabilization tax cut	Tax cut $69.3[d]	+29.6	0	−23.3
7. Balanced stabilization offsets	Tax cut $18.5[d] New government programs $18.5	+ 0.4	−0.8	− 3.1

SOURCE: Tables 1 and 2, Chapter 8.

NOTE: Defense cut based on READ disarmament model—consisting of $21.6 billion in defense purchases from the private sector, and $10.4 billion cut in expenditures in defense personnel. Tax cuts assumed to be across-the-board on personal income tax.

[a] *ex post* based on minimum impact estimate.

[b] Minimum estimate. Maximum estimate is up to double this figure.

[c] Minimum estimate after correction for the monetary expansion resulting from use of the surplus to reduce the national debt (as explained on page 282).

[d] *ex ante*.

likely to be of secondary importance. In any case, Table 1 is concerned primarily with *fiscal* offsets.

As there indicated, the first type of policy (or absence of policy) which would provide *no* offsets to the defense cuts would produce minimum declines of $37 billion in GNP and 2 million in employment—even after allowance for the stimulating effects of substantial reduction in the national debt. With larger multipliers, which are well within the range of possibility, the declines might be up to twice these figures. Moreover, since 46 per cent of the net defense cuts would occur in the first three years, and since the disarmament announcement effects might crowd into this period a part of the impact of cutbacks scheduled to occur later, it is possible that in the absence of offsets, disarmament could provoke declines in GNP of $15 to $20 billion a year for the first few years. This would clearly involve a serious depression, though not of the 1929–1932 magnitude. It is hard to believe we would be so foolish as to let this happen.

A more likely danger is that we would seek at least a balanced budget. As is indicated in Table 1, policies 2 and 3, which achieve a balanced budget by means either of full tax cuts, or of partial tax cuts supplemented by new government spending programs, would lead to minimal contractions of $8 to $12 billion in GNP and 2 to 3 million in employment—with up to twice these estimates a possibility. While such results would not constitute a depression, they would imply a recession or a significant interruption in economic growth.

Even worse results would flow from a formula, likely to be very popular politically, by which the "savings" from defense cutbacks would be split evenly three ways: among tax cuts, new government programs, and the creation of a budget surplus for reduction of the national debt. This would be formula 4 in Table 1, and the effects, as shown, would be a $15 to $30 billion decline in GNP and a 2 to 4 million rise in unemployment—which would rank, I suppose, as a fairly serious recession or a mild depression.

Policies 5 and 6, aiming to stabilize the economy solely by means of tax cuts, are revealed by Table 1 to be rather impractical. The former would stabilize GNP but still permit a decline of 2 to 4 million in employment. The latter would require tax cuts and deficits so large (of approximately $70 billion and $23 billion, respectively) as probably to be outside the boundaries of serious political discussion.[4]

It is the last alternative in Table I, which I have called the "Balanced Stabilization Offsets Program," which appears to me as offering the preferred solution. This is a program which provides tax cuts about equal in size to the new government expenditure programs, the total of the two being somewhat (about one-seventh) in excess of the $32 billion defense cutback they are designed to offset. Such a program prevents any significant decline either in production or in employment. It shares the benefits of the cutback equally between the taxpayers and the community desiring expanded welfare programs, and it involves a budget deficit which does not seem large by the standards of recent experience and current planning.[5] The obstacles to the adoption of such a policy will be discussed later.

THE PROPENSITY TO REDUCE THE NATIONAL DEBT
AND MONETARY POLICY

The crucial factor in how well we handle disarmament impacts may very well be what I have elsewhere called the "propensity to reduce the national debt out of defense savings."[6] A public opinion survey

---

[4] It would also most probably give rise to severe sectoral inflation, since it would produce a sharp rise in GNP with no rise in employment.

[5] Such a program would have the additional advantage over programs envisaging a shift of all released defense resources to private use in that it would pose a less severe structural problem. On the basis of the input-output tables shown in Chapter 5 it appears that a shift of $32 billion of defense expenditures into business investment and personal consumption (in their 1961 proportions) would leave over 1.25 million workers without jobs because of the lower labor requirements in the sectors of expanding demand. On the other hand, under a balanced offsets program with half of the defense cuts shifted to new government programs, this sort of difficulty would be minimized because of the relatively high labor absorption capacities of the nondefense government programs.

[6] See "The Propensity to Reduce the National Debt Out of Defense Savings," Proceedings of the American Economic Association, *American Economic Review Supplement,* March 1961.

kindly undertaken for READ by George Katona[7] disclosed a strong public sentiment favoring use of a "savings" from defense cuts to reduce the national debt, with 20 per cent of a general sample favoring it as the *best* use of such savings, and another 15 per cent naming it as their second choice. One might surmise that a sampling of newspaper publishers or Congressmen would find even higher percentages favoring this use of defense savings. Yet, from the point of view of the economist, such an approach may present serious dangers.

The most immediate danger is that it encourages delay in adopting offsets to the defense cuts, since it appears "conservative" to see how much of a budget surplus will actually materialize before deciding how to distribute it. However, the failure to adopt tax cuts or new nondefense expenditure programs immediately may itself have severely restrictive effects. This is because the economy responds sharply not only to actual cuts in defense expenditures, but to *cuts in defense orders*. Thus, for example, in 1953 there was a decline of 4.3 per cent in industrial production between the second and fourth quarters, although the rate of defense expenditures had declined by only a trivial $0.5 billion. What had declined sharply was defense obligations for hard goods, which had dropped $2.8 billion within six months, thereby stimulating a $9.7 billion drop in new orders received by the durable goods industries.

As a result of this sensitivity of the economy to defense plans, as well as to actual defense expenditures, any "wait-and-see" philosophy in disarmament adjustment courts considerable danger of provoking an unnecessary recession before a response is prepared. (Ironically, this may extinguish much of the anticipated surplus!) The difficulties of achieving a sufficiently prompt response are compounded by the cumbersome and slow-moving machinery of Congressional decision-making—emphasizing, as it necessarily does, the long-term advantages and disadvantages of particular changes in taxes and expenditures and the compromising of the numerous special and sectional interests that may be affected.

Aside from the important matter of timing, a policy of utilizing

---

[7] Thanks are again extended to Professor Katona and the Survey Research Center at the University of Michigan for assistance in this very important matter.

defense savings to reduce the national debt does involve positive attempts to attain a budget surplus by holding back on offsets, whether in the form of federal nondefense expenditures or of tax cuts. Insofar as this aim is successful, and a budget surplus is attained and used for debt reduction, what are the effects?

Budget surpluses are widely viewed as an element in national saving, and their use for debt retirement as a stimulus to private investment. To what extent does this mitigate the deflationary impact ascribed to them in our model? In our analysis we wish to make a sharp distinction between *running* a budget surplus on the one hand, and *using* the surplus to retire debt on the other. A budget surplus per se, with an accumulation of cash in the Treasury or of government deposits in the bank, is, at that stage, unquestionably deflationary: The government, thereby, takes more out of the private income stream in taxes than it puts back by its own purchases and other payments.

The process involves a transfer of privately-owned cash or deposits to government accounts, with an increase in Treasury cash holdings, or in government deposits in member banks, or in Federal Reserve banks. Since private cash or deposits, are part of the money supply, but Treasury cash holdings and United States government deposits are not, the result of the process is to reduce the money supply. However, the *use* of the surplus or accumulated Treasury cash or government deposits—to repurchase and retire government securities—may have partially offsetting effects.

It is unnecessary to repeat the thorough, original, and definitive discussion of the mechanics and effects of debt reduction provided by Warren Smith in Chapter 8. Some of the main conclusions seem to be: (1) Debt redemption—except for Federal Reserve-held debt—restores the money supply (which had been depleted by the surplus) but reduces the supply of securities.[8] (2) It has many minor effects, but its chief effects are to drive up the price of bonds

---

[8] This restoration of the money supply (and of bank reserves) will, however, occur and endure only if the banks wish to remain "loaned-up," and if there is sufficient will to borrow on the part of the public. Either or both of these prerequisites may be lacking in the event of a recession (such as might be created by budget surpluses), and it is this possibility that makes monetary expansion a somewhat unreliable counter-deflationary instrument.

and to lower interest rates. (3) This would fully offset the deflationary impact of the initial destruction of income by the running of the surplus only if investment were much affected by a decline in interest rates, which does not appear to be the case. (4) On a rough estimate, the stimulus exerted by lower interest rates and monetary ease, when the national debt is reduced, may offset 23 per cent of the deflationary impact of the cutback in defense expenditure. (5) To offset the remainder of the deflationary impact would, on a similarly rough estimate, require a rise in the money supply 2.34 times as large as the defense cuts—which could be produced by open market purchases of .351 the size of the defense cuts, and/or by reduction in the rediscount rate or reserve requirement.

Even so, Smith admits these estimates may give an unduly favorable impression of the capabilities of monetary policy. I am possibly even more skeptical than Smith on this point, and consider the capacity of an expansionist monetary policy to offset the effects of severe deflationary fiscal measures is not yet proven.

The 1945–1948 adjustment, while aided by liberal bank credit, was sustained by the working out of the inflationary potential contributed by wartime deficit financing, and did not offer a test of what monetary policy could do in a basically deflationary context.

The post-1953 adjustment offered a sterner test, which was either by-passed or failed. As previously indicated, fiscal policy was primarily deflationary in this period, with an $11.5 billion budget surplus from 1955 to 1957. Monetary policy part of the time added to the deflationary pressure and part of the time opposed it, but not very successfully.

While there was a decline in reserve requirements, and in 1954 and 1955 a temporary decline in the rediscount rate, over the whole period from mid-1953 to the latter part of 1958, the Federal Reserve Banks increased their holdings of government securities by only $2 billion, and the money supply was expanded by only $16.2 billion—far less than would have been required, on Professor Smith's "monetary trade-off" formula, to offset the restrictive impact of the fiscal policies adopted. As a result there was a protracted interruption of industrial growth after the end of 1955 —to which we have already referred.

Since 1958, heavy reliance on monetary expansion has been precluded, in any case, by balance-of-payments difficulties. As is pointed out by E. M. Bernstein, recorded and unrecorded outflows of short-term funds accounted for $4.8 billion of the balance-of-payments deficits of 1960 and 1961,[9] that is to say, for three-quarters of the total deficit. He estimates that a reduction in short-term interest rates, consequent upon a substantial increase in bank reserves, could readily lead to a further capital outflow of $2 billion. On the other hand, a budget deficit of $6 billion would, he believes, increase our outpayments by only about $200 million for additional imports. Deficit financing, rather than monetary ease, is therefore, in his opinion, the course which a nation like ours, with inadequate growth but balance-of-payments difficulties, ought to pursue. This also appears to be the burden of the message on this subject in the *Thirty-Second Annual Report of the Bank for International Settlements.*[10]

Would disarmament itself sufficiently improve our balance of payments so that full reliance could again be placed on monetary policy? It now seems that disarmament will not so dramatically improve our balance-of-payments position as had been widely assumed—particularly in the early stages when adjustment policies will be most needed. This is because: (1) We will be vigorously cutting back our overseas military forces, expenses, and foreign procurement *before* disarmament begins, leaving less of a decline to occur under disarmament; and (2) the remaining overseas foreign bases, and overseas military expenditure, and defense-support aid will not be eliminated in the early stages of disarmament,[11] whereas our now rapidly expanding commercial exports of armaments will end immediately. (See Chapter 13.)

We conclude that a policy of monetary expansion has not yet shown sufficient potency, nor is it likely to be applied with suf-

---

[9] E. M. Bernstein, "Two Basic Problems of the U.S. Economy," *Quarterly Review and Investment Survey,* New York: Model, Roland and Stone, First Quarter 1962.

[10] June 1962, pp. 20–24.

[11] In the READ model, overseas bases would be *denuclearized* early, but retained to deter limited war until an IDO police force was ready to take over this function.

ficient vigor, to be relied upon to offset the deflationary impact of fiscal adjustment policies (such as 1 and 4 in Table 1) that involve substantial budget surpluses.

Could monetary policy, nevertheless, render helpful assistance in less difficult situations? Certainly it could. The true strength of monetary policy lies in its flexibility, the speed of its application, and its relative freedom from political constraints. It can, therefore, make a major contribution by providing minor and frequent adjustments required to offset temporary excesses or deficiencies of demand arising from inevitable mistakes and misjudgments in the application of fiscal policies, or from the relatively slow-moving and ponderous character of fiscal measures.[12]

Another important function for monetary policy during disarmament is to make sure that any deflationary impact arising from the *financing* of a budget deficit is offset by monetary expansion. Thus, the expansionary effect of the $3.1 billion deficit involved in our example of a balanced-offsets fiscal policy might be substantially diminished if the Treasury merely sold additional bonds to the public or to the commercial banks, since such sales would reduce bank reserves and the money supply. This offsetting monetary effect could and should, itself, be nullified by Federal Reserve System open-market purchases of government securities, or by a lowering of reserve requirements or rediscount rates. Such action should be viewed not as an independent monetary initiative, but as the implementation of the monetary side of the conditions required to make an expansionary fiscal policy fully effective.

To undertake these balancing functions in a period of disarmament adjustment, however, two conditions would have to be met: (1) Fiscal policy would have to provide adequate offsets for any major deflationary impact, leaving monetary policy with only a moderate field for stimulative action; and (2) the level of demand created by fiscal measures would have to be high enough so that even in periods of relative monetary ease, interest rates would be

---

12 Monetary policy would undoubtedly continue to enjoy this advantage in flexibility even if, as would certainly be desirable if not positively necessary, fiscal policy were also made more flexible by incorporating some formula, based on administrative flexibility in its application, e.g., along the lines of the "income tax holidays" suggested below.

well up to, or ahead of, the rates prevalent in other industrial countries, thereby safeguarding our balance-of-payments situation. Obviously, such a policy requires the abolition of both the national-debt ceiling, and of the interest-rate ceiling on government securities, which hamper the forthright use of fiscal and of monetary policies respectively.

STRUCTURAL ADJUSTMENTS

Our economy is remarkably capable of overcoming structural obstacles in the presence of adequate over-all demand. This was well demonstrated, both during World War II and in the period immediately after it, when enormous changes in labor force, in industrial and skill patterns, and even in regional distribution of population occurred with startling rapidity and extraordinarily little friction and hardship. With order books bulging, American manufacturers showed great willingness, ingenuity, and competence in expanding production, entering upon new types of production, hiring new, unskilled, and even migrant workers, breaking down traditional job skills into simpler elements, and providing on-the-job training and upgrading. We heard no complaints at that time about automation and deficiencies in advanced skills as sources of structural stagnation; demand was high enough to break down structural barriers to full utilization of labor and capital.

Such conditions of inflated demand seem unlikely to recur, however, in the absence of war; and in the meantime, there has been a considerable increase in the structural immobility of the factors employed in the defense activity. Whereas defense production in World War II, and even in the Korean War, was not too different from production for civilian end-uses, defense production has subsequently become much more highly specialized and differentiated. A shift of released resources from defense to conventional non-defense uses, would today be more difficult and involve more waste of valuable capabilities than in the past. It is also likely that it would encounter stronger resistances than in the past, because the persons involved are more highly skilled, more well-to-do, and more articulate, and because the whole defense effort no longer has the temporary makeshift character that it used to have, but is solidly entrenched as an enduring component of our normal peacetime economy. It would be less likely, therefore, to accept a solution by which its source of support were cut off with no reasonably satisfactory alternative opportunities provided.

While structural problems, therefore, possess an independent importance, they are, nevertheless, of clearly subordinate significance when compared to the fundamental problem of maintaining adequate demand. If demand remains slack, there is little point in worrying about structural problems. What is the advantage in turning a discharged Marine sergeant into an unemployed laboratory assistant—or even into an employed laboratory assistant, if this is attained only by keeping an existing laboratory assistant out of a job? Does it really help to transfer an unemployed airplane worker from Wichita to Chicago, thereby bringing the average unemployment rates of the two cities closer together, if both those cities have unemployment well above the acceptable minimum?

Clearly, if at the time disarmament began, we still had a national unemployment rate of 5.5 per cent, and with 8 per cent of total labor force time being lost as a result of unemployment or involuntary part-time employment, we could expect to see a bitter struggle of displaced defense personnel and munitions workers to find new jobs. Under these conditions, both the will and the resources would be lacking to do a good job on structural problems. From the point of view of social justice, the man who has been a victim of involuntary unemployment for several years would appear to have at least as good a claim for extended unemployment benefits, and retraining and relocation assistance, as the man who until yesterday was working at excellent wages in a defense plant. No retraining or relocation program could change the essential conditions enough to make a real dent on the problem. Under these conditions, structural adjustment programs would be felt to be what they really were, and what they are today—essentially palliatives, designed to give hope and to signify society's concern, but without the capability of curing the real evil.

It is only under conditions of substantially full employment and full utilization of capacity that policy on structural adaptation suddenly assumes importance. For, under these conditions, a reduction in structural immobility may actually increase the use of resources; and any reduction in the difficulty of making transitions does not merely benefit one individual or firm, or community, in favor of another, but reduces the delays and costs of the changeovers, and makes possible a more exact and appropriate matching of desires, capabilities, and opportunities.

The general policies appropriate for reducing structural immobility have often been described. Adolf Sturmthal, in Chapter 11, has provided a detailed discussion of structural adjustment policies in relation to the labor force, and there is no need for elaboration here. It may be of interest, though, to note that certain steps are within the capability of the individual defense contractor. Companies could vest pension rights, provide company-wide rights of transfer, provide extended coverage for group insurance, hospitalization, and similar perquisites, and could even undertake to maintain them in force for a limited period in the event of involuntary temporary layoffs. Companies in defense industries could easily set up special contingency reserves for demobilization changeovers, and might appropriately negotiate with their unions for payroll deductions to be entered in such funds out of which subsidiary unemployment compensation benefits or termination allowances might be paid in the event of disarmament. With the cooperation of the government, contributions into such reserves might be tax deductible and allowable as a regular production cost in defense contracts. Possibly the principle could also be established that a proportion of all contracts, e.g., 0.5 per cent to a total of $1 million a year, should be allowable as extra cost to all prime contractors for the conducting of research on their conversion, diversification, and marketing problems in the event of disarmament—such studies, to qualify for cost treatment, having first to be approved by the Economics Division of the Arms Control and Disarmament Agency.

Similar studies, similarly coordinated by the ACDA, could fruitfully be undertaken by the various branches of the armed services and of the defense departments, covering the postdefense missions of public importance to which they might make a particular contribution.

In making such studies it is clearly unnecessary to try to foresee in detail just what each factory will do and where each worker will go. We can expect most of the necessary shifts in a private enterprise economy to be made more or less spontaneously. Businesses that are losing defense contracts will seek to exploit opportunities in other areas. United States workers, who are exceptionally mobile, can be counted on to seek out and find many of the new jobs that will be made available. A substantial share of workers in the defense industry would have less than average difficulty in finding alternative jobs, since an unusually high proportion of them are highly skilled and have scientific, engineering, and other advanced technical training. As may be noted in Table 5, Chapter 2, about 1.33 million of the 6.25 million persons likely to be released from defense-dependent employment as a result of disarmament are in the professional and technical category, or have been managers, officials, and proprietors.

Structural problems may assume more of a regional than an industrial or vocational character. The potential disarmament impacts on different geographic areas varies widely. This point is illustrated in Tables 6 and 7 in Chapter 2. In the past, solutions would have been sought primarily through relocation of unemployed workers; now it seems more likely that a wholly different emphasis would be found suitable, in view of the fundamental changes in cost structures which have been occurring.

With the rapid rise in the cost of community facilities (housing, mass education and health facilities, and so on) relative to the cost of factories and equipment, with the lower proportionate costs of transportation and power, and with the increased rate of obsolescence in plant and equipment, the case becomes more and more persuasive for aiding new industry to enter areas where there is an existing skilled labor force, rather than seeking to move unemployed workers to areas with idle manufacturing facilities. This is the course followed by various European programs for structurally depressed areas, and new United States legislation in this field takes the same approach.

There is little question that industry can be motivated to enter areas where there are sizable and durable cost advantages, as illustrated by the acceleration of the southward movement of United States industry in recent decades, and the recent success of Puerto Rico and several other relatively underdeveloped areas, in drawing additional industrial investment by means of incentive schemes.

However, the advantages have to be apparent on a *net* basis, after taking account of the additional expenses of plant relocation, labor relocation or retraining, additional tranportation costs of raw materials, components, and final products, absence of well-developed feeder industries, and frequent lack of educational, cultural, and other amenities for the managerial staff and their families. Furthermore, decisions of this sort occur rather slowly. It takes time for industry to evaluate the new incentives and the other pros and cons involved in major relocation decisions. In a disarmament context, it is unlikely that normal area redevelopment policy could attract new industry quickly enough to assure a smooth transition. Some of the cost advantages of lower wages and lower property values, for example, would appear only after the migration of some of the most energetic and adaptable of the workers, a growing demoralization of the rest, and a thorough deflation of local property values. This process is not only a traumatic experience for those involved, but more important, it also destroys much of the inherent value of the community as a successful "going concern" with a well-balanced labor force, a demonstrated expertise in making a line of products currently in demand, and an unimpaired morale. To conserve these values, it is necessary to have new, alternative programs to feed into the existing situation as old ones are completed. The new programs need not be military programs, but, as we shall see, may have to be rather different from ordinary commercial work.

Geographic structural problems largely overlap those of industry. The heart of the problem is in the aerospace-nucleonics-electronics complex, which now accounts for roughly four-fifths of all procurement and R&D. It is clear that this immense industrial empire has no normal civilian demand in prospect for any substantial fraction of its potential output, and no easy way to convert to the production of standard commercial items without losing much of its unique capability. In sharp contrast to defense industry in World War II, and even in the Korean War, this industrial complex has grown up in a permanent defense production environment. It never really "converted" from production of civilian items; it has little or no experience of such production and no plans to return to such production. Entry into such an environment would not involve reconversion, but radical diversification into largely unfamiliar lines. There is, for the first time in United States history on any substantial scale, a "permanent war industry" type of organization.

The description of the distinguishing characteristics of defense industry in Chapter 4, written by an economist who was also an official in one of the leading defense firms, provides a helpful insight into the structural and managerial characteristics of defense firms and of the environment within which they function, setting them apart to some extent from private firms working in standard commercial markets.

This is essentially a "bespoke" business, in which the product is not made until after it is sold; hence, the firms engaged in it have often demonstrated an inadequate appreciation of and competence in the whole marketing side of business, which in many commercial lines becomes the dominant factor. Defense firms are, moreover, geared to dealing with a single customer, the United States government, and are accustomed to investing a large amount in preparing bids and accepting low-margin initial orders as a way of getting essential experience and know-how which will later qualify them for larger and more profitable orders. They usually operate under limited profit potentials (with renegotiations where the firm's prices have proved to provide too much profit), but also with a degree of flexibility in the estimating of costs. They are, and must be, quality-conscious and innovation-oriented to a degree that would be unsettling if not indeed ruinous in most civilian lines; this is correlated with a lower emphasis on costs. Primacy is given to meeting exacting technical standards, and costs are permitted to rise to the extent necessary to achieve those standards; in civilian industries the priorities are usually the other way around. Controls are exercised largely by the administrative process, including more or less continuous oversight by procurement officials, rather than by the test of the market and capacity of competitors to beat the price on a standardized item.

The defense forces and defense agency personnel also have changed since World War II. Except for the draftees, they are no longer primarily a group of civilians hastily assembled for defense duty on an emergency basis, but a dedicated professional group with a lifetime commitment to their jobs. All this changes the situation in important ways. It means that these industries and these jobs will be much more difficult to abolish than in the past, because they are now the permanent careers of those who are in them. This does not mean that disarmament is impossible, or that the possibilities of peace are threatened by the vested interests of an unholy alliance of generals and war contractors. It does mean that to redefine the content of many defense jobs will be a far easier and more constructive solution than to abolish them. It also means that planning for a constructive use of the new expertise and professional career commitments which have been developed as an essential part of the national defense effort becomes one of the important guiding objectives of disarmament adjustment policy.

There is one type of structural-adjustment problem that will have to be taken into account in plans for employment adjustment, and that is the varying quantities of employment associated with a given volume of final output. As the Leontieff-Hoffenberg chapter (5) has shown, shifts of output from defense activity to other types of activities may lead to varying amounts of labor displacement, dependent on the labor-absorption characteristics of the alternative expenditures. In general, public expenditures on goods and services seem to provide the most employment, and investment activities and non-agricultural exports in support of international development also absorb more labor than increases in consumer expenditure.

In the event of a crash disarmament program where the maintenance of an adequate level of employment would be an overriding factor, considerations of this sort would play a major role in policy-making. They would not, of course, be so important in the case of a slow disarmament such as is envisaged in the READ model. Under such a program, more emphasis could be placed on facilitating the movement of resources into sectors with the biggest expansion potential and which are likely to make the largest long-run contribution to the achievement of our national goals.

A FORWARD POLICY FOR OPTIMUM ADJUSTMENT

As earlier indicated, I consider the balanced-offsets fiscal policy (Program 7 in Table 1) the only reasonably satisfactory fiscal solution. Sensible as this sort of adjustment policy seems to me, I am under no illusions about the difficulties it may have in obtaining acceptance. To a good many persons it will appear positively scandalous that in a period of drastically reduced government expenditures, it is not possible to obtain a surplus for debt reduction or, at the very least, to run a balanced budget. This is one of those cases where common sense speaks with a loud voice, but is nevertheless wrong. The fact is that a period of large and rapid defense cuts is a particularly bad time to try for a budget surplus or even a balance, because the downward multiplier offsets of cuts in defense spending are large[13] and even the announcement effects create downward pressures before the decline in actual spending. Thus, a surplus or even a balanced budget will be achieved in such a situation only at an unnecessarily low level of national income and employment.

If, to avoid this terrible waste of human resources, it were decided to attempt to apply a Balanced-Offsets policy, we would encounter three main types of obstacles: (1) the resistance to a budget deficit, (2) the disbelief in the efficacy of tax cuts, and (3) the political opposition to expansion in federal nondefense programs. Let us very briefly consider whether and how they may be overcome.

---

[13] Leslie Fishman, in Chapter 10, asserts that government financing of defense plants and of their feeder industries implies a much lower multiplier for defense expenditures than usually assumed, and that, therefore, personal tax cuts in amounts equal to (or even less than) defense cuts should provide adequate offsets. I feel that his argument is sufficiently novel to deserve additional discussion, but so far I disagree. Only a limited part of the defense program now consists of procurement—about 40 per cent in 1960—and this includes large amounts of R&D. The extent to which government subsidized plants during the period of expansion of defense actually may not be determining in deciding on the likely impact during defense cuts, once these plants have been largely depreciated. The bulk of defense expenditures now is based on current payrolls for the armed forces, defense departments, or defense contractors. The multiplier effects of defense cuts comes largely from the decline in expenditures by those now on these payrolls. In the Suits' econometric model, a reduction of $1 billion in government purchases from the private economy reduces GNP by $1.3 billion, which is already a very low multiplier, and a reduction of $1 billion in the government's payroll reduces GNP by $1.9 billion, while a compensating $1 billion drop in income taxes raise GNP by only $1.1 billion. The disparity in the multiplier effects on employment is even worse.

On the irrational fear of budget deficits, I find the situation is rapidly improving. In 1962, the Chamber of Commerce, the Committee for Economic Development, and other business groups definitely came out for tax cuts, despite the enlarged budget deficits they would cause. When Thomas S. Lamont, vice chairman of the board of the Morgan Guaranty Trust, can say, as he said recently: "I do not like, but I do not fear, what may be a temporary increase in the budgetary deficits resulting from gradual tax reduction. The threat of debilitating inflation, when and if it arises, can be met,"[14] I am encouraged to believe that public acceptance of what most economists would regard as a sensible view of budget deficits cannot be too far off.[15] And by the mid-sixties, a deficit of $3 billion will hardly look frighteningly large. Moreover, the economist can make the perfectly sound point that such a budget deficit could be appropriately interpreted as the price being paid for having half the offsets in tax cuts, instead of having them all in new government programs, which would require no deficits. The deficits would basically reflect the fact that tax changes have a lower multiplier than do changes in government expenditure.

As for the second difficulty, the disbelief in the efficacy of the tax cuts dies hard. It is sustained by an attitude of radical empiricism, not to say skepticism, which would be analogous in physics to a disbelief in the possibility of an atomic explosion until the moment the first bomb was exploded in Los Alamos. A deficit-financed tax cut in 1963, if it occurs, may be of great value to the nation by demonstrating the workability of such a device for raising expenditure—such demonstrative effects could be of even greater importance than the immediate effect on our growth rates.

The sort of tax reduction required for the purpose of quickly raising nondefense expenditure as an offset should have the following characteristics: (1) be administratively simple to apply

---

[14] In a speech to the Annual Meeting of the New England Council, in Boston, Friday, November 16, 1962.
[15] The important shift in business thinking, which left most Congressmen (and some older economists) behind, was helped by the widespread, popular discussion of a tax cut. See E. Benoit, "A Tax Cut Now?" (pro) and Senator Douglas (con) in *The New Republic,* August 13, 1962.

and remove; (2) have the minimum possible effect in changing the burden of taxation, as between the various interest groups, so as to avoid the need for Congressional controversy over who gets the advantages; and (3) be clearly marked as temporary, and intended to stimulate the economy, rather than to influence the distribution of income.

I suggest that these criteria might be met by what I call "income tax holidays." These would exempt all individuals and corporations from income or profit taxes for one or more pay periods as required. Administration would be extraordinarily easy. Withholding taxes would simply be stopped for a designated two week payroll period; at the end of the tax year, when making out their tax returns, individuals and corporate taxpayers would be allowed to reduce their tax obligations by a corresponding fraction (i.e., 2 weeks/52 weeks equals 3.8 per cent). No changes in normal tax or withholding rates would be required, and the "holiday" could be renewed as often as experience showed it to be necessary and desirable, as indicated by current data on personal income, production, and sales, which revealed whether current growth was in line with national targets. Decisions on when to declare such tax holidays could be by presidential order subject to some formula limitations and annual maximum. Such a program would give fiscal policy a flexibility now sadly lacking: Decisions could be made with respect to small rather than large amounts, and on the basis of current observations rather than on the basis of predictions, which are always subject to differences of opinion.

But the major difficulty faced by the balanced-offsets policy selection is the big increase in federal nondefense expenditure programs that is called for. Federal nondefense expenditures on goods and services were, in 1961, $8.7 billion; and transfers to state and local governments were $7.0 billion—a total of $15.7 billion. While there is considerable popular desire for additional public programs, there would be great political difficulty in raising federal nondefense purchases and grants to state and local governments substantially and quickly. To raise them by $18.5 billion—as required in our model under the balanced-offsets policy—would imply a 118 per cent increase beyond the 1961 level.

There has been heated political opposition in the past to increases in these expenditures. This opposition has inspired much propaganda, exaggerating the extent of such increases. In fact, federal expenditures for nondefense goods and services, deflated for price increases, were lower in 1961 than in 1939; indeed, on a per capita basis, they were 42 per cent lower. Adding federal grants to state and local governments, also deflated, there has been a significant decline since 1953; the per capita total in 1961 was 11 per cent below the 1953 level. Taking real nondefense expenditures for goods and services at all levels of government (federal, state, and local), we find that they have fallen between 1939 and 1961 from 16 per cent to 11.5 per cent of GNP; that is to say, by one-third in their weight in the total of goods and services. Those facts, so in conflict with current stereotypes, are little publicized. They suggest both that the priorities in this neglected sector are urgent, and that the political resistances to meeting them are strong.

The resistance is explained, or at least rationalized, by the fact that most nondefense types of government expenditure fall within fields which are reserved to state and local governments under our federal constitutional structure. While federal grants-in-aid have been expanding (they rose $4.7 billion in constant 1961 dollars between 1946 and 1960), there is resistance to too rapid an expansion because: (1) This has redistributionist aspects inasmuch as income is thereby transferred from the wealthier to the poorer states; (2) the state and local governments are often so poorly organized and administered, that their capacity to handle large additional grants with economy and efficiency is questionable; and (3) the state and local governments themselves may resist the minimum federal oversight required to assure the responsible expenditure of the funds. While such difficulties are only "administrative" and hence "frictional," they are, nevertheless, important, and do place very real limits on the possible tempo of increase in federal grants-in-aid.

The solution here proposed rests on a rather novel basic orientation to the whole problem. In effect, disarmament would force us to make a tremendous choice between returning to the *status quo ante,* or pushing forward to something new and better. In most discussions of disarmament adjustment, the problem has been thought of more or less in terms of getting back to where we were before, with a minimum of hardship. This approach ignores the tremendous transformation in the nation since we engaged in a full-sized defense effort on a more or less permanent basis. Too many new potentialities have been created that could not now be given up without grave loss. The defense program has financed a large part, and the most dynamic part, of our research and development and educational effort. If we will tomorrow be living in an age of jet travel, space exploration, telstar world communication systems, nuclear energy, miniaturized advanced electronic gadgetry, etc., it will be largely due to past defense research. The values for civilian life created by this defense research will have paid for the whole defense program many times over. To cram ourselves back into the dimension of the pre-defense era makes no sense; even if it were possible, it would betray too many potentialities. The question is: Can we have the economic benefits of big-defense without having to have defense itself. Can we have roast pig without (at the least the risk of) burning down the house? I think we can, but we shall have to organize not only a "moral equivalent of war" but an "economic equivalent of defense."

While we have indicated in Chapter 12 the large potentials of expanded government expenditure in more or less traditional fields, it is helpful also to envision the opportunities for *novel* programs which would have the triple advantages of: (1) avoiding the constitutional and traditional obstacles to federal expenditure and the opposition of entrenched vested interests; (2) providing a use for the special type of resources released from defense industries; and (3) making a strategic contribution to the nation's long-term growth, and to its foreign policy goals. I will provide three illustrations of the type of program I have in mind. These are programs which can be begun immediately, or have already begun, and which can be enlarged as needed during disarmament.

The first illustration of what I am talking about has particular significance in that it offers opportunities immediately, before disarmament starts, and may even play a key role in enabling disarmament to become possible. I am referring here to the use of electronic and other techniques for the purpose of disarmament monitoring, verification, and inspection.

The situation now prevailing is illustrated by the following report from a high official in a corporation that is a major defense contractor: A scientist in their employ hit on a principle which might, he thought, be applied to the problem of detecting metal objects buried beneath the ground, and asked whether he should pursue this line of investigation; he was told not to, since the company could think of no possible market for such a device. Clearly, if the United States government had managed to convey to all defense contractors its strong interest in negotiating a sound disarmament agreement as fundamental to United States security, the company in question would have realized the vast potential significance of a device to detect buried stocks of weapons. But if the United States government wishes to convince defense contractors on this point, a few public statements to the press, in the United Nations, etc., will not be enough. To the business community, money talks far louder than official pronouncements. Only if we begin to fund our interest in disarmament inspection in significant amounts will the reality of our national interest in disarmament be recognized and accepted on the operating level and disarmament "taken seriously" as a fundamental part of our whole national security program. There is perhaps no other single type of measure that the United States government could take—including the whole range of diplomatic initiatives—that would, in the long run, more effectively impress on the nation, and indirectly on the world, the sincerity of our interest in disarmament and the strength of our conviction that preparations for peace offer economic opportunities no less attractive than those provided by preparations for war.[16]

From the point of view of industry, this is an area where any expertise acquired may have a long-term payoff. If disarmament does not occur, there will almost have to be some type of arms control which will rely heavily on such techniques; and if disarmament does occur, there will be a continuing R&D program by the international

---

[16] Fortunately, a beginning is already being made. Arms control or disarmament studies have already been commissioned in General Dynamics, North American Aviation, Lockheed, Douglas, United Aircraft, General Electric, Bendix, Boeing, and Raytheon. In view of the enormity of the problems we confront, however, it is puzzling that the ACDA has been so modest in its requests to Congress for research funds, and it appears uncertain whether larger funds for disarmament research are actually needed.

disarmament organization (costing in the READ model $3 billion a year, of which $1 billion would be supplied by the United States) which will deal in good part with inspection problems and techniques. The achievement of an advanced capability in this area could turn out to be a very valuable investment for a defense producer when his strictly military lines are phased out.

The second example is the obvious one of the space program. Several highly-placed government officials I have talked with are already well aware of the value of the space program offset to defense cutbacks and are beginning to think of it much in that light. The "fit" with the missile industry, in respect to resources utilized and skills required, is too obvious to miss. What is not always understood by the general public is the extent to which such a program gives collateral support to a variety of other programs, and a stimulus to the development of R&D resources which will later become available to other programs as well. The main value of the program, indeed, is likely not to be anything we shall bring back from the moon or other planets, but the incidental discoveries we will make about our own world and the ways to utilize it more effectively. Already, information gained in connection with space research has had valuable benefits for water purification, metallurgy, communication techniques, information storage and retrieval, solar energy and other unconventional energy sources, observation of body changes under stress (as during surgery), the production of antidepressant drugs, and many other fields of primarily earthly significance.

Would we not make even more progress if we applied the same research funds to the direct pursuit of the terrestrial improvements mentioned? Not necessarily. One needs to get outside the framework of routine assumptions and standard questions. Sometimes, this is best achieved by tackling novel problems and tracing out the side implication of results for the standard fields, thereby casting wholly new light on them or making possible the development of new instruments or techniques with the aid of which formerly stubborn problems can be readily resolved. Moreover, it is a fact that only a really big challenge can win sufficient public recognition to attract the necessary funds. Such funds can often then be utilized to support collateral research on problems, e.g., water purification, which are of far more immediate importance but have been unable on their own to win adequate public support.

Looking to the future, there may be other national R&D programs recognizable as having great national importance, and capable of stimulating popular imagination and winning enthusiastic popular support.

Another program of this sort, which may develop in time into a sort of parallel with the space program, is the program of world economic development. Like the space program, it is related both to defense and to foreign policy and is, hence, appropriately a matter of federal concern. Like the space program also, it could develop ultimately into a very large program, drawing heavily upon our best domestic talents. To do this, it would be necessary to broaden the program beyond the limited and politically difficult concepts of aid and charity and get it into the more exciting context of world-wide investment in wealth production.

When so viewed, it will become apparent, I think, that there are major technological barriers to the success of this enterprise which we have not yet solved, and that a major R&D program on these barriers to development will need to be mounted before we can use our foreign aid as much more than palliatives, genteel subsidies, and ways of exerting political influence.

The sort of R&D programs that come to mind in this connection include the following: (1) the use of teaching machines, and television-radio networks to achieve breakthroughs in world education (both elementary and advanced) as well as to promote the acquisition of skills and the cultivation of new, popular attitudes essential for effective industrialization; (2) the desalinization of water, and other techniques of aridity control and restoration of desert areas, including improvements on existing techniques of irrigation and reforestation and river valley development; (3) new approaches to tropical nutrition, including not only standard types of agricultural improvement but also the investigation of such food sources as algae, fish meals, yeasts, and hydroponics, as well as new extractive methods of converting plants directly into proteins and oils, and the synthesizing of key elements deficient in tropical diets —along with improved techniques of food storage and distribution; (4) new approaches to tropical medicine, emphasizing not only the

300 - EMILE BENOIT

gross problems of morbidity, but the more subtle problems of impairment of human energies; (5) basic research on the problems of overpopulation and the development of improved techniques of controlling family size useful for rural and low-income populations and compatible with various moral and religious attitudes; (6) creation of standardized components for on-site assembly by unskilled labor into simple homes, schools, offices, and factories; and possibly also for farm implements, power systems, and simple types of industrial machinery; (7) development of small package power units of rugged design capable of operating economically for long periods with minimum maintenance requirements and the development of unconventional power sources—solar batteries and cookers, fuel cells, wind machines, etc.—for special development purposes.

An R&D program which tackled fundamental matters of this sort would not only put economic development in a new and more hopeful perspective; it would, to a considerable extent, utilize United States resources within the United States and avoid the "giveaway" overtones which, up to now, encourage people to regard the program as essentially a burden, rather than as an exciting investment in the future. It is of first importance in this connection that we, ourselves, could benefit from important breakthroughs achieved in the program, even though the primary purpose of the plan would be to help others.

Moreover, like the space program, this would be a program which could utilize to good effect much of the personnel and other resources released by disarmament, and utilize them on a project of fundamental significance, the importance of which, for the welfare of the nation and the world, could be dramatized and made readily understandable to all.

A forward-looking policy such as I have described would visualize the disarmament adjustment problem not as essentially one of finding a place to park the released resources and keep them from becoming a nuisance but, rather, as a once-in-a-lifetime opportunity to apply some highly valuable, although specialized, resources to carefully selected alternative uses in which they could contribute more effectively to the highest-priority needs of mankind.

Appendix

THE BURDEN OF NATIONAL DEFENSE[a]

(*Dollars in millions*)

	DEFENSE EXPENDITURES, 1958			ARMED FORCES, 1960	
	TOTAL (INCLUDING U.S. MILITARY AID)	U.S. MILITARY AID[b]	TOTAL FROM DOMESTIC RESOURCES AS PER CENT OF GNP	THOUSANDS OF PERSONS	PER CENT OF POPULATION
WORLD, TOTAL	$114,650		9.4	19,087[c]	0.7[c]
INDUSTRIAL PRIVATE ENTERPRISE ECONOMIES, TOTAL	60,289		8.0	5,515	1.0
NORTH AMERICA, TOTAL	47,243		9.9	2,609	1.3
United States	45,503		10.2	2,489	1.4
Canada	1,740		5.4	120	0.7
EUROPE, TOTAL	12,625		5.1	2,746	1.1
Austria	73		1.5	50	0.7
Belgium-Luxembourg	375	$ 40	3.2	123	1.3
Denmark	143	25	2.9	44	1.0
France	3,355	122	7.1	1,026	2.3

301

	DEFENSE EXPENDITURES, 1958			ARMED FORCES, 1960	
	TOTAL (INCLUDING U.S. MILITARY AID)	U.S. MILI-TARY AID[b]	TOTAL FROM DO-MESTIC RE-SOURCES AS PER CENT OF GNP	THOU-SANDS OF PERSONS	PER CENT OF POP-ULATION
Federal Republic of Germany	1,631	108	3.1	260	0.5
Italy	1,035	100	3.9	400	0.8
Netherlands	436	48	4.5	135	1.2
Norway	143	51	3.7	40	1.1
Sweden	514		4.8	75	1.0
Switzerland	236		3.1	d	
United Kingdom	4,684	78	7.4	593	1.1
FAR EAST, TOTAL	421	139	1.5	160	0.2
Japan	421	139	1.5	160	0.2
CENTRALLY PLANNED ECONOMIES, TOTAL	49,211		15.9	7,990	0.8
EUROPE, TOTAL	47,111		17.9	4,990	1.5
U.S.S.R.	45,000		20.0	3,623[e]	1.7
Albania	11[f]			21	1.3
Bulgaria	200[f]			100	1.3
Czechoslovakia	620[g]		5.0	150	1.1
East Germany				65	0.4
Hungary	179[h]		3.5[h]	75	0.8
Poland	511		3.8	200	0.7
Roumania	375[f]			200	1.1
Yugoslavia	215	17	7.3	556[i]	3.0
FAR EAST, TOTAL	2,100			3,000	0.4
Mainland China	2,100[j]		4.6[k]	3,000	0.4
PRIMARY PRODUCING ECONOMIES, TOTAL	5,150		3.2	5,582	0.4
LATIN AMERICA, TOTAL[l]	1,151		2.7	823	0.4
Argentina	184		3.5	127	0.6
Bolivia	4	m	2.0	12[n]	0.4
Brazil	409	19	3.2	227	0.3
Chile	98	6	3.5	33	0.4[o]
Colombia	54	3	2.2	16	0.1
Costa Rica	2		0.5	1	0.1
Cuba		2		18	0.3

| | DEFENSE EXPENDITURES, 1958 | | | ARMED FORCES, 1960 | |
	TOTAL (INCLUDING U.S. MILITARY AID)	U.S. MILI-TARY AID[b]	TOTAL FROM DO-MESTIC RE-SOURCES AS PER CENT OF GNP	THOU-SANDS OF PERSONS	PER CENT OF POP-ULATION
Dominican Republic	30	1	4.6	16	0.6
Ecuador	19	2	2.3	4	0.1
El Salvador	7		1.3		
Guatemala	10	m	1.5	8	0.2
Haiti	6	m	2.3	4	0.1
Honduras	5	m	1.4	3	0.2
Mexico	70		0.8	300	0.9
Nicaragua	8	m	2.8	3	0.2
Panama	1		0.3	3	0.3
Paraguay	9		4.0	6	0.4
Peru	48	5	3.7	32	0.3
Uruguay		5			
Venezuela	187		3.1	10	0.1
EUROPE, TOTAL	621		3.3	707	1.4
Finland	64		1.7		
Greece	152[p]	116	5.2[p]	158	2.1
Iceland					
Ireland	22		1.3	9	0.3
Portugal	86	18	4.2	79	0.9
Spain	297	50	3.4	461[i]	1.5
AFRICA, TOTAL	432		3.0	c	c
Ethiopia	16	7	1.8		
Ghana	10		1.0		
Liberia	1	m	0.8	3	0.1
Libya	4	1	3.4		
Morocco	87	1	5.8	50	0.5[o]
Nigeria	13		0.5		
Somali Republic	1		1.9		
Sudan	10		1.2		
Tunisia	11		1.5		
Union of South Africa	73		1.5[q]	10	0.1
United Arab Republic (Egypt)	206		6.1[r]		
NEAR EAST, TOTAL	1,572		3.2	c	c
Afghanistan	19	m	3.1		
Ceylon	13		1.1	8	0.1

303

| | DEFENSE EXPENDITURES, 1958 | | | ARMED FORCES, 1960 | |
	TOTAL (INCLUDING U.S. MILITARY AID)	U.S. MILITARY AID[b]	TOTAL FROM DOMESTIC RESOURCES AS PER CENT OF GNP	THOUSANDS OF PERSONS	PER CENT OF POPULATION
India	656		2.1	500	0.1
Iran	187[s]	82	6.6[s]	130	0.6
Iraq	114	11			
Israel	149	m	7.6		
Jordan	52[t]	5	29.7[t]		
Lebanon	21[u]	2	3.9[u]		
Nepal	3		0.7	6	0.1[v]
Pakistan	187[w]	x	3.4[w]	103	0.1
Turkey	171[y]	225	4.4[y]	500	1.9
FAR EAST, TOTAL	787		4.8	2,681	0.7
Burma	112		10.3	100	0.5
Cambodia	34[z]	6	7.7[z]	28	0.6
Indonesia	281		5.5	200	0.2
Korea, North				536[c]	
Korea, South	170[aa]	260	7.6[aa]	600	7.4
Laos	14[bb]	7	14.3[bb]	29	1.5
Malaya				15	0.2
Mongolian Republic				350[c]	
Philippines	90[cc]	20	1.8[cc]	32	0.1
Taiwan		200		157	1.5
Thailand	86[dd]	19	3.9[dd]	134	0.6
Viet Nam, North				350[c]	
Viet Nam, South		47		150	1.1
OCEANIA, TOTAL	587		3.6	61	0.5
Australia	502[ee]		3.8	48	0.5
New Zealand	85[ee]		2.7	13	0.5

a This table was prepared by Mary Painter, on the basis of national budgets, International Cooperation Administration unpublished data, and other sources. The estimates are intended only as rough approximations.

b Average of fiscal years 1958 and 1959.

c The totals of the number in the armed forces are the sum of the figures for each country for which the data were available. The calculation of the armed forces as a percentage of the population includes only those countries for which the data for both the armed forces and the population were available (i.e., it excludes the Mongolian Republic, North Korea, and North Viet Nam). The world total and the total for primary producing countries include the countries in Africa and the Near East for which the data were available, but the totals for these two regions are not shown. The exclusion of a number of countries for which data are lacking would make only relatively small changes in the larger totals, but would make important changes in the regional totals. For example, in Africa, both Ethiopia and Egypt have significant armies. South of the Sahara, the armies are probably small in relation to the population, but the total population is very large. Nigeria alone may have some 40 million inhabitants. And none of the former French colonies are included. In the Near East, data are missing on Israel and the major Arab states. Thus, any total given for these two regions might be seriously misleading.

d Switzerland has no standing army, but has universal compulsory military service.

e As of January 1960. By the law of January 15, 1960, the forces were to be reduced to 2.423 million, or 1.1 per cent of the population.

f Budget for 1955.

g Planned expenditures for 1958.

h Appropriation for 1955. The budget since that date has been cut drastically.

i As of July 1959.

j Budget.

k Estimate for 1957. GNP in 1957 at 1952 prices inflated to 1957 prices by the ratio of national income in 1957 prices to national income in 1952 prices.

l Armed forces figures are for 1956.

m Less than $500,000.

n Average of estimate of 10,000 to 15,000.

o Population of 1959.

p Includes $14 million budget support from the United States. If this were excluded, defense expenditures would be 4.7 per cent of GNP.

q Percentage of national income for the year ending June 30, 1958.

r Percentage of 1956 GNP, increased to allow for a rise in cost of living between 1956 and 1958; any increase in the volume of output since 1956 is not included.

s Includes $38 million budget support from the United States. If this were excluded, defense expenditures would be 5.2 per cent of GNP.

t Jordan received from the United States and other countries a total of $40 million budget support which was not allocated between defense and other government expenditures. If it is assumed that budget support was distributed evenly over all expenditures, defense expenditures from Jordan's resources would be $20.5 million, or 11.7 per cent of GNP. If all the budget support were allocated to defense, the defense expenditures from Jordan's own resources would be $12 million, or 6.9 per cent of GNP.

u Lebanon received from the United States and other countries a total of $17 million budget support which was not allocated between defense and other government expenditures. If it is assumed that budget support was distributed evenly over all expenditures, defense expenditures from Lebanon's own resources would be $17 million, or 3.2 per cent of GNP. If all the budget support were allocated to defense, defense expenditures from Lebanon's resources would be $4 million, or 0.7 per cent of GNP.

v Population of 1954.

w Includes $21 million budget support from the United States. If this were excluded, defense expenditures would be 2.9 per cent of GNP.

x Data classified.

y Includes $44 million budget support from the United States. If this were excluded, defense expenditures would be 3.2 per cent of GNP.

z Includes $16 million budget support from the United States. If this were excluded, defense expenditures would be 4.1 per cent of GNP.

aa Includes $64 million budget support from the United States. If this were excluded, defense expenditures would be 4.8 per cent of GNP.

bb Includes $13 million budget support from the United States. If this were excluded, defense expenditures would be 1.0 per cent of GNP.

cc Includes $12 million budget support from the United States. If this were excluded, defense expenditures would be 1.5 per cent of GNP.

dd Includes $7 million budget support from the United States. If this were excluded, defense expenditures would be 3.6 per cent of GNP.

ee Budget for 1960.

Index

61; location of, 199–200, 288–289; profits and diversification of, 81–82, 83; redeployment in, 42–49; sales and diversification of, 81–82, 83; *see also* Defense industries; Firms; Military organizations

Inflation, prices and, 168

Input: disarmament effects on, 89–98; of military organizations, 7

Inspection systems, 50–65; aerial inspection, 58–60; citizen supervision of, 63; costs of, 54–55, 63–64, 228, 296–298; error and violation problems, 53–54; high-altitude missile testing, 56–58; for industrial plants, 60–61; for military installations, 61–62; for military research and development, 62; for nuclear testing, 55–56, 58; personnel needs in, 55, 56, 59, 61, 62, 63, 64–65

Interest rates: ceilings on, 153–154; construction and, 139–141; debt retirement and, 134–136, 136–137, 163–164, 168, 282; expenditures and, 146; investment and, 138–143; savings and, 137, 138; tax reduction and, 168

International affairs: internal effects of disarmament, 240–245; *see also* Foreign aid

International police force, disarmament violation and, 53–54

Investment: consumer spending and, 177–179; consumption and, 206–207; debt retirement and, 136, 137, 164, 180, 282; defense spending and, 174–175; defense *vs.* private, 176; factors in, 205; Federal spending and, 180; interest rates and, 138–143; private, economic effects of changes in, 103–107; tax reduction and, 161–162, 178–179

Labor force: disarmament and adjustment policies for, 287–291; displacement with disarmament, 195–196; growth of, 183; hours-of-work shortening, 198–199; military organizations and, 7–8; mobility of, 186–189, 197–198, 288; occupational changes in, 187–189; occupational retraining, 189–191, 199, 201; organization of market, 184, 185–186; personnel costs of military, 67–68; personnel needs for inspection systems, 55, 56, 59, 61, 62, 63, 64–65; placement of, 186; *see also* Employment; Unemployment

Latin America, economic effects of disarmament on, 242–243

Liquidity, economic, disarmament approach and, 166–168

Manpower Development and Training Act of 1962, 200, 201

Market: debt reduction and, 165, 166; increased federal spending and, 166; organization of labor, 184, 185–186; research and development cutbacks and, 121–125

Military Assistance Program (MAP), 233–234, 240

Military organizations: characteristics of, 290–291; competition of, 9–10; declining value of exploitation and, 16–17; employment in, 38–39, 40–41; expenditures of, 67–72, 75–79; firms contrasted with, 7–8; foreign economic development and, 267–268; industrial distribution of defense production, 72–75; inspection of military installations, 61–62; product of, 10–11; redeployment in, 42–49; research and development inspection, 62; size and heterogeneity of, 13–14; social system of, 9–11; viability of, 11–13, 14–16, 17

Mobility of labor force, 186–189, 197–198, 288

Money: debt reduction and, 165, 166; deflationary effects of disarmament, 132–133; expansion and debt-retirement supplement, 143–146; fiscal and monetary adjustments to disarmament, 131–156, 276–285; income and demand for, 142–143; supply, debt retirement and, 133–136, 281–285; trends in supply of, 273

Monopoly of military organizations, 9

Multilateral disarmament, 30

Mutual deterrence system, 16

Natural resources, conservation and development programs, 209–210

National defense, classical theory of, 14–16

Nuclear weapons: cost of test ban inspection system, 55–56, 58

Occupations: changes in, 187–189; redeployment and, 44–45; retraining in, 189–191, 199, 201

Operations and maintenance costs of military, 68, 75

Output: capital and, 254–258; disarmament effects on, 89–98; employment and, 291

Payoffs in disarmament bargaining, 18–21, 21–22; power and, 22–23, 26–27; revolution in system of, 17

Power: payoffs and, 22–23, 26–27; redistribution of, 22–23